Critical Muslim 52

Genocide

Critical Muslim is published quarterly by C. Hurst & Co. (Publishers) Ltd. on behalf of and in conjunction with Critical Muslim Ltd. and the Muslim Institute, London.

All editorial correspondence to Muslim Institute, Canopi, 7-14 Great Dover Street, London, SE1 4YR
E-mail: editorial@criticalmuslim.com

The editors do not necessarily agree with the opinions expressed by the contributors. We reserve the right to make such editorial changes as may be necessary to make submissions to *Critical Muslim* suitable for publication.

C. Hurst & Co (Publishers) Ltd., New Wing, Somerset House, Strand, London, WC2R 1LA

ISBN:9781911723851 ISSN: 2048-8475

To subscribe or place an order by credit/debit card or cheque (pounds sterling only) please contact Kathleen May at the Hurst address above or e-mail kathleen@hurstpub.co.uk

A one-year subscription, inclusive of postage (four issues), costs £60 (UK), £90 (Europe) and £100 (rest of the world), this includes full access to the *Critical Muslim* series and archive online. Digital only subscription is £3.30 per month.

A Cataloguing-in-Publication data record for this book is available from the British Library

Critical Muslim

Subscribe to Critical Muslim

Now in its thirteenth year in print, *Critical Muslim* is also available online. Users can access the site for just £3.30 per month – or for those with a print subscription it is included as part of the package. In return, you'll get access to everything in the series (including our entire archive), and a clean, accessible reading experience for desktop computers and handheld devices — entirely free of advertising.

Full subscription

The print edition of *Critical Muslim* is published quarterly in January, April, July and October. As a subscriber to the print edition, you'll receive new issues directly to your door, as well as full access to our digital archive.

United Kingdom £60/year
Europe £90/year
Rest of the World £100/year

Digital Only

Immediate online access to *Critical Muslim*

Browse the full *Critical Muslim* archive

Cancel any time

£3.30 per month

www.criticalmuslim.io

CM52

AUTUMN 2024

CONTENTS

GENOCIDE

GENOCIDE

INTRODUCTION: HERE WE GO AGAIN

C Scott Jordan

At 3:15 pm on 11 April 1945, a detachment of troops from the US Army entered the main gates of Buchenwald Concentration Camp just outside the central German city of Weimar. The troops were given a hero's welcome: the camp had been liberated. In July 1937, Nazi forces began the construction of Buchenwald. It was one of the first and largest of the Nazi concentration camp complexes constructed within the Altreich, the territory which belonged to Germany before Adolf Hitler began his game of annexations. The camp's beginnings were rather simple. A place to intern suspected communists and their sympathisers. Eventually, the camp hosted approximately 280,000 prisoners, a European union of Jews, Poles, Slavs (of all kinds), Romani, the mentally ill, the physically disabled, those labelled 'sexual deviants' (largely homosexuals, trans individuals, and gender queers), and all other such political prisoners or prisoners of war the Nazis would prefer to not have to think about ever again. While the Nazis kept good records, their method of labelling the fate of their captives made totalling up causalities a less than straight-forward task. Best estimations show that 20 percent of those detained were killed, some 56,545 souls. Upon their liberation, the surviving prisoners made a collage of handwritten signs, repeating a phrase in a variety of languages. That phrase was 'Never Again'.

Of all the possible words these freed prisoners could have come up with after years of torture and, for many, the complete loss of hope, this pairing might seem an odd choice. The phrase comes from an epic 1927 poem penned by the Israeli poet Yitzhak Lamdan. *Masada* tells the tale of the siege of Masada, one of the last battles of the First Roman-Jewish War taking place during the first century. Zionists hold this event and Lamdan's poem as one of the finest displays of Jewish bravery exemplified by a rebel group holding out against the onslaught of Roman troops. It is not a tale without its controversies. First off, the heroism of the rebels is derived from their last desperate act, where they all committed collective suicide instead of allowing themselves to be taken as slaves. And this particular group of Jewish rebels were not without their own faults, by today's standards they would easily gain the label of 'terrorist' from various political commentators. Of course, nationalist movements are not known for holding back on exaggeration and Zionism is certainly no exemption in this regard. Much of the tale of Masada has fallen into the realm of mythology, but both Lamdan's usage as well as the prisoner's choice of the phrase 'never again' is curious. It hits much harder than say 'Remember the Alamo' or 'In Flanders Field', but lacks the notion of sacrifice conveyed in these statements. Instead, it denotes that not only did something bad happen, but someone bad also allowed this to happen. Perhaps memory is not enough to make a hero, but action. Of course, what action to take remains something we are left to figure out. For the prisoners of Buchenwald, their hope is that you would not forget what happened here and that you will always stand against fascism. Today, in that same spot, a stainless-steel plate resides, kept year-round at 37 degrees Celsius, the temperature of human skin.

The quote itself and the sentiment surrounding it went from the immortalisation offered by a physical monument to the life given by popular parlance with the adoption of the Universal Declaration of Human Rights in 1948 and the spirit that birthed the European Union. It bears as many meanings as it has invocations, closely following many of the worst things humans have ever done. It can be said to be a promise, a vow, a pledge, and while the Romanian American writer Elie Wiesel, a survivor of the Buchenwald camp, affirms all this, his greatest hope is that 'never again' would not be allowed to become a slogan, what we might today call a 'buzzword'. Wiesel, interestingly, sees it as a 'prayer'. Perhaps that is easier. You see, then it is not our fault for breaking or defying a commitment we made. Instead, 'never again' can simply remain, like so many others, another unanswered prayer. The allowance of genocide remains one of those arguments the atheist presents me to which I have not yet discovered a suitable response.

As it stands, mathematically 'never again' is equal to or lesser than forty-seven years. Although it was not decided until 2007, the International Court of Justice found that the crimes committed, beginning in 1992, by Serbian, Montenegrin, and Bosnian-Serb leadership against the Muslims of Bosnia & Herzegovina were, in fact, genocide. This is the first time an international court ruled that a genocide had been committed, violating the Convention on the Prevention and Punishment of the Crime of Genocide or, simply, the Genocide Convention, which came into effect in 1951. Of course, since then numerous other cases can and have been made. And hardly any of the nations that exist today have a historical closet empty of skeletons. More accurately, they have a historical closet filled with a mass grave or two of one ethnic group or more of peoples deemed unworthy of personhood somewhere along the line. Yet only a handful of cases have been brought up before international courts. And every time something truly awful happens, again a flurry of 'never again's are released. And more genocides are committed. Why?

Well, to begin, genocide is a hard thing to pin down. A large portion of this issue discusses mere definition. And this is not a bad thing, this is a conversation that, especially now, needs further elucidation and critical analysis. If the definition is too loose, then genocide loses the sting that it must uphold when it comes up. The stakes are that genocide could become, in Hannah Arendt's phrasing 'banal' or even normal – far from the worst thing that one group of humans could do to another. This is something that cannot be abided. Yet, if we are too uptight and conservative to ever use the term for the horrors we continue to perpetuate, the same fate could meet the word genocide – it in turn becomes a historical thing that humans used to do to one another. The assumption would be that we are now more sophisticated, when in actuality, we have done nothing worthy of elevating our ethical stature, in this regard. And the best part of this balancing act is that it is virtually impossible to please everyone. Some pretty horrible stuff may not make the cut. And often, when an accusation of genocide it made, whether or not it fits the definition, it is almost certain that whatever is happening is pretty bad – and likely evil. Quickly we begin to feel we are on mission impossible.

This seemingly unsolvable puzzle is further perplexed by the common lens many of us are using to grapple with genocide – the ongoing situation in the Gaza Strip. Indeed, the actions Israeli forces are taking against the Palestinian people is fresh on all our minds and is a major focal point amongst the articles in this issue. But is it too fresh? Do our emotions and terror blind us beyond the capacity for rational thought? Are we doomed to only be able to give solid analysis on genocide once the dust has settled and the whole scenario can be played over and over until sense is made. Maha Sardar observes that it is important for us to reflect on the history of genocide but that while hindsight reveals many details, we should all be held to a higher ethical fortitude when it comes to deciphering right from wrong in terms of current events.

Martin Shaw, evaluating whether what is happening in the Gaza Strip can be considered genocide, takes on this enigma by dissecting the idea of genocide from the beginning. Starting with Raphael Lemkin, the man who coined the term 'genocide', Shaw traces the word's role in the establishment of the United Nations and the post-World War II world order. Noting the controversy over 'genocides' usage and application, he highlights a few important points. Shaw differentiates physical destruction from social and cultural destruction while also seeing them as important shades of genocide. The crux for him is that genocide comes with a historical momentum, genocides do not simply rise 'out of the blue' and that the case must be made from the position of the 'policy' of one group in targeting and exterminating another. Interestingly this does not allow genocide to be a passive action, and indeed, one does not accidentally commit genocide or happen to genocide as a means to a better end. The most troubling conclusion Shaw reaches is that, no matter whether an incident is found to be genocide or not, the courts can only act so fast and without buy-in from the major powers, which keep such forces as the United Nations Security Council from acting, the whole discussion is for not. Sardar concurs with Shaw on this last point, noting that 'the only "lessons learnt" from what has come before, seems to be the ease with which states can dissemble and distort reality to avoid confronting what is happening before their eyes'.

'Never again' is not the only phrase in danger of becoming a buzzword for political expediency. Genocide too is always under threat of sharing this fate. This was the fear that permeated the first case of genocide brought to the UN stating a breach of the Genocide Convention. In 1951, the Civil Rights Congress of the United States launched a petition against the US for its treatment of black Americans. The international courts feared this was a misuse of the treaty's intention and threw out the petition. We have more recently witnessed this with Russia using accusations of genocide against the Ukrainian government as justification for its full-scale invasion in February 2022. Over Gaza, Sardar points out that whether to call it genocide is not determined by any standard of a definition, but instead by one's political beliefs. And the will of states can have an incredible impact on the political beliefs of the citizenry, as well as the ignorance they bear. We can easily utter genocide when it wins us votes or if we need to justify using our abundantly resourced military. Genocide can just as easily be made unspeakable, *verboten*, when the indicting fingers point back at us or at our allies. Postnormal times has us sometimes practicing both approaches simultaneously, without any time to realise what a contradiction we have found ourselves in.

Abdelwahab El-Affendi demonstrates this contradiction masterfully when he examines western laws against 'Holocaust denial' juxtaposed to the banning of the use of the word genocide in reference to the situation in Palestine. El-Affendi makes this double-standard starker by noting that historical occurrences were not as well documented as what is happening today, so if the historical discussion cannot be had, how is one able to watch television or look at social media and deny what is right there for all and sundry to see. The key take away is that denial is an important rhetorical tool. 'Never again' is an incredibly powerful narrative. Rhetorical denial is essential to keep that narrative alive. The point of the narrative is to justify history, in short to allow us to feel good at the end of the day without focussing on the calculus of tabulating the 'goods' and 'horrifying evils' committed along the way. If Israel were to be seen as perpetrating a genocide, then the last eight odd decades would have been for not and we are right back to the antisemitic square one of the Jewish question. Ironically, these are the same people who cannot differentiate a member of the Jewish faith from a Zionist, from someone who is for or against the rationale that gives us the contemporary State of Israel — all three are indeed different ideas people may hold that need not be mutually exclusive. Speaking ill of one or all of these entities need not be a simple, black-and-white case of antisemitism. So, in opposing such a myopic view, every genocide must be seen in its own context.

Liam Mayo looks at narratives around genocide in a broader sense. Instead of whether or not an event is a genocide and using the rhetorical tool of genocide or denial narratives to justify further actions, Mayo watches how history has flown from one catastrophe to the next, building a narrative. So instead of the Holocaust as this monolithic horrible thing, it is actually the horrifying result of modernity. But Mayo expresses the equal importance of the long view narrative and the personal narratives of those who lived through such awful things. Commentators, primarily on one side of the argument, prefer to remove the personal narratives from events so that a cold calculous can be used to determine if actions taken are fulfilling imagined principles that do the truly abominable, such as justifying war, killing, and some really disgusting stuff. Mayo wonders if we have fallen into a trap of modernity, by which we roll from catastrophe to catastrophe and, as long as the slightest bit of progress is made, we call that a win and prepare to start the whole cycle again.

At least in terms of genocide, and I would add to this all other horrible stuff we do to one another, it is time to break that cycle. Richard Appignanesi's eloquent examination of evil as a 'gratuitous act' strikes the nail on the head, waking us from any delusion that this cycle must be our fate for the greater good. For Appignanesi, evil is evil for it is without reason. For the sake of progress, modernity has tossed out transcendence – Nietsche's death of God – opening the gates for 'religious arbitrariness' that, in lieu of reason, allows evil to run amok, unabated. Under these conditions, genocide is not simply allowed or excused, it is normalised.

So, what are we to do? Sardar rightly states that genocide must stand 'at the very pinnacle of crimes against humanity'. People are dying. There is no progress in that. 'An allegation of genocide is an allegation of a total departure from the norms that all of us, states and individuals, purport to value; it is an allegation of the abandonment of civilisation for barbarism.' A definition and internationally recognised standards are necessary, but they will require debate, controversy, and further discourse. For the international courts to do their job without losing their dignity in the process, they need time. Time was not a luxury for the Tutsi or the Bosniaks, and it remains one unavailable to the people of Gaza, the Rohingyas, or the numerous other peoples around the world under threat of extermination. Further historical investigations can progress our understandings of our capacity for sickening displays of inhumanity and provide us a foundation for making sure such dark acts cannot again be repeated.

Although a grotesque industry of exploitation has been made out of this argument, it is important to begin with the Holocaust. The Holocaust is the gold standard of genocides. A mark of distinguishment for which no human should be proud, nevertheless, it was the most despicable display of blatant and unrelenting genocidal policy. This was the historical moment when a parent catches a child doing an act, where recognition is instantaneously transmitted that what was done was wrong and with that knowledge, we have a duty to do better. The Holocaust was unlike any other moment in history and did fundamentally shake the world order to the core. We can say a multiplicity of events led to the creation of the post-war world order, but, if we are to be honest with ourselves, it was the Holocaust that broke the camel's back. There is a very good reason that Godwin's Law – the law around internet conversation that states the longer a chat continues, the probability that someone will be compared to Hitler and the Nazis approaches one – exists in our contemporary world. The Nazi policy explicitly targeted the Jewish people of Europe – and it should be emphasised that the Romani, Slavs, queer identifying peoples, disabled persons, and other political, ethnic, and religious groups were also targeted by these policies. No time was wasted on assimilation or 're-education'. All of these folks were literally striped of their humanity, along with their clothes, and sent to die on a truly industrial scale. This term gets used a lot today and I'd argue, inappropriately. Yes, advanced weapons deliver death on an 'industrial scale', but the industrial scale of death inside Nazi concentration camps does not have innocent bystanders. It was a literal assembly line of humans being lined up to be shot, to be hanged, or to be gassed to death by Zyklon-B. Remove the pest by any means necessary, spare no expense. Time is money, another day, another dollar. Now that it has happened, we as the international community know where the low bar sits. There it is for us all to look at – no shortage of documentation there. Today, we certainly have not lost our desire to dehumanise and kill off 'others'. But now there are rules. Theoretically, now we know better. You cannot simply wipe a population off the planet.

You send them to refugee camps, you put great effort into proving their lack of humanity or capacity for civility, you send them to re-education camps. If you bomb them you have to say you are bombing terrorists. Now you have to meticulously and carefully commit cultural genocide in order to get rid of those pesky others. Genocide today is hard work.

That is thanks, in no small part, to the efforts of activists and legal specialists who have shaped the post-war international order. Although they seem impotent, the United Nations, the Security Council, the International Criminal Court, the International Court of Justice, the Universal Declaration of Human Rights, the Genocide Convention, these are victories for humanity. Their failure was not in ill-conception, but in underestimating the true depravity us human being are more than capable of attaining. It is incorrect to think that we are in postnormal times and therefore genocide is an amplified part of this condition. Genocide is not postnormal. It is, as you will read in the following pages, very normal. It is a residual of the passing epoch that we have yet to cope with. It is a vestigial contradiction of modernity that we must seek to transcend. As we continue to navigate postnormal times, I hope that in arriving in the next epoch, whatever we may call it, that we can look back at 'Never Again' and experience the shame we should feel over our capacities as humans and dispel our prideful need for power, territory, and progress. Let us vow to be better to one another. Let us not waste this opportunity.

GENOCIDE, THEN AND NOW

Maha Sardar

In Spring 146 BC, Roman forces led by Scipio Aemilianus breached the walls of Carthage, spending the next seven days systematically destroying the city and killing its inhabitants; the small number who survived were sold into slavery. A decade on, the years 132 to 136 BC saw mass killings and starvations of the Jewish people in the province of Judea, as retribution for their revolt against Roman rule. By order of the emperor, Hadrian, the name of the province was changed from Judea to Syria-Palaestina, an effort to erase the bond between the Jews and the land. It seems to me that the human story has not changed much since then.

A millennium later, the armies of Genghis Khan set out to bring an end to the Tatar people, ordering the execution of their men and the sexual enslavement of their women. A few hundred years down the road the Spanish are wiping out the indigenous people of South America. The Americans are annihilating the Red Indians – the Wounded Knee massacre being the most noted. Move on a few hundred years and we find Americans massacring the Moros in the Philippines. The French are slaughtering the people of Algeria. The Portuguese are committing structurally determined mass violence in Mozambique. The British are committing massacre upon massacre throughout their empire. Hitler oversees the Holocaust in Europe.

More recently, we have the My Lai (America, again) massacre. The Hutu people in Rwanda kill every Tutsi they can. Daesh massacre and rape the Yazidi people. The Darfuris in Sudan endure twenty years and counting of systematic extermination, rape, forced transfer, and torture. And in Gaza the 'most moral army in the world', as described by the former Israeli Defence Minister, Avigdor Lieberman, and the current Prime Minister Benjamin Netanyahu, shows that its morality permits displacement, mass starvation, targeted killings of civilians, mass deaths of children, sexual violence, and the destruction of all means of life for an entire people.

Human history is plagued with stories of mass murder and exterminations. As an optimist, I think that the stories about people and societies recorded in the history books that I read growing up show an abiding good in the human spirit. What you might simply call humanity. But I am forced to admit that there is significant evidence that my optimism is misplaced. As my reading matured, I mulled over what stories tell us about what it means to be human. I was captivated by novels with evil characters – Iago of *Othello*, Richard III, Count Dracula, Professor Moriarty, Milady of *The Three Musketeers*, even Napoleon in *Animal Farm*. But this was balanced by Plato's *The Symposium* and *The Republic*. My copies of J S Mill's *On Liberty* and Voltaire's *Candide* were among my most thumbed and worn. Not to forget the humanity that one finds in Rumi's *Masnavi* or Attar's *Conference of the Birds*. But after visiting sites of genocides in Bosnia, Cambodia and others, and living through and learning about genocide in Rwanda and Myanmar, it is difficult to fathom that human beings can be reduced to such a level of barbarity that their humanity all but evaporates. I am horrified by the very idea that some humans think they are superior to others. Indeed, all humans are equal, 'but some are more equal than others' as Orwell put it.

Society after society has persuaded itself that the 'enemy' is less than human, and requires domination, humiliation, and ultimately annihilation. What causes one group to see another as lesser, as lacking even a minimum of human dignity; this impulse towards hatred, this willingness to degrade the other as subhuman, and so to justify its eradication? And, just as importantly, what can we do about it? How can we protect what are the most vulnerable groups across the globe – the minorities, the displaced, the refugees, the marginalised - from becoming the victims of genocide and other crimes against humanity? Thinking about these issues, I became fascinated with the notion of human rights, and the idea that there are certain rights inherent to all human beings, regardless of who they are. These enquiries ultimately led me to become a human rights lawyer. For me, human rights are not just a utopian and idealistic set of philosophical values. They are, or should be, practical constraints which protect humanity today from the worst transgressions of human dignity, and so maximise our collective ability to become fully human.

Origins

The United Nations' 1948 Declaration on Human Rights begins by recognising 'the inherent dignity and of the equal and inalienable rights of all members of the human family'. This is a social and political declaration as much as it is a legal one. One way in which the international community of states has sought to give it some force is by the imposition of a treaty of binding and enforceable international obligations. One such obligation is the prohibition on committing acts of genocide, today located in the 1948 Convention on the Prevention and Punishment of the Crime of Genocide.

Although genocide has its roots in the writings of Søren Kierkegaard, Friedrich Nietzsche, and Fyodor Dostoevsky, it was the horrors of the Second World War which led to focussed thinking. The term itself was the construct of one man, the Polish Jew and jurist Raphael Lemkin. He fused the Greek term *genos* (race or tribe) with the Latin suffix *cide* (killing) to make the modern word, *genocide*. In Lemkin's definition, genocide is 'the destruction of a nation or of an ethnic group' or, more precisely, 'a coordinated plan of different actions aiming at the destruction of essential foundations of life of national groups, with the aim of annihilating the groups themselves'.

Lemkin was explicit that while his term genocide was a 'new conception', it did not describe novel behaviour. As he put it, this was a 'new word, coined by the author to denote an old practice in its modern development'. Genocide, in Lemkin's conception, was aimed at the 'disintegration of the political and social institutions, of culture, language, national feelings, religion, and the economic existence of national groups, and the destruction of the personal security, liberty, health, dignity, and even the lives of the individuals belonging to such groups'. Interestingly, Lemkin himself was not wedded to the term genocide, but also proposed the term *ethnocide* as an equivalent alternative.

Lemkin's purpose was to break away from the conception of war as an act committed by states against one another, and to recognise that states at times waged war against peoples, not other states. He gave as examples, amongst others, the devastation of Carthage, the Roman destruction of Jerusalem, the Christian crusades, and the wars of Genghis Khan. While mass killings were of course part of Lemkin's conception of genocide, they were not its only component. Lemkin observed the political, cultural, economic, biological, physical, moral, and religious domination and subjugation of a people as all-encompassing elements of the term.

Writing, as he was, in the early 1940s, Lemkin's preoccupation was with the crimes of the Nazi state and its Holocaust in Europe. Part of his purpose was to give shape to, and pin down, what had previously been described, by Winston Churchill, as 'a crime without a name'. It is perhaps surprising then to know that genocide was not amongst the charges of which Nazi leaders were convicted at Nuremberg. Reference was made to the term in the indictment and in several of the prosecutors' speeches, but not in the Tribunal's statute or its final judgment. Nonetheless, the term quickly took root and was adopted by the UN General Assembly in 1948 on the Convention on the Prevention and Punishment of the Crime of Genocide. It was further promoted by thinkers such as French philosopher Jean-Paul Sartre, who in his 1968 book *On Genocide* represented the Vietnam War as a form of colonial genocide.

The Convention both prohibits acts of genocide, which it labels a 'crime under international law', and commits signatories to take steps 'to prevent and to punish' the commission of that crime. It defines the term 'genocide' as meaning any one of five identified acts 'committed with intent to destroy, in whole or in part, a national, ethnical, racial or religious group'. These five acts being (a) killing members of the group; (b) causing serious bodily or mental harm to members of the group; (c) deliberately inflicting on the group conditions of life calculated to bring about its physical destruction in whole or in part; (d) imposing measures intended to prevent births within the group; and (e) forcibly transferring children of the group to another group.

The main feature that distinguishes the criminal offence of genocide from those of crimes against humanity, war crimes, or other offences such as unlawful killing is the requirement to prove that the perpetrators possessed 'the intent to destroy, in whole or in part, a national, ethnical, racial or religious group'. The International Criminal Tribunal for the Former Yugoslavia (ICTY) and the International Criminal Tribunal for Rwanda (ICTR) have called this requirement genocide's special intent or *dolus specialis*. The ICTR, in the case of Rwanda, found that Mayor Joseph 'Kanyabashi's spoken words encouraging the population to search for the "enemy" and "clear bushes", being references to killing Tutsis, evidences Kanyabashi had the requisite intent to destroy, in whole or in part, the Tutsi ethnic group'. Similarly, in the case of Goran Jelisić, the Bosnian Serb war criminal who was found guilty of having committed crimes against humanity, the Appeals Chamber held that evidence that the defendant 'referred to a "plan" for eradicating (prominent Muslims)' and expressed a desire to 'cleanse… the extremist Muslims and balijas like one cleans the head of lice' provided a basis for a finding 'beyond a reasonable doubt' of intent to destroy the Muslim group in the town of Brčko.

The acts thus described are of such obvious abhorrence that the International Court of Justice (ICJ) has suggested that, even without the Genocide Convention, their prohibition would form part of the customary law of nations. They are universally and rightly considered one of the most – if not the most – heinous and unjustifiable acts that might be perpetrated by one group against another. Insofar as there is a hierarchy of crimes against humanity, genocide sits at its apex.

Politicisation

This classification of genocide as the worst of all crimes gives it a singular rhetorical force. An allegation of genocide is an allegation of a total departure from the norms that all of us, states and individuals, purport to value; it is an allegation of the abandonment of civilisation for barbarism. It is no wonder then that the decades since 1948 have seen accusations and rejections of genocide fall largely along political lines. States find it in their interests to highlight some incidents of mass violence as genocide, whilst minimising others. When military intervention wants justification, use of the term is encouraged; where there is no willingness to intervene, the term is discouraged.

Hence, the United Nations, conscious of the politicisation of the term, instructs its staff: 'It is extremely important that United Nations officials adhere to the correct usage of the term, for several reasons: (i) its frequent misuse in referring to large scale, grave crimes committed against particular populations; (ii) the emotive nature of the term and political sensitivity surrounding its use; and (iii) the potential legal implications associated with a determination of genocide. This note aims to provide guidance on the correct usage of the term "genocide" based primarily on legal rather than historical or factual considerations'. No legal term has caused more controversy.

Strive as the UN might, it is not possible to employ the term genocide without affording 'historical or factual considerations' a central role. Genocide is not a legal construct existing independently of fact and place; it is the label we give to describe real conduct, occurring inevitably in a particular historical and cultural context. Responsible use of the term can only be grounded in factual and historical awareness.

The UN's drive for a neutral and independent use of the term, though subject to its own faults, is nonetheless a welcome counterweight to the nakedly political way in which states use and misuse the term genocide. Before 1990, the Cold War's geopolitical dynamics (1945-1989) revealed the stark cynicism with which states approached allegations of genocide. As human rights scholars Paul Bartrop and Samuel Totten observe, 'the USA and USSR seemingly turned a blind eye when their allies committed genocide, and each was largely restrained from intervening in genocides outside their sphere of influence by the unstated but very real threat of retaliation from their superpower rival'. As a result, 'genocide was perpetrated almost with complete impunity during the Cold War period'. The United Nations, shackled by the prevailing realpolitik, proved largely ineffective in preventing genocide during this time.

Since then, the politicisation of genocide has only deepened, particularly as Gulf States and emerging industrial powers assert their growing geopolitical influence. The mass killing of around 300,000 Black Africans in Darfur by the Sudanese government during the 2000s was for years considered by many countries to be a 'conflict' rather than a 'genocide', despite the one-sided nature of this 'conflict' in terms of casualties and resources. In recent months, as the hostilities have reignited the UN Special Advisor of the Secretary-General on the Prevention of Genocide, Alice Wairimu Nderitu, said that in Darfur there are 'circumstances in which a genocide could be occurring or has occurred'. Arms sales continue to flow into Sudan from around the world to support Sudan's genocidal conduct, despite a UN embargo. To deny a genocide is taking place can be profitable for those who benefit from trade with its perpetrators.

Similarly, when the UN Human Rights Council voted not to debate China's treatment of the Uyghurs and other Turkic Muslims, China became emboldened, declaring it a 'victory'. Shamefully, many of the dissenting votes came from majority Muslim countries. Some states continue to maintain that China's treatment of the Uyghur ethnic minority does not amount to genocide – despite the mass arbitrary imprisonment of hundreds of thousands of members of the Uyghur ethnic minority in the Chinese region of Xinjiang, the demolition of half of the region's mosques and many important sacred sites, the sending of detained parents' children to orphanages, and intrusive mass surveillance.

An assessment by the United Nations OHCHR suggests that the Chinese regional authorities are explicitly committed to a policy of 'de-extremification', where 'primary expressions of extremification' include 'spreading religious fanaticism through irregular beards and name selection' – in other words, visible signs of Muslim religious identity. Human Rights Watch have given examples of China's stated policy goals of 'sinicising' Islam, which include ensuring that Uyghurs 'have correct views … on ethnicity, history and religion', forced sterilisations of Uyghur women, and their policy of detaining Uyghurs on a massive scale for arbitrary reasons including being born between certain years, having too many children or wearing a veil. This is clearly aimed at the forced assimilation and eventual extinction of the ethnic minority. It is difficult to see any justification, beyond political cynicism or wilful blindness, for attempts to defend this conduct as anything but genocide.

The second half of the twentieth century saw more clear incidences of genocides – in Cambodia, Bosnia, and Rwanda – each raising questions both about the definition and the response of the international community.

Cambodia

The massacre of Cambodian citizens conducted by the Khmer Rouge (1975–1979) provides a striking example of the difficulties posed by the definition of genocide. While the Convention applies to acts of destruction targeted against 'national, ethnical, racial or religious groups', it does not per se cover politically motivated mass violence. For that reason, the 'killing fields' of Cambodia were argued by some to constitute systematic political slaughter rather than a genocide. Although ethnic groups were targeted, there were also killings of Cambodians by other Cambodians, based on a perception of social class, who were deemed to be a threat to the incumbent Khmer Rouge, led by Pol Pot. It took until 2018 for this debate to be settled, when the Extraordinary Chambers in the Courts of Cambodia (ECCC, or more commonly called the Khmer Rouge Tribunal) began to make findings not just of war crimes, but of genocide, against the key perpetrators of the mass killings in Cambodia.

Despite attempts to avoid the label of 'genocide', the regime systematically exterminated up to three million people, specifically targeting intellectuals, the educated, ethnic Chinese, Vietnamese, and Cham Muslims—70 to 80 percent of whom were annihilated. While some might question why it matters what precise legal term we apply to these atrocities —whether 'genocide', 'crimes against humanity', 'war crimes', or violations of the Geneva Conventions—this labelling does matter. The defendants have persistently sought to deny the genocide charge, offering legal arguments to differentiate it from other crimes against humanity. For the victims, however, it is crucial that their suffering be recognised for what it truly was: not mere cruelty, but genocide—the deliberate targeting of a group deemed inferior.

Whatever the resolution of that debate, the example of Cambodia shows how far the international community's rhetoric and condemnation of genocide is so rarely matched by action. It took the international community almost thirty years to act despite reports of the massacres reaching the outside world. As early as 1973, the US consul in Cambodia reported villages being wiped out, information that reached Washington in 1974. In that report, Kenneth Quinn, a US foreign service officer, likened the Khmer Rouge's programs to those of Nazi Germany and the Soviet Union. Cambodian refugees in Vietnam reported genocidal acts to Charles Twining of the US embassy in Thailand, detailing mass executions by teenage boys using garden tools, starvation of children, and asphyxiation of Buddhist monks.

Having failed to take steps to prevent, or even limit, the genocide, the UN belatedly stepped in to assist its punishment, supporting the Cambodian government in creating the ECCC to investigate the mass murders. Although Pol Pot himself escaped conviction by the expedient of dying before he could be charged (a popular routine of dictators, followed also by Chilean military dictator Augusto Pinochet in 2006), nine individuals ultimately faced indictment, with only five of those cases then reaching the ECCC, and just three leading to convictions. Even in what we might today call a quintessential image of genocide, conceptual complexities, legal difficulties, and the snail pace of international action have all collaborated to frustrate recognition and punishment of the perpetrators.

It is easy to become entangled in legal intricacies and overlook the profound human realities that these legal frameworks are designed to protect. Just 17 kilometres from Cambodia's capital, Phnom Penh, lies Choeung Ek, once a tranquil longan orchard. Before 1975, this orchard must have been a peaceful expanse of greenery and fruit-bearing trees. The site still exudes a certain serenity, with its lush trees still bearing longan fruit. But this calm is tainted by the chilling truth that in 1975, this orchard was transformed into the infamous 'killing fields' of the Khmer Rouge, where thousands were buried in mass graves. An orchard one day, a graveyard the next. From 1975 onwards, over 17,000 people—men, women, and children—were executed or buried here, their lives brutally cut short by the Khmer Rouge's merciless pursuit of ideological purity. When I visited in 2017, I stood before the towering stupa filled with the skulls of the victims. The earth itself continues to yield bones as it shifts.

Bosnia

A little over a decade after the Cambodian genocide, the world saw in the early 1990s ethnic cleansing in Bosnia, another grim chapter in human history. The path to genocide (1992-1995) began with restrictions on employment, free assembly, and communication for ethnic groups. This escalated into a systematic, state-sanctioned and driven campaign to eliminate the targeted populations. Croats and Muslims were interned in concentration camps and starved, with 100,000 Bosnians murdered within a year. Those expelled from the territory commonly faced rape and murder; some victims were dismembered with chain saws. The atrocities in Bosnia received extensive and graphic coverage in the West but despite the global awareness, international intervention was sorely lacking.

A feeble UN Protection Force was eventually positioned in Bosnia to protect non-Serbian Bosnians. They failed spectacularly in their mission. The height of the atrocities was the massacre in Srebrenica, where around 8,000 Bosnian Muslims (mainly boys and men) were murdered by the Army of Republika Srpska (VRS) under the command of General Ratko Mladić. They were 'raped and bayoneted, throats cut and shot. The killings were systematic, men were separated from women: the women were raped then killed'.

The International Criminal Tribunal for the former Yugoslavia (ICTY), established in 1993 to prosecute war crimes committed during the Yugoslav Wars, determined in 2001 that the Srebrenica killings, compounded by the mass expulsion of Bosniak civilians, constituted genocide. The same conclusion was reached by the International Court of Justice in 2007. Senior officers in the Bosnian Serb army bore the brunt of the responsibility. However, the UN and its Western allies also shouldered some blame for failing to protect the Bosniak population in Srebrenica, designated a 'safe area' by the UN Security Council in 1993. In a critical review in 1999, UN Secretary-General Kofi Annan admitted, 'through error, misjudgement and an inability to recognise the scope of the evil confronting us, we failed to do our part to help save the people of Srebrenica from the (Bosnian) Serb campaign of mass murder'.

Once again, the international community moves itself to condemn genocide only long after the atrocities have unfolded yet stands idle while the horrors are being committed. The UN's retrospective on its own failures serves as a grim postmortem not only of its actions but also of those who perished as a consequence.

In Sarajevo, a little north of the Latin Bridge there is in an old warehouse, a Museum of Crimes Against Humanity and Genocide, established in 2016. I visited recently, during a trip to the city. The first room provides an overview of Yugoslavia's disintegration, laying the groundwork for the horror that followed. Deeper into the museum, the exhibits became personal: a worn jacket, a guitar, a little girl's shoes — each item a silent witness to the lives that were abruptly shattered. The implements of torture, firsthand journals recording the descent into brutality; all are testament here of what passed in Bosnia in the early 1990s. But this genocide is not lost to the depths of time, surviving only in the archaeologist's perspective, of tales teased out of stationary objects. The museum is not only a host of objects, but shows videos of the bombing of Mostar, recording forever the motion of human destruction.

The museum's latest addition, *Footsteps of Those Who Did (Not) Cross* displays personal belongings of those who were killed by Bosnian Serb forces in July 1995, alongside items from survivors. It holds hundreds of pieces of footwear found along the treacherous route from Srebrenica to Nezuk, also known as the 'march of death'. These shoes were worn by boys and men, walking towards what they hoped was safety, only to be met with massacre. It is the story of the Bosnian genocide, but also of countless other slaughters perpetrated by one race against another.

These vigils are critical, offering a moment for people to pause, reflect, and honour the dead. In Bosnia, remembering serves not just to preserve the past, but as a defence against those who would manipulate history for their own ends. As I wandered through Sarajevo, I saw signs declaring, 'we must not forget' plastered across a city still physically and emotionally scarred by the trauma of genocide. The city's cry, a desperate plea from a community abandoned by the world, is a powerful reminder that their suffering must never be erased. As Elif Shafak poignantly expressed, 'not to be able to tell your story, to be silenced and shut out, therefore is to be dehumanised'. Bosnia, like Germany, bans the denial of its genocide. Certain strains of humanity, if allowed to prosper, will not flinch from the horrors of the past, but embrace them as their own.

Rwanda

When Belgium withdrew from Rwanda in 1962, it left behind two rival tribes: the majority Hutu and the minority Tutsi. In April 1994, the aircraft carrying Rwanda's president, a Hutu, was shot down in the air. The president – Juvénal Habyarimana – died, along with every other passenger. From this spark blazed what we today call the Rwandan genocide (7 April – 19 July 1994), with 800,000 Tutsi and moderate Hutus brutally killed: 'raped, mutilated, and slaughtered with grenades and machetes. In many cases, they were herded into churches and hacked to death'. Of these deaths, around 500,000 were Tutsi – about 77 percent of their total population.

In the early days, reporting of the events in Rwanda dismissed the genocide as fighting between rival tribal factions. The warning signs were there. Both Rwandan and international human rights organisations forewarned of the upcoming genocide, as did state diplomats. Canadian General Romeo Dallaire, head of the UN peacekeeping force, sent daily warnings of the genocide to the UN, but they were ignored. France, Belgium, and the US evacuated their citizens but refused to help the Tutsi survivors.

Early and decisive international intervention could have stopped the genocide, but global leaders rejected this option. Archives released by Human Rights Watch depict how international leaders for weeks declined to use their political and moral authority to challenge the legitimacy of the genocidal government in Rwanda. No action was taken to limit the radio programmes used to incite Hutu to slaughter.

In stark contrast to the Cambodian genocide, where the US freely made accusations of genocide, in the case of Rwanda, as Eric A. Heinze explained in a 2007 article in *Political Science Quarterly*, 'US officials went to great lengths in the semantical charade to avoid the rhetoric of genocide'. And, as an American official wrote in a 1994 briefing on Rwanda: 'be careful. … Genocide finding could commit USG [the United States Government] to "do something"'. Admit that a genocide is ongoing, and you must surely act to do something about it – if not military intervention, then at least an embargo or trade sanctions – both as a matter of law and basic humanity. In international law, where the principal actors are not individuals, but national governments with obligations to their own people (and sometimes their own pockets), justice takes a back seat to self-interest.

Eventually, once the genocide was committed and hundreds of thousands already dead, the UN Security Council in 1994 created the International Criminal Tribunal for Rwanda (ICTR), which indicted ninety-three people. The first conviction issued by the Tribunal came on 2 September 1998. Among those eventually convicted were Jean-Paul Akayesu, a former mayor, and Jean Kambanda, the former Rwandan Prime Minister. The conviction of Akayesu marked 'the first in which an international tribunal was called upon to interpret the definition of genocide as defined in the Convention for the Prevention and Punishment of the Crime of Genocide'. This was a hollow victory for a society that was already left devastated and traumatised by genocide.

Gaza

And now, against this horrific background, we must ask: is Israel's conduct in Gaza a 'war' or genocide?

At the very least, it is uncontroversial to say that since October 2023 the world has witnessed unimaginable scenes of horror taking place in Gaza. Parents clinging onto their headless children's bodies. Dusty grey corpses pulled out of rubble. Generations of families wiped out instantly. Children with sniper wounds to their head and hearts. Charred and limbless corpses. Mass graves. As Philippe Lazzarini, Commissioner-General of the United Nations Relief and Works Agency for Palestine Refugees in the Near East (UNRWA), put it: this war 'broke all the superlatives'.

The official estimate of the Palestinian health authorities by 10 September 2024 was that more than 41,000 people had been killed, with another 10,000 missing and more than 95,000 injured. About 40 percent of all those killed have been children. Those not killed by air strikes face famine and starvation. Taking account of these second order effects of war, medical professionals have estimated that the true death toll is likely to be orders of magnitude above the current official figures. The authoritative journal *The Lancet* estimates that if we include unidentified deaths, deaths by starvation, and 'slow deaths', the total figure could be 186,000. Not only life has been rendered terrifyingly fragile, so has infrastructure. More than 70 percent of Gaza's houses have been destroyed, along with every one of its universities and the majority of its schools and hospitals.

Israel has, in the course of proceedings against it in the International Court of Justice (ICJ), acknowledged what it calls 'humanitarian suffering' in Gaza, and 'tragic and agonizing civilian casualties'. The ICJ, when ordering interim measures to protect the population in Gaza on 26 January 2024, described the situation as 'catastrophic', noting that 'many Palestinians in the Gaza Strip have no access to the most basic foodstuffs, potable water, electricity, essential medicines or heating'. It reiterated that message again on 28 March 2024 and 24 May 2024, each time indicating further interim measures, and observing 'the worsening conditions of life faced by Palestinians in Gaza, in particular the spread of famine and starvation'. Israel's case in the interim relief proceedings has been that these are the regrettable and inevitable consequences of 'urban warfare against a genocidal terrorist organization', and it has done everything it can realistically do to mitigate it. It is not, therefore, difficult to say that the result of Israel's war in Gaza has generated conditions antithetical to human life.

The controversy is over the 'intent' component of the genocide definition, that is whether Israel is carrying out its war with the intent of achieving the total destruction of Gaza's population. For Israel and its supporters, it is both absurd, offensive even, to accuse the world's only Jewish state of genocide. The former UK Prime Minister, Rishi Sunak, suggested that there was a 'horrific irony' in the ICJ ruling against Israel on interim measures to prevent genocide. The implication was that it was unthinkable even to suggest that Israel's conduct might be characterised in this way. For this outrage in its purest form, one need look no further than Israel's submissions to the court in the ICJ's proceedings. South Africa's case is not only, in Israel's pleading, unjustified and wrong, but is 'outrageous', 'bellicose and offensive' and a 'morally untenable attempt to prevent Israel from exercising its inherent right to defend itself', by a state seeking to support 'its ally Hamas' via 'shrill' submissions.

Outside the proceedings, Israel openly accuses the court of antisemitism for daring to entertain, let alone agree with, South Africa's submissions. In response to the ICJ's recent decision, in separate proceedings to the genocide case, that Israeli policies and conduct in the Occupied Palestinian Territory amount to systemic discrimination and apartheid, the chairman of Israel's Foreign Affairs and Security Committee decried the court was 'hijacked by Islamists and their supporters' and 'turned from a court of justice into a court of empowering and encouraging terrorism'.

There is ample evidence to support South Africa's case that what Israel is carrying out is not a programme of legitimate self-defence in response to the atrocities of 7 October 2023 but a campaign of genocide. As it was put by Irfan Galaria, an American doctor who worked in Gaza delivering aid in January 2024, what is happening in Gaza is 'not war – it was annihilation'. When a state makes impossible demands of civilians to evacuate from northern to southern Gaza on foot within twenty-four hours, only to then proceed anyway to bomb the areas to which evacuees were sent and were told were safe; when a state cuts off all but token access to aid and resources, even in defiance of ICJ orders; when a state destroys the infrastructure necessary for the maintenance of society, in schools, hospitals, universities, government buildings, water facilities; when a state targets NGO aid deliveries; when soldiers film themselves shooting children playing football and roaming houses to destroy possessions of civilians; when all of this is what Israel and its soldiers are doing, the simplest explanation is that its war is driven by the singular intent to destroy the Palestinian people in Gaza.

But the accusation of genocidal intent does not need to rest just on inference. There is example after example of Israeli officials, soldiers and prominent civilians making clear their attitude towards the Palestinian people in Gaza. On 4 November 2023, an Israeli army general stated in a public video that whoever 'returns here, if they return here after, will find scorched earth. No houses, no agriculture, no nothing. They have no future'. Israeli army soldiers have been filmed in December 2023 chanting may 'their village burn, may Gaza be erased', that 'there are no uninvolved civilians', and that they were there to 'wipe off the seed of Amalek'. That last chant followed from Benjamin Netanyahu's statements, both publicly and in letters sent to members of the armed forces, likening the conflict to that between the Biblical Israelites and the Amaleks, where the Israelites set out to 'spare no one, but kill alike men and women, infants and sucklings, oxen and sheep, camels and asses'.

This rhetoric of total eradication does not arise in isolation but must be seen in the context of Israel's treatment of the Palestinian people over the past hundred years, rightly recognised by Amnesty International in 2022, and by the ICJ in 2024, as apartheid. Israel's protestation that its leaders and soldiers' words are taken out of context, or that it is doing everything it can to minimise civilian casualties and suffering, would be absurd in any event, in the face of the mounting evidence. In the context of apartheid and decades of illegal settlements seeking to drive the Palestinians out of their land, they represent a perverse distortion of reality.

Israel's attempt to paint the accusations against it as antisemitic notwithstanding, many human rights experts have used the word genocide without hesitation. Francesca Albanese, the UN Special Rapporteur, asserted that there are 'reasonable grounds to believe that the threshold indicating the commission of the crime of genocide against Palestinians as a group in Gaza has been met'. The director of the New York office of the

UN's High Commissioner for Human Rights, who resigned in protest at the inadequacy of the UN's response to events in Gaza, termed the Gaza crisis as a 'textbook genocide'. On 14 January 2024, the Special Rapporteur on the Right to Health, Tlaleng Mofokeng, characterised Israel's occupation as 'genocidal'. On 27 February 2024, Michael Fakhri, the UN Special Rapporteur on the Right to Food, declared that Israel is 'intentionally' starving Palestinians, describing it as 'a situation of genocide'.

A comprehensive legal analysis was recently published by the University Network for Human Rights, a coalition of universities and academics who examined Israel's actions since 7 October 2023 in their historical context. The report unequivocally concludes that 'Israel's actions in and regarding Gaza since October 7, 2023, violate the Genocide Convention. Specifically, Israel has committed genocidal acts of killing, causing serious harm to, and inflicting conditions of life calculated to bring about the physical destruction of Palestinians in Gaza, a protected group that forms a substantial part of the Palestinian people'.

Israel of course still has its defenders. American President Joe Biden has refused to acknowledge that Israel is committing genocide. Germany likewise remains steadfast in its support of Israel, with German Foreign Minister Annalena Baerbock proclaiming 'in these days we are all Israelis'. Rishi Sunak did not elaborate on why he considered it a 'horrific irony' for Israel to be accused of genocide. Presumably he had in mind the misplaced notion that, the term genocide having been coined to describe the treatment of the Jewish people, it is inconceivable that the Jewish state (as Israel describes itself in its Declaration of Independence) could itself ever be guilty of that crime. The sinned against, it is suggested, do not sin themselves. But, as the British journalist James Butler observes 'it is a sad but abundant historical irony that past oppression can be invoked as a guarantor of moral righteousness, a permanent exculpation, once power is finally attained'. If there is any irony here, it is in the perpetration of genocide, not its accusation.

Notable and respected legal personalities in the UK have spoken out repeatedly to defend Israel's actions as legitimate self-defence. However, the evidence for genocide is overwhelming. But the defence of Israel, and turning a blind eye to genocide, is an ideological stance. Nothing will persuade an ideologue to acknowledge what is unfolding in front of their eyes. As the *Guardian* columnist Arwa Mahdawi asks:

> Would video evidence of a Palestinian being raped by Israeli soldiers at Sde Teiman, a military prison that resembles a torture camp, make any difference?… that's no biggie…

> How about reports from US doctors that Israeli snipers are shooting Palestinian children in the head while they play in the street? This isn't something that highly trained snipers can accidentally do — it is seemingly deliberate. But again: not a big deal…How about the videos on social media of Palestinian children with their heads blown to bits by US-made weapons? Or the recent video of a little girl killed by shrapnel while rollerblading in northern Gaza, still wearing her pink rollerblades when pronounced dead? The videos of Israeli soldiers burning copies of the Qur'an and desecrating mosques? Again: nothing here so disturbing that it stops the members of the Biden administration from sleeping at night.

Similar conclusions have been expressed in op ed pieces in the respectable Israeli left-wing newspaper *Haaretz*, or in the reports and documents by B'Tselem, the Israeli Information Centre for Human Rights. In a recent opinion piece in *Haaretz*, Israeli journalist and author Gideon Levy laments that 'Israel is turning, with alarming speed, into a country that lives on blood. The daily crimes of the occupation are already less relevant. Over the past year, a new reality of mass killing and crimes of an entirely different scale has emerged. We are in a genocidal reality; the blood of tens of thousands of people has flowed'. He concludes, 'this is genocide, even if it does not meet the legal definition'. The spirit of 'Jewish supremacy', notes another *Haaretz* opinion piece, is alive in 'mainstream Israel'; 'Israeli's Dehumanization of the Palestinians has reached a new height', says another.

'Social death'

Dehumanisation is the keyword here. The genesis of genocide is often dehumanisation—the systematic stripping away of the human qualities of a person or group. This process is not just a harbinger but a crucial instrument in the execution of genocide. By denying the humanity of the targeted group, perpetrators create a moral and psychological framework that justifies and facilitates extreme acts of violence and brutality.

Historically, both propaganda and discriminatory policies have been central in dehumanising those marked for extermination. During the Holocaust, Nazi propaganda grotesquely portrayed Jews as 'vermin' and 'subhuman', cultivating widespread hatred that paved the way for their systematic annihilation. In Rwanda, the Hutu extremist radio station RTLM referred to Tutsis as 'cockroaches', inciting ordinary citizens to partake in the mass slaughter. The International Criminal Tribunal for Rwanda, in its judgment against Kayishema and Ruzindana, for example, considered derogatory language in its assessment of intent: utterances by the Defendant that referred to Tutsis as *inyenzi* ('cockroach'), 'dirt . . . to be removed', and 'Tutsi dogs', constituted evidence of specific intent to commit genocide. In contemporary times, troubling echoes of this dehumanisation are heard in Israel, where the Defence Minister describes Palestinians as 'human animals' and the Heritage Minister, mooting the possibility of using nuclear weaponry in Gaza, talks of the 'monsters in Gaza'.

This attitude of dehumanisation does not spring up out of nowhere. It is the result of decades, sometimes centuries, of 'othering', from the levels of high policy to everyday cultural content. Where Hollywood presents Arabs as consistently villainous, often a threat to society or connected to terrorism, this is both a symptom of, and cyclically contributes to, the dehumanisation of the group. Nor are these attitudes limited to fiction. One need only compare the reporting of many western media outlets on the war in Ukraine with their reporting on Afghanistan, both the capture of the country by the Taliban and the plight of the refugees thus engendered. The attempt of some journalists to justify this by explaining that Ukrainians, unlike Afghans, are 'civilised' and 'look like us', was grossly offensive but unsurprising. So, when Israeli officials call for 'total annihilation' of Gaza, talking of a battle of 'civilisation against barbarism', dehumanisation rings in every word.

Dehumanisation strips individuals of their humanity, making it easier for perpetrators to justify and carry out mass killings. Often it is most immediately apparent in the rhetoric used by one group about another. But dehumanisation can also manifest through bureaucratic and systematic measures that reduce individuals to mere statistics or objects, eventually banished to a 'social death'. The theory of 'social death,' coined by sociologist Orlando Patterson, provides a profound perspective through which to understand the mechanisms and consequences of genocide. 'Social death' refers to the condition in which a group of people is systematically excluded from the social fabric of society and deprived of their identity, community, and humanity. It is the idea that someone can be identified and treated as if they are ontologically deficient; they are not seen as being 'fully human'.

Thus, a genocidal society cannot be understood through the lens of rational self-interest. The Chinese state is not meaningfully threatened by Uyghur groups, even from the small terrorist organisations responsible for some attacks in the first years of the twenty-first century. Rather, the presence of bearded, visibly Muslim men who are still Chinese citizens threatens the highly curated psychic space of Chinese political discourse, the idea of a unified national society. In the same way, the population of Gaza seems to represent a threat to the psychic space of Israeli public discourse, at least in terms of the pronouncements and anxieties of its government. As the Palestinian writer Raja Shehadeh states, 'the very high human and material cost of the war in Gaza proves that what Israel fears from Palestine is Palestine's very existence'. The destruction of Palestinian life serves to demonstrate the power of the Israeli state, enforcing 'social death' as a means to reinforce the stability of a threatened social structure.

All of this is nothing new. In 1290, when Edward I published a decree requiring the expulsion of all Jews from the Kingdom of England, he did so in a society which demonised and dehumanised Jews as ritualistic child murderers, as an 'alien, evil, antisocial, and anti-human creature, essentially subhuman'. The Atlantic slave trade justified itself via its conception of African slaves as a mentally inferior variety of humanity. The Nazis portrayed Jews as rats, lice, cockroaches, foxes, and vultures, incapable of ordinary human feeling. US soldiers in Abu Ghraib tortured, raped, and desecrated Iraqi prisoners, treated them like dogs, dragging them about on leashes or piling them naked together, and then posing behind them with a beaming grin.

The capacity to reduce the perceived 'other' to object or animal – less than animal even – seems a constant feature of human nature.

Coda

Reflecting on the current situation in Gaza, I was struck by a poignant line from Alex Garland's recent film *Civil War*, where Lee Smith, a war photographer, laments: 'every time I survived a war zone, I thought I was sending a warning home, "Don't do this", but here we are'. This sentiment mirrors the grim reality of the genocide in Gaza. Despite the harrowing lessons of history, the world continues to witness the systematic persecution and mass murder of populations. The only 'lessons learnt' from what has come before seems to be the ease with which states can dissemble and distort reality to avoid confronting what is happening before their eyes.

Genocide stands at the very pinnacle of crimes against humanity. There is no more heinous act, in the international plane, than the targeted and systematic destruction of a people. But the moral righteousness that western states wear so easily when (rightly) condemning Russia's actions in Ukraine, to the point of accusing Russia of genocide (Ukraine's case against Russia in the ICJ is supported by the US and UK among others), becomes unthinkable when the perpetrator of genocide is their ally. The events of Bosnia, Rwanda, Cambodia, and many others are a stark reminder of the catastrophic consequences of delayed international intervention. We must not stand by idly as passive observers. We cannot complain that we did not know what was happening; each day brings a relentless stream of horror and destruction, instantly broadcasted through social media reels. Genocide is being live streamed before our eyes.

The warning signs have long been there, echoing through the rhetoric of Israel's leadership. This ideological drive to erase Palestinian life is a tragic manifestation of the use of the 'socially dead' to bolster the stability of a threatened social structure. The idea that the wholesale destruction of Palestinian lives, as nothing more than state power acting in self-defence, is a chilling reflection of this genocidal intent.

The international community is rising. Mass protests in support of Palestine continue to take place; students are protesting on university campuses demanding disinvestment from Israel; people are boycotting brands that support Israel; there is mounting evidence and a growing chorus of respected international human rights lawyers, academics, and experts who have labelled the atrocities in Gaza as genocide. Even the editors of Wikipedia voted in favour of renaming an entry 'Gaza genocide' removing the words 'allegations of'. But the wheels of international justice turn slowly. We await the final determination of South Africa's case against Israel at the ICJ, a process that could take years. Meanwhile, the suffering continues, unabated.

Those speaking out against Israel's actions do so at their own peril. In an era where dissent is often met with vilification, smear campaigns, and, in some cases, legal repercussions, the courage required to speak truth to power has never been more evident. Activists, journalists, lawyers, and even politicians who dare to condemn the atrocities are frequently labelled as antisemitic or accused of undermining national security. This alarming effect is not only a barrier to free speech but also a dangerous obstacle to justice. The voices of those who bear witness to the suffering and call out the injustice are vital in breaking through the narrative that seeks to justify or obscure the realities on the ground. Yet, these voices are often drowned out by a campaign to delegitimise their concerns. Despite this, the rising global outcry, seen in mass protests, campus movements, and legal challenges, serves as a testament to the growing recognition that what is happening in Gaza cannot be ignored or excused.

The tragedy in Gaza is not just a moment in time but a devastating chapter in the ongoing story of human cruelty. The international community's failure to act decisively would be a betrayal of what are meant to be its fundamental and universal principles. The haunting images and stories from Gaza, Sudan, Myanmar (and many more) should serve as a dire warning: genocide is not a relic of the past to be reflected upon in a museum or memorial after the fact. From the times of the Romans, it has been a continuous present and urgent danger.

It is time we write a different human story.

THE POLITICS OF GENOCIDE

Martin Shaw

The Israeli destruction of Gaza has returned the world's focus to the idea of 'genocide'. South Africa has brought a case against Israel to the International Court of Justice (ICJ), under the Genocide Convention, and while the court will not come to a final ruling on this for some time, it said in January 2024 that there were 'plausible' risks of genocidal harm to Palestinians in Gaza, and has since issued a series of instructions to prevent this. Israel has largely ignored these, instead continuing to kill and starve the civilian population, but the Gazans' suffering and the plausibility of the genocide charge are having political consequences. The credibility of the West's claim to stand for a 'rules-based' world order has been severely damaged in the eyes of the rest of the world as well as of many within the West itself.

Muslims have naturally been among those outspoken about the suffering of their coreligionists, and for some Gaza may appear to fit a pattern of Muslim victimhood, alongside the harm being inflicted by the Chinese regime on the Uyghurs, by the Myanmar military on the Rohingya and, not so long ago, by Serbian nationalists on Bosniaks and Kosovars. Does this mean Muslims are particularly prone to having genocide committed against them, or is there a more complex pattern in which Muslims are sometimes the perpetrators as well as the victims of genocide? What, indeed, is the definition of genocide that would enable us to answer these questions?

The term 'genocide' was coined in 1944 by Raphael Lemkin, a Polish Jewish lawyer, to describe the deliberate destruction of ethnic and national groups. Although later it was often equated with the Nazis' extermination of European Jews, Lemkin saw the idea as describing the 'crippling' of groups and societies as well as the killing of their individual members, and he applied it widely to Nazi policies towards the occupied peoples of Europe during the Second World War.

Lemkin's goal was for the emerging United Nations to adopt a law prohibiting the deliberate destruction of peoples, and remarkably this was achieved with the adoption of the Genocide Convention in 1948. This document defined the crime of genocide as certain acts 'committed with intent to destroy, in whole or in part, a national, ethnical, racial or religious group, as such'. The acts included not only killing or physically harming members of a group, but also 'deliberately inflicting on the group conditions of life calculated to bring about its physical destruction in whole or in part'.

While it is valuable that the chief prosecutor of the International Criminal Court (ICC) is seeking to indict Israel's leaders for war crimes and crimes against humanity, Lemkin's rationale insists that genocide should be the primary framework within which to analyze their acts. For Lemkin, the perpetrators' *overall* policy towards the target population is as important as their specific crimes. 'Taken separately,' he suggests, 'all these acts are punishable in the respective codes; considered together, however, they should constitute offences against the law of nations by reason of their common feature which is to endanger both the existence of the collectivity concerned and the entire social order.'

From this perspective, the comprehensive harm of the kind we see in Gaza (killing, wounding, torturing and starving people, and destroying hospitals and schools, and so on) raises a question beyond that of which excessive military tactics might constitute specific crimes. It raises the question of whether the perpetrator state or armed group has a *general* policy that regards the civilian population as an enemy to be destroyed. This conclusion, with regard to Gaza, would be difficult to avoid, based on the evidence – even if Israeli leaders had not frequently proclaimed exactly that general genocidal intention. Moreover, although the Convention specifies that genocide is a crime 'whether committed in time of peace or in time of war', it is noteworthy that Lemkin originally analysed it as a policy not only of war, but also of military occupation – which, from a legal point of view, is what Israel has maintained in Gaza as well as the West Bank since 1967.

The scope of genocide remains, of course, contested, with many tying it narrowly to mass killing and extermination. There is a tension in the Convention between the idea of genocide as the destruction of a society, including its social organisation and culture, and the specific emphasis on 'physical' destruction in one key clause. However, as Israel has clearly aimed since October 2023 to destroy Gaza, in the sense of crippling its society and reducing its people to a state of helplessness, and since it has used both direct killing and starvation to achieve this, its actions appear well within the scope of the legal definition. In this context, the permanent expulsion of the surviving population from northern Gaza, which Israel began to carry out in late 2024, constitutes another method of the ongoing genocide.

It is difficult not to be shocked by the growing chasm between, on the one hand, the two international courts' attempts to apply international law to Israel's assault, and on the other, the attitudes of Western governments. The United States has sought to discredit the activities of both courts – with some in Congress even attempting to sanction the ICC prosecutor – and the soon-to-be-indicted war criminal Benjamin Netanyahu received standing ovations when he addressed a joint session of Congress. Meanwhile both the United Kingdom and Germany intervened to prevent judges issuing the warrants the prosecutor has requested, although the new UK government has withdrawn its intervention. Most Western states have also ignored, if they have not actively opposed, the interim measures adopted by the ICJ in the genocide case.

The situation is hardly unexpected. The Gaza genocide has not arisen out of the blue, but is the culmination of what historian Rashid Khalidi has called 'the hundred years' war on Palestine'. Once the Zionist movement first promoted systematic settlement in Palestine in the early years of the twentieth century, with a view to establishing a Jewish state, and certainly since the British government's Balfour Declaration in 1917, it became increasingly apparent that Zionism posed an existential threat to Palestinian Arab society. Indeed, Zionists soon proposed 'transferring' the Palestinians to other Arab lands in order to eliminate them from Palestine – an incipiently genocidal idea, even if the term for it had not yet been invented.

Both Britain, as the mandatory power in Palestine until 1947, and the UN itself in that year's partition plan, played a part in creating the situation in which Israel forced the majority of Palestinians out of the territory it conquered in the 1948 war. It can be argued that this forced removal, accomplished through massacres which terrorised the population into flight as well as by a determined refusal to allow most to return, was a process of genocide – since the Zionists forcibly destroyed the existing Arab society – and that the term 'ethnic cleansing', now sometimes used as a description of this, is euphemistic.

Though the Genocide Convention was being drafted during the very months in which the Palestinians were being forced out, attempts to raise the plight of the Palestinian population were unsuccessful. Indeed, the forced removal of populations was deliberately excluded from the means of genocide listed in the Convention, and not only because of Palestine. In 1947–48, the British were also overseeing a much larger and even more disastrous partition in India, where millions were forced to move, and hundreds of thousands of Muslims, Sikhs, and Hindus were killed by militia linked to rival Indian and proto-Pakistani nationalist parties as they sought to assert control over newly designated borderlands. Meanwhile, the USSR ratified its wartime mass expulsions of Chechens and others 'in perpetuity' only two weeks before voting for the Convention. Czechoslovakia, Poland, and Yugoslavia were expelling millions of German civilians from their territories at the same time.

Therefore, forced removal – the prime means by which ethnic and national groups were being deliberately destroyed in the late 1940s – was consciously omitted from the convention designed to prevent the deliberate destruction of such groups. Even Lemkin, who was lobbying for the Genocide Convention, did not want the ongoing expulsions to interfere with its adoption. Not surprisingly, therefore, there were soon signs that the great powers who drove its adoption did not regard it as applying to themselves or their allies. As the USSR and the Western states were already engaged in the opening stages of the Cold War, this meant that the Convention was largely stillborn, and the international criminal court that was envisaged to enforce it was not created for another half century.

Given this historical background, it is not surprising that the Gaza genocide has failed to force the hands of Western governments, even if it has embarrassed them and exacted some political costs, particularly from centre-left leaders. Israel-Palestine may be a tiny place with a very modest population, but its symbolic significance has been magnified through three quarters of a century of conflict. Over this period, the US and major European states have staunchly supported Israel and their media and public spheres have been thoroughly permeated with ideas prioritising Israeli security concerns over the Palestinians' demands for justice. The Hamas attack on southern Israel on 7 October 2023, with its brutal civilian hostage-taking and killing, was in this sense perfectly primed to reinforce pro-Israeli orientations in Western governments and elites. It is actually more surprising that some Western states – like Spain, Norway, and Ireland – have moved substantially towards a pro-Palestinian position in the last nine months than that the major players have not.

However, the politics of genocide cut more than one way. If the refusal of Western governments to challenge Israel's criminal assault on Gaza exposed their hypocrisy – since they had backed Ukraine against Russia's comparable attack, and Biden even called it 'genocide' – so the failure of many of Israel's critics to challenge Russia suggests a comparable problem. Even South Africa, hero of the Global South and international law when it comes to Palestine, is compromised on Ukraine, with the historic links of its liberation movement to the former Soviet Union apparently counting in favour of Putin. Yet in Mariupol, Ukraine had experienced something like Gaza, in the service of a (re)colonisation project broadly comparable to Israel's in Palestine.

Likewise, the reluctance of some critics of Israel – not only in governments, but also in Palestine solidarity movements – to address the brutality of Hamas's assault only reinforces the idea that 'genocide' is a purely political construct, not an objective standard for law, morality, and politics. Ironically, Israel itself was reluctant to label Hamas's killings genocide, we can only assume because they perceived that this would open the door for accusations about their own much greater onslaught. Only when defending Israel against South Africa's charge in the ICJ did its representatives actually say that, if anyone had committed genocide, it was Hamas.

Indeed, in order to understand genocide in this case we need to grasp it as a dialectical process. Zionist colonisation, like many other settler-colonial projects, had set up a potential for genocide in Palestine; the Nakba had partially actualised that; and Israel's ongoing dispossession of Palestinians and – according to the ICJ in July 2024 – increasing 'annexation' of their territory extended this Nakba, even as extreme-right ministers openly proclaimed their intention to complete it through the forcible removal of more Palestinians. In this sense, Israel had set up a genocidal *structure* in its relations with Palestinians, and Hamas, rather than pushing back against this structure, embraced it, carrying out its own genocidal massacres of civilians in the kibbutzim and music festival of Israel's south. Although there was an unplanned, demotic element in some of the killing – as there has been in Israel's – the evidence is that – also as in the Israeli case – the genocidal drive came from the leadership.

Accounting for the atrocities of Hamas (and the other armed Palestinian groups that joined it on the seventh of October) is not only necessary for an adequate response to Israel's genocide, it is also necessary for *understanding* it. The murderousness and callousness of the Israeli government and army in Gaza, apparently supported by most of the Israeli population, is a direct response to the brutality and humiliation that Israel experienced at Hamas' hands, which continues to have major consequences. To those of us who study genocides, this is a familiar pattern – especially in colonial situations, they are often 'countergenocidal', as colonial powers respond to genocidal attacks on their own civilians with exponentially greater violence. The pattern of violent response in Israel's previous attacks on Gaza, from 2008–2009 onwards, had been controlled by the brutal logic of 'mowing the lawn'. With 7 October, any restraint was abandoned.

7 October and Gaza have activated not only the material but also the ideological structure of genocide in Israel-Palestine. The Nazis' extermination of the Jews, constructed as the Shoah or Holocaust, has not only been made foundational to modern Jewish identity – where it draws on thousands of years of persecution – but it is also the defining case of the entire global discourse of genocide, even in much of academia. The recognition of the new Gaza genocide as a second and even worse Nakba now strengthens Palestinians' own narrative of genocide; but in the resistance to this we can see not only the material links of Israel to the Western system of power, but also the ideological formation of whole generations of political and media elites.

If Palestine plays a unique symbolic role for Muslims, it is clearly not the only place in which questions of genocide arise for them. As I have noted, there are other major cases of systematic dispossession, expulsion, and atrocity against Muslim populations by non-Muslim regimes, which are often considered genocide – even if, because these cases mostly centre on forced removal, the label is sometimes withheld by those who consider that 'ethnic cleansing' is a separate phenomenon rather than a dimension of genocide.

Religious discrimination is clearly a significant aspect of these and other cases of genocide, and the Genocide Convention, as we have seen, specifies 'religious groups' as one of the four types which are protected. However, there is considerable confusion about the status of these categories: not all populations that are attacked in a genocidal manner can be fitted easily into them – for example, the International Criminal Tribunal for Rwanda had to rule that the Tutsi, the main targets of the 1994 genocide, were a protected group, although they did not correspond to one of these types.

Moreover, genocide scholars have concluded that populations are attacked according to how the perpetrators define them, not because of how they might be ascribed in an 'objective' legal or sociological classification. The chief perpetrators of genocide are opportunistic political and military leaders, whose ideologies are notoriously flexible. In attacking a population, they generally define it as a political and military enemy, often for exaggerated 'security' reasons – as Israeli leaders do when they represent even Palestinian children as potential terrorists. The genocide scholar Dirk Moses calls this kind of attempt to future-proof states against enemy populations the pursuit of 'permanent security'.

Therefore, while religious discrimination is often part of genocide's ideological mix, it is not usually central: although the victims may be Muslims or members of another religion, they are not attacked as a religious group. Because it is operating with the extant law, the ICJ has to classify populations according to the Convention's categories, and it considers the Palestinians as a national group rather than as members of a religious group. This is obviously plausible, since Israel regards Palestinians as an enemy primarily because of their presence in the 'Land of Israel' and their competing national claims to the land. Yet it is an ideological bonus for Israeli propagandists to represent Palestinians as adherents of an allegedly fanatical Islam, as it is for Hamas – for whom Israeli civilians are enemies primarily for being 'settlers' on Palestinian territory and citizens of the occupying state – to stigmatise Israelis as Jews, evoking widely-held antisemitic views.

Only where the perpetrators are an avowedly religious organisation with a strict ideology are religious reasons likely to be central to a genocidal project. Thus the 'Islamic State' movement, with its extreme interpretation of Islam, has widely been considered to have committed genocide on religious lines against the Yazidis, as well as to have practiced radical discrimination against Christians, Shia Muslims, and others who not accept their particular version of Islam.

'Islamic State' is, therefore, the exception that proves the rule that while religion often enters into how states and armed organisations define populations as enemies to be destroyed, other factors are decisive. The 1915 Armenian Genocide is widely considered one of the major modern genocides, and the Ottoman regime partly identified Armenians and other Christians as enemies through their religion. But the genocide took place in the context of the First World War struggle between the Ottoman and Russian empires, and was the culmination of decades of nationalist political struggles during the long dissolution of the Ottoman state – in which expulsions and massacres were also committed (albeit on a lesser scale) by Christian nationalists, for example in the Balkans.

Likewise, the widespread massacres during the 1947 Indian Partition, also widely considered genocidal, in which victims on all sides were certainly targeted on the grounds of religion, were part of the political struggle between the two main parties, Congress and the Muslim League, provoked by the League's determination to establish a separate Muslim state, and the chaotic way in which the British carried out the partition. Similar massacres occurred, and are also often considered from a genocide perspective, in the 1971 war in East Pakistan which led to the establishment of Bangladesh, but here religious identification was less central.

Similarly, during the Bosnian War (1992–1996), Serbian nationalists invoked Orthodox Christianity and Croatians Catholicism, but the Bosnian government, which most Bosniaks (Bosnian Muslims) supported, defended a plural, multi-religious and multi-ethnic state. Serbian and Croatian nationalists utilised religious themes while carrying out genocidal expulsions and massacres of Bosniaks, but they did not act for narrowly religious reasons.

Iraq is another example in which religion was used for political purposes, where the dictatorship of Saddam Hussein, based on the Sunni minority of the population, attacked groups that it saw as threatening the regime, carrying out the chemical massacre of Kurds at Halabja in 1988, widely considered an instance of genocide, and destroying the society of the Marsh Arabs. Similarly, it brutally repressed the Shia and Kurdish uprisings in 1991, in the aftermath of the regime's defeat by a US-led coalition, provoked by its annexation of Kuwait the previous year. When the US returned to overthrow Saddam in 2003, politically empowering the parties of Iraq's Shia majority, the Sunni-based resistance to the US occupation (especially al-Qaida in Iraq, the forerunner of the 'Islamic State') increasingly directed their violence against the Shia. The resulting low-level civil war in Baghdad between Sunni- and Shia-based militia, in 2005–2007, had a genocidal character, as it saw both sides attempt to destroy the opposing civilian population in the areas they controlled, expelling and committing atrocities against them.

The sectarianisation of political and armed conflict which we see in these examples, in which genocidal violence is frequently inflected with religious ideas, is not of course unique to the Middle East or the Muslim world. Nor is the hostility of sectarian-defined actors always directed solely against adherents of other religious ideas. In Bosnia, the genocidal attacks by Serbian and Croatian nationalists aimed to destroy plural urban centres as well as Bosniak communities. In Indonesia in 1965, Islam was part of the nationalist and anti-Communist ideology of the army officers and local militias who massacred hundreds of thousands of Communists together with ethnic minorities, like the Chinese, who they identified with Communism.

In the end, while perpetrators of destructive violence may often identify their targets in something like – or a combination of – the UN Convention's 'ethnic', 'national', 'racial', and 'religious' categories, the best way to understand genocide is always as a political and military project in which a state or armed group treats a civilian population (rather than another armed organisation) as an enemy to be destroyed. Indeed, since genocide is political, many have proposed that 'political groups' – a category which, like forced removal, was removed from the Convention during the drafting process – should also be considered victims of genocide.

The controversy over including 'political groups' is one of the longest-running among genocide scholars. If genocide usually has a political rationale, it is logical for the scope of genocide to include the destruction of social and political movements, as well as ethnic, national, and religious groups – even if the Convention does not include this. Indeed, historically there have been close links between authoritarian regimes' destructions of political movements and of ethnic enemies. In the 1920s, the Italian Fascist movement destroyed the labour and socialist movements, before eventually carrying out genocidal massacres as part of its imperial project in Abyssinia (Ethiopia). The Nazis destroyed the German working-class movement, in significant part physically as well as organisationally, before proceeding to the genocide of the Jews and others in their conquest of Europe. In the 1930s, Franco's military rebellion carried out what the historian Paul Preston has called a 'Spanish Holocaust' of the left, killing up to 200,000 people.

Indeed, genocidal power often labels political and social opponents as ethnic or religious enemies, aiming to convert political conflict over its rule into ethnic and religious struggle. A prime example of this is the Syrian regime of Bashar al-Assad, which responded to a peaceful revolution in 2011–2012 with massacres of civilian protestors. Assad's campaign sectarianised the struggle, with even more extreme and indiscriminate violence against the majority Sunni areas which protested than in Alawi and Christian areas, as he tried to consolidate the regime's support among minorities. Like the earlier conflict in neighbouring Iraq, the civil war became increasingly genocidal, with both the regime and what became 'Islamic State' deliberately killing members of opposing civilian populations.

The return of genocide, therefore, is a return of the *idea*: the *reality* of genocide had never gone away. I have not even mentioned other countries like Sudan and Ethiopia about which plausible allegations of genocide have been made even in the months during which Gaza has suffered total destruction. Neither of these situations have received even a fraction of the extent of worldwide recognition of genocide that Gaza has had. Gaza even seems to have taken away attention from Ukraine, where Russia's attack is continuing, although official Western attitudes towards Ukrainian suffering are far more supportive than they are of Palestinians.

My conclusions are therefore straightforward but troubling. Genocide remains a global problem with many manifestations. Gaza's terrible plight has drawn attention to it, and that attention should extend to all the ongoing cases of genocide. It is encouraging that the two international courts have acted on Gaza, albeit too slowly and at times timidly, but the opposition to them by some major states and the failure of the Security Council to act forcefully show that international law is not sufficient to stop genocide. That remains a political task for everyone in world society who sees the problem for what it is, among whom I hope we can include the readers of *Critical Muslim*.

GRATUITOUS ACTS OF EVIL

Richard Appignanesi

Genocide. When did such a momentously devastating evil first enter history? Has it always preyed on us? A browse of Wikipedia tell us that Polish lawyer Raphael Lemkin coined the term genocide in 1944 in his book *Axis Rule in Occupied Europe*. He considered genocide a 'crime of crimes' and 'the epitome of human evil'. And now it appears on Europe's doorstep. Israel stands accused before the International Court of Justice of conducting genocidal warfare against the Palestinians of the Gaza Strip while in pursuit of retaliation for the massacre of Israeli citizens on 7 October 2023 by Hamas. Israel has turned the Holocaust into a secular synagogue where the world has been induced to expiate its guilt. The moral alms-giving of that war-time guilt has been depleted in the ruins of Gaza. Hamas strategists must nevertheless accept some blame. Surely they must have foreseen Israel's predictable response under Prime Minister Benjamin Netanyahu's extreme right-wing crony government. Israel and Hamas are locked in grotesque mirror asymmetry of mutually willed destruction.

Is genocide a crime attributable alone to modernity? First, imagine the prerequisite system necessary for it: the constant and perpetual dehumanisation of the victims – men and women, old and young, children and disabled – to prepare for the efficient bureaucracy and war machine to take over, the herding or transporting of the victims, the purpose-built torture chambers, the assembly-line killing, the disappearance of evidence. Second, and having stressed *imagine*, the occurrence is *unimaginable*. This realisation is not second place but primary and of outweighing importance to long-term history. Imagination is what perished irretrievably in the Holocaust and the genocides that followed. Genocide requires credicide, death of belief, or rather, active killing of belief.

Genocide is in the end incommunicable. *How could it be?* Note the ambiguity of that question. We have not the succumbed imagination to answer its truth from the abyss. It is a product of our contemporary cultural disablement; and it has a long root in history. To mull over genocide, we need to examine evil as gratuitous act.

Let's step back to go further.

What has Jung accomplished to assist our comprehension of evil? Perhaps to prepare the groundwork of a *Tractatus Analytico-Theologicus*? That would indeed be an incomparable project, as though the paragon of theologians, St Thomas Aquinas, the 'Angelic Doctor', were endowed with the psychoanalytical genius of Sigmund Freud to equip an amalgam between them of the one's *Summa Theologica* and the other's psychoanalytical theories of the unconscious as a new investigative tool of existential exploration. Jung does not claim that instrument but nevertheless plays upon it namelessly and no less grandly. He has engaged God in a tragic mission of analysis. I say tragic, a much-misused word. It should mean what Aristotle understood of it in ancient Greek drama, the catastrophic fall of a superior being, a king, for instance, like Oedipus, who mistakes his character flaw of hubris for his own preponderant authority. Tragedy is foreseen but not preventable by the prophetic enclosure of *eironeia*, irony, wrongly taken for sarcasm in the modern idiom, in true Greek sense gives forewarning of a fate that cannot be averted and in that sense is an 'unspeakable utterance'.

The fall of God is surely that of a tragically hubristic 'superior being' in the scope of *eironeia*, though in this instance of a Judaic testamentary variety in which God is placed beyond reach of blasphemous utterance as the literally 'unspeakable' Yahweh. It is altogether forbidden to *say* him. Jung's extraordinary missionary endeavour of analysis is to extract from God himself his own blasphemic utterance of unconsciousness, which is the revelation of his humanly implicated in*humanity*. This is no concession to the crude binary paradox whether God 'made us' or we 'made him up', a Janus-faced indecision that entraps us in the toils of fiction. We can overcome that sterile undialectical entanglement by reconnoitre with God's immanent power of negative self-disposition. What does that mean? Simply, it is Jung's insight of God's existence in unconsciousness which moreover is the source of our consciousness of the question of evil posed by Job's torment (what for is human life victim to evil? Whereby does our existence sustain evil? Questions which look to some likelihood of God's permanence for authorisation).

In this space of reciprocally plaintiff mirrors, Jung identifies the occurrence of a psychodynamic transference in which god discloses – or more accurately mortgages – an historically pivotal 'love of humanity'. The mortgage clause of redemption is time sensitive, however. Jung makes abundantly clear and discomfitingly plain that our ingenuity has furnished us with nuclear and biochemical forces and now our own godly hubristic Anthropocene climate change to cause the terminal Holocaust of human life. Humankind has a choice at this juncture either of self-transcendence or suicide. We have long superseded the antiquated quandary of 'nature-versus-nurture', as Jean-Paul Sartre well said: 'What we call freedom is the irreducibility of the cultural order to the natural order.' Beyond the boundary of culture there is no such thing as 'nature'. It has been manufactured culturally by our guilty conscience. Our unnaturalness was dramatised by the Biblical myth of Genesis which recounts the first humans' eviction from Paradise as a fall from the original state of nature to our present sinful condition. No one lives in nature, not the Kalahari Bushman any more than the Wall Street banker. Both are practical mechanics of culture. Progress has been fossil-fuelled (oh, the supreme irony of 'fossil', a condition towards which we speed) to arrive at the Anthropocene Age of consumers in a fatally toxified artificial paradise.

Doom-saying is tedious. I stick with Samuel Beckett's final postponement of the end as approved by Shakespeare's *King Lear*: 'The worst is not, so long as you can say, this is the worst…' We can benefit to our great advantage that has never yet been properly fathomed by Jung's disclosure of a peculiarly *dispossessive* deity in unconsciousness. Put this another way, we can speak – and in fact we have always spoken of it without being aware – of the *no-thingness* of God. This allows us the good riddance of Kant's factiously vexing antinomy, that pitfall of the human mind whereby arguments for the proof and disproof of God's existence are constrained to contest each other equally, endlessly and undecidedly. The none thingness of God is instead consistent with both the contradictory standpoints of apophatic and cataphatic theologies, and perhaps surprisingly with atheism. I shall explain. Apophatic theology, from the Greek *apophemi* or 'denial', is a negative theology whose austere mystical approach to the existence of God is by denying that the human faculties can ever know the divine attributes. Rather than this *via negativa*, cataphatic theology takes a positive line of deductive reasoning to certify the proof of God's existence, demonstrated in the Aristotelian manner by St Thomas Aquinas in his *Summa Theologica*. Atheism's blunt denial of God's existence would seem to make it the odd man out. And yet what all three share is agreement that God is no thingness, that is to say, *unobjectifiable*. Whether we disclaim admission of God's knowable attributes apophatically, or comply with Thomism's voluminous reasonings on the divine characteristics that are in the end ineffable, or simply embrace atheistic disbelief, it makes no existential difference; in the end as in the beginning, alpha and omega, God is nothing accessible. 'I don't care' or 'I don't know for sure', the positions of indifference and agnosticism, lack vigour. Such lassitude of mind in climacteric modernity, tranquillised by liberal humanism, has made it itself unresponsive to admit the non-fungible reality of evil. Why so?

Despite whatever best efforts of negative or positive theologies or the refutations of atheism, God must remain *unsubstantiated*. An absentee, it appears, who evades hypostatisation. A corrective link to Jung's essence of God in unconsciousness is missing from these perspectives of an unsubstantiated God. But that is a difficulty of comprehension that I shall have to amend as I proceed and in the meanwhile, deal with God's evasion from the labouring conscious mind.

The embargo on the hypostatisation of God comes down simply to this. *The absence of God is coincident with the absence of evil.* This dual interdependent deficit is explained because neither God nor evil is a thing. God is a question of immaterial faith, therefore. But what of evil? Is it also a question left to a 'matter of faith'? The question is senseless in our day. An internationally respected cognitive scientist, and a long time friend of mine, recently expressed his cultural dismay in an email to me: 'we abandoned our tired old Christian-based culture in the sixties – dumped it completely and suddenly. cold turkey, in a stupid and indiscriminate manner. I don't know of any other society in history that has cut off its entire historical foundation with such casual idiocy...'

God has effectively vanished from the West's secular conception of itself in modernity. Some may once have feared that God's extinction would permit unrestricted evil. It was not anticipated that his incognito departure would simply make evil a random anomaly of no more interest to human affairs than the rare sighting of Halley's comet crossing the sky. Why should

Lucy Letby, a thirty-four-year-old neonatal nurse, kill eight babies and attempt the murder of ten others in a Cheshire hospital between 2015 and 2016? She is no 'Mrs Hyde' monster but a personable vivacious blonde and blue-eyed English rose of the suburbs. Why should Dr Harold Shipman, an affable and trusted physician, administer fatal doses of diamorphine to murder an estimated 250 of his mostly elderly female patients in the course of a practice extending from 1977 to 1998? (One possible motive was Shipman's forgery of Kathleen Grundy's will assigning assets of £386,000 to him, a blunder that led to his arrest, and possibly some thefts of jewellery from other victims. Otherwise his actions seem motiveless.) Why did they do it? *Because they could*, is the unconditional answer. To enjoy the exquisite libertine pleasure it gives them and delight in the havoc of grief inflicted on families – that is their reason. Is there reason for the evil imposed on the innocent casualties in the grotesquely named 'theatres of war' in Yemen, Syria, Sudan, Gaza, and elsewhere?

We are left in a state of secular bereavement with Hannah Arendt's 'banality of evil'. But no need to grieve the derelict end of iniquitous deeds if we accept the therapeutic consolation, such as Arendt alleges, that evil only serves to de-humanise the person so judged; it demonises rather than acknowledges the common level of the evil-doer. I am ill at ease with any reduction of evil to the excusable commonplace, which encourages the socially sponsored alibi that can shrug off personal responsibility. So too, by impersonal equivalence, evil can also finish as the occurrence of mere happenstance, a news item that shocks and is soon forgotten.

I am struck by a feature of evil that is overlooked. Evil has no temperature of intimacy. I do not mean simply being impersonal but as though freeze-framing its apparent proximity to us and yet entirely eluding our grasp. Like a weightless object of a sort that disappears into quicksand without leaving ripples. It lacks the trace of warmth that normally attaches to the intimate rub of the human act. I will raise an objection to my own view by reminder of the serial killers Ian Brady and Myra Hindley, who collaborated in sexual intimacy to commit the 'Moors Murders' between 1963 and 1965, atrocities in which five youngsters from ten to seventeen years old were sexually abused, tortured, and killed. In one case, the ten-year-old Lesley Ann Downey was posed for pornographic photographs and her screams recorded on audio-tape. Her body and those of the other four were buried on Saddleworth moor some distance outside Greater Manchester. Brady, of fatally arrogant intelligence, imagined himself a Nietzschean Übermensch, beyond good and evil, and a disciple of the Marquis de Sade; his partner Hindley credited him with a mesmeric Svengali-like hold over her, as though she had 'slept walked' into their crimes to which she confessed only having witnessed but never in partaking. I cannot detect anything like warmth of intimacy in the coupling of this Sadeanist pair. Nothing that relieves them of cold, detached indulgence in evil for evil's sake. Verdicts of psychopathological disorder are pointless to decipher their motivation.

In the Gospel of St Matthew 5:45, we read the wisdom of Christ to the multitude: 'For He maketh His sun to rise on the evil and on the good, and sendeth rain on the just and on the unjust.' There is an element precisely of that inescapable eventuality which dictates the choice of evil. What do I mean by asserting this inevitable 'possible happening'? How can the possible ever be regarded as inevitable? To unravel that paradox requires providing an explanation of evil. The problem of evil I am led to see is this: to secure individual anchorage for evil in historical reality. One could easily retort that evil has always constantly been committed in history. Surely this doesn't explain the problem. I agree, it doesn't, but serves to identify the proportions of the problem. The evils one hears of in history are consigned to calamity that seems to fall in us by chance like accidently destructive forces of nature. There is something inhumanly incidental to Hitler's colossal evil or others like him empowered for more or less notoriously titanic misdeeds. As the cliché saying has it: 'killing one person makes you a murderer; causing the death of a hundred thousand makes you a statesman'. Calamitous occurrence takes evil out of the ordinary and places it in the exceptional category. And yet, at the same time, paradoxically, evil on a mindlessly incalculable scale, such as we saw in the case of that bureaucratic nonentity Adolf Eichmann, banalises its performance. Calamity and banality do not explain evil – they explain it away. And that is the problem of evil's dead-end collision with the inexplicable.

My purpose must be to cast light on modernity's progressive disinculpation of evil by submission to banality and calamity. These two are modernity's Scylla and Charybdis, the twin maritime hazards of Greek mythology that between caused the wreckage of voyaging ships. Let us examine this alternant binary of banality and calamity more closely. Banality extenuates evil as the commonplace byproduct of someone's un-mindfulness. Evil results from thoughtlessness snared in a web of circumstance. Calamity is no less a circumstantial entrapment in extreme eventfulness, history, so called after its post scripted occurrence. History is never seen to happen ahead of one but always behind one's back. Jean-Paul Sartre matches it with gnomic dark humour to an existential 'blow-back'. 'It is not true that History appears to us as an entirely alien force. Each day with our own hands we make it something other than what we believe we are making it, and History, backfiring, makes us other than we believe ourselves to be or become.' Even the illustrious Great Actors of history are only hanging by their fingernails to history's sheer cliff face in the paranoid delusion of belief that they are always in the right. There is always a charlatan aura of gambler staked to anyone who brags, 'I've made history!' As Napoleon's wise Corsican mother Letizia responded to his imperial coronation in 1804, 'Provided it lasts!'.

Banality and calamity are a dissatisfying bipolarity which distracts from a focal account of the evil *act*. Both are cancellations of the act to impersonality, viewed from either end of the telescope, either too sizably little or too big for proper qualified ascription to a person. My leverage to extricate the vitally begotten individual from the bipolar pincers of impersonality may seem eccentric, if not to say fallacious, which is to correct history with fiction. My defence for resorting to fiction is that history cannot foretell but is always posterior and conformable to events: whereas fiction particularly of an exceptional ulterior sort can be prophetic. Aristotle had already lectured in around 330 BC on literature's superiority to history. 'The poet and the historian differ in this: one communicates events that have actually happened and the other those kinds of events that might happen. Because of this, poetry is more philosophical and serious than history.' The proof will be seen as I survey the gratuitous act of evil intermeshing with literature's foretelling of history.

André Gide (1869–1951), the French novelist and Nobel Laureate, offers the ideal fiction paradigm as someone long intrigued by the gratuitous act of evil, an immoralist and delinquent performance of the chance deed without moral consideration. Gide welcomed the feral truancy of the motiveless act to break out of the classic mould of French literature which had excelled in formulaic moral psychology since the days of Corneille, Racine, and Pascal with its curtsy to austere decorum. He was readied for radical dissidence by familial Protestant descent, turning atheist against his devout gentry kin and confessing his homosexuality in autobiographical writings, graphically in *Si le grain ne meurt* (If it Die) in 1926 (in which he reports his meeting with Oscar Wilde and his obnoxious lover 'Bosie'), and also in 1926 *Corydon* a Socratic defence of pederasty which tagged him thereafter as a 'corrupter of the youth'.

Gide nurtured his savage idea from 1905 to its maturity as a novelist in 1914, *Les Caves du Vatican* (The Vatican Cellars) which he declared a *sotie*, harking back to a popular Renaissance genre of farce which parodies a world governed by fools. The novel pivots on a motiveless act performed by a protagonist, Lafcadio, who while journeying through Italy satisfies his 'desire to impinge on the fate' of his travelling companion, Amedeé, by hurling him off the train. This is Lafcadio's second gratuitous act: the first when he saved two children from a burning house. (Goodness too it seems can occur gratuitously; and indeed the act of charity, unless it is thoughtless, so to speak, has no merit if done for social applause or one's heavenly reward. The gratuitous doing of good must be understood as a self-sacrificial action as opposed to closure in self-indulgent evil.) The fact of his good deed contradicting the other evil one he has committed is of no consequence to Lafcadio without interest in the moral values of good and evil. He acts totally on impulse by taking advantage of whatever chance that arises uninhibited by any moral code. He is in Gide's definition of *l'homme disponible*, the available man prompted by possibility and what he feels spontaneously true to his nature. I recall Walter Benjamin's acute observation on the 'destructive character': 'because he sees ways everywhere, he always positions himself at the crossroads. No moment can know what the next will bring.' Destruction dogs the steps of the wayward and always available man. 'What exists he reduces to rubble, not for the sake of the rubble, but for the way leading through it. The destructive character lives for the feeling, not that life is worth living, but that suicide is not worth the trouble.' The destructive character's cynically weary rejection if suicide will presently be seen apropos. Gide's remark in his *Journal* in 1909 that 'there is no difference in essence between the honest man and the knave', exemplifies the particular nature of Lafcadio's destructive character available to possibility.

Is it Gide himself who risks duplicity as he errs in a hall of mirrors? He proved farsighted in plucking gratuitousness from the very air of the zeitgeist. André Breton, pontiff of the Surrealist movement, in his *Second Manifesto of Surrealism*, 1929, promoted the gratuitous transgression as an axiom of true Surrealism:

> The simplest Surrealist act consists of dashing down the street, pistol in hand, and firing blindly, as fast as you can pull the trigger, into the crowd. Anyone who, at least once in his life, has not dreamed of thus putting an end to the petty system of debasement and cretinisation in effect has a well-defined place in that crowd, with his belly at barrel level......let us not lose sight of the fact that the idea of surrealism aims quite simply at the total recovery of our psychic force by a means which is nothing other than the dizzying descent into ourselves, the systematic illumination of hidden places and the progressive darkening of other places, the perpetual excursion into the midst of forbidden territory.

Breton's provocation assails us repellently now for other reasons than his shock tactic. Terrorism has made commonplace the unpredictable random killings of bystanders in large numbers, 9/11 being the apogee of multitude slaughter. A sad fact of our social media culture is that even such spectacular atrocities are barely, or for long, newsworthy. Nevertheless we should not lose sight of the bewitching power of aestheticised terrorism. 11 September brought home to us an outrageous aesthetic strangeness. It caused the German avant-garde composer Karlheinz Stockhausen's awed wonderment at the 'masterpiece' perpetrated by Al-Qaeda artistry. For him, Mohammed Atta's orchestration of planes crashing into Manhattan's Twin Towers must be deemed:

> The greatest work of art that is possible in the whole cosmos...You have people concentrated on one performance, and then 5,000 people are dispatched into eternity, in a single moment. I couldn't do that. In comparison with that, we're nothing as composers.

Stockhausen went online hastily to apologise for his indiscretion. He pleaded a misunderstanding; but the offence is nevertheless a naïve confession of aestheticism entirely in keeping with Stockhausen's megalo-Wagnerian excesses as a late modernist composer. I point to *The Helicopter String Quartet* premiered in 1995, which demonstrated his own grandiose airborne ambition. Each player of the quartet ascends in a separate helicopter, flying to patterns directed by the score, and their performances are relayed back to the audience on the ground. A craving for the postmodern sublime exposes its finality on September 11. He should not have apologised for blurting out the truth. It was a sincere admission of exhausted virtuosity – and the endgame is terrorism. Mohammed Atta's 'Manhattan Requiem', could be said to be a gratuitous act of evil; but we teeter on the cliff edge of indecision whether it is commitment assignable to religious belief, political strategy or some other delusion of purpose. I will wager that today commitment is obscure to – *and obscures* – those who fanatically vow to it.

Gide's fascination with the unmotivated free act stayed with him as an *idée fixe* for a decade, until again peaking in another novel, *Les Faux monnayeurs* (The Counterfeiters, 1925) whose unusual aleatory structure has absorbed the chance feature of the gratuitous action. One has a sense of a moral parallelism that Gide draws between freeing himself from his upbringing under the watchful eye of a Calvinist God and liberating his characters in the novel from authorial predestination by adopting a Cubist-style of multiple viewpoints which allows a pluralistic competition of voices – a circle, as it were, with not one but numerous detached centres. He was assisted along this route of choral-voiced dissonance by the supreme master of that form of novelistic pluralism, Fyodor Dostoevsky (1821-1881), directed to what the Russian semiotician Mikhail Bakhtin (1895-1975) identifies in Dostoevsky as the 'dialogic or polyphonic style' of contradictory viewpoints rather the monological 'omniscient author' mode of narration. To cite Bakhtin: 'A person has no sovereign internal territory, he is wholly and always *on the boundary*; looking inside himself, he looks *into the eyes of another* or *with the eyes of another*.' Something else other than 'dialogism' endorsed Gide's enthusiasm for Dostoevsky. Something of an affinity which seems altogether at odds with Gide's willingness to jettison the Christian faith. He could not have chosen a more antipodean model than Dostoevsky, obsessed with the 'insulted and injured' Gospel Christ, but at the same time tormented by the itching bedbugs of sinfulness, guilt and corrosive atheistic doubts; a contradictory soul, arrested and subjected to mock firing-squad execution for his membership in the illegal Petrashevsky circle of socialist utopians, imprisoned four years in a Siberian gulag, exiled six more years, only to stoop on his release to kiss the 'Little Father' Tsar's tyrannous hem and thereafter become a pan-Slavic ideologist, anti-Semitic Russian fanatic. And precisely because he was so narrowly focussed on Russia's unique destiny, because he was 'acutely conscious…of the danger to any country in too marked Europeanisation' – in Gide's own words – he was able prophetically to envisage the lineaments of the Bolshevik conspirators in his novel *The Possessed* (also titled *The Demons*) in 1872, a near half-century before Lenin's arrival from Switzerland in a sealed train at the Finland Station in 1917 to veer the course of the February Revolution towards a conclusive Bolshevik *coup d'état*. 'The whole of *The Possessed* prophesies the revolution of which Russia is at present in the throes.' I quote from Gide's *Addresses on Dostoevsky* first delivered in Paris at the Vieux Colombier School of Dramatic Art in 1922 and published in 1923. The Russian author had entered Europe's literary bloodstream at the turn of the century. Friedrich Nietzsche encountered Dostoevsky's work in 1886 and referred to it in *The Wagner Case*, *Twilight of the Idols* and *The Antichrist*, all written in 1888. 'Dostoevsky was the only psychologist from whom I had anything to learn. He belongs to the happiest windfall of my life,' he wrote to the Danish critic Georg Brandes who had championed Nietzsche and introduced him to Scandinavia in the 1880s. 'A happy windfall', if one can call it that, more a crossbreeding of two non-conformist minds psychologically aligned by the modern epochal phenomenon of God's ending: for Nietzsche, the annunciation, 'God is dead'; for Dostoevsky, in consequence of it, 'everything is permitted'; and for both, fears that the abyss of nihilism would engulf decaying European civilisation.

A volatile suffusion of fury for God and Russia under threat of nihilism – and at the same time a desperate scission of the two within his own soul – informed Dostoevsky's vision in *The Possessed*. Here is Ivan Pavlovich Shatov in the novel (as quoted by Gide) who has repudiated his earlier socialist convictions at university to embrace Russian Orthodox Christianity and the Slavophile reform movement of *Pochvennichestvo*, 'return to the soil', which rejects nihilism, Marxism and liberalism and had Dostoevsky's sympathy, speaking to the charismatic villain Nikolai Vsevolodevich Stavrogin: 'the people is the body of God. Every people is only a people so long as it has is own God and excludes all other gods on earth irreconcilably... If a great people does not believe that the truth is only to be found in itself...if it does not believe that it alone is fit and destined to raise up and save all the rest by its truth, it would at once sink into being ethnographical material, and not a great people...A nation which loses this belief ceases to be a nation.' To which Stavrogin concludes: 'An individual out of touch with his country has lost God.'

Gide continues in this vein: 'What would Dostoevsky think of Russia today and of her people? It is a painful speculation...Did he apprehend, was he able to foresee her ghastly torments? In *The Possessed* we find all the seeds of Bolshevism. You need only listen to Shigalev's exposition of his theory and the admission he makes at its close: "I am perplexed by my own data and my conclusion is a direct contradiction to the original idea with which I start. Starting from unlimited freedom, I arrive at unlimited despotism."' Who is Shigalev?

A theorist in Pyotr Stepanovich Verkhovensky's secret anarchist groupuscule with plans of a monomaniacal system for the post-revolutionary re-organisation of mankind. Dostoevsky modelled Verkhovensky's character on an anarcho-nihilist agitator and Marxist sympathiser Sergei Nechayev (1847-1882) who organised the murder of a former member of his conspiracy, Ivan Ivanov in 1869 for alleged desertion to Orthodoxy and Tsarism, just as Verkhovensky plans in the novel to kill Shatov on a similar renegade pretext. I am not aware that Dostoevsky red Nechayev's inflammatory *Catechism of a Revolutionary* (1860) but he was certainly deeply concerned by the infectious Nechayevite style of terrorism that was filtering into student radicalism at the turn of the 1870s.

Nechayev portrays the ideal revolutionary in his *Catechism* as an ascetic immoralist, a doomed man who has severed all links to the social order and all ties to the entire civilised world of which he is a merciless enemy who continues to inhabit it with the sole purpose of destroying it. He allies himself with the savage world of the violent criminal, the only true revolutionary in Russia. His purpose is to penetrate all social formations; but, above all, no matter how tiny the core of followers, the aim is to aggravate the miseries of the common people, so as to exhaust their patience and incite them to rebellion. This last agitational principle of stimulating the people out of complacency to outright revolution was Lenin's beacon light, as he put it, 'the worse, the better' for ripening the social conditions of revolution. Lenin prospered exceptionally by maintaining his disciples' faith in the 'Bolshevik' nucleus, a term meaning 'majority' (as in *Bolshoi*, 'big, great, grand'), a misnomer for a small almost negligible fractional Marxist party. The pay-off on Lenin's gamble – the Bolsheviks capture of an entire and huge backward country – encouraged subsequent delusionary hopefuls of similar success in overturning the social order by disseminating chaos and violence, extending from the syndicalist Georges Sorel to the Italian pioneer Communist Antonio Gramsci and reaching ahead to 1969 and the Black Panthers in America and the terrorist Red Brigades in Italy. Dostoevsky is therefore spot on to animate his Frankenstein creation Verkhovensky with a Nechayev-like giddy boast, 'there's going to be such an upset as the world as the world has never seen before… Russia will be overwhelmed with darkness, the earth will weep for its old gods,' only in the end to cause mayhem in the teacup-sized town of Tver and its Caulin textile mill. And yet, in the future backlight cast by the triumph of Lenin's apparently delusional 'Bolshoi' aspiration, it does not now look like Dostoevsky was simply lampooning Verkhovensky's deception to motivate his miniscule cell by pretence that it is connected to the Central Committee of a vast clandestine organisation which will topple Tsarism and establish socialism. Not a parody but a prophecy! Dostoevsky was unlikely to know that Nechayev always kept near him the inspiring images of Maximilien Robespierre and St Just, the Jacobin architects of the Great Terror that indubitably overwhelmed the French Revolution with the sanguinary darkness of the guillotine. And we can perceive in that sombre frenzy of revolutionary terror the dead-hand control that leads Shigalev's utopian plan of 'unlimited freedom' to arrive at 'unlimited despotism'.

In 1973, a hundred years after the appearance of Dostoevsky's demonic anarchist intriguers, Aleksandr Solzhenitsyn (1908–2008), a survivor of eight years' Siberian Gulag imprisonment, published *The Gulag Archipelago*, secreted in Paris. By his conversion in the Gulag from the Soviet Union's undisputable dogma of 'scientific socialism' to the old pre-revolutionary faith in Orthodox Christianity, by his profound attachment to the soil of Russian values and rejection of Western liberalism, Solzhenitsyn closes the circle as spiritual great grandson of Dostoevsky and as a writer likewise committed to Russia's troubled destiny. Troubled not least by its resentment at Western Europe's ingratitude and disavowals of its debts to Russia's protection dearly paid for by Russian sacrifice. Two memorials of Europe's amnesia: the crushing defeat inflicted on Napoleon's Grand Armée at Borodino; or nearer in failed memory, breaking Hitler's back at Stalingrad. Christian Europe's unacknowledged debt to Russia is declared in Andrei Tarkovsky's 1975 film, *Mirror*, in which the child Alyosha reads from Aleksander Pushkin's 1836 letter to Pyotr Chaadayev: 'it was Russia, it was her boundless expanses that swallowed the Mongol invasion. The Tatars dared not cross our western borders and leave us in their rear. They retreated to their wastes, and Christian civilisation was spared. To achieve this aim, we had to lead an entirely individual existence, which, while leaving us Christian, nevertheless made us utterly alien to the Christian world... You say that our source, whence we drank Christianity, was impure, that Byzantium was contemptible, and so on. Ah, my friend, was not Jesus Christ himself born a Jew, and was Jerusalem not talked of everywhere? But does this make the Gospel less amazing?... As regards our being a historical nonentity, I definitely cannot agree with you... do you not see that there is something important in Russia's position today; something that will astound the future historian?' Do I hear Verkhovensky's reprise of Pushkin's prediction that Russia 'will astound the future historian'?

Gide quotes Dostoevsky, a 'veteran European Russian' to describe himself, and lets Andrei Petrovich Versilov, a dissipated landowner and rogue in Dostoevsky's novel *A Raw Youth* (1875), speak for him: 'The highest Russian thought is the reconciliation of ideas, and who in the whole world could understand such a thought at that time? I was a solitary wanderer: I am not speaking of myself personally – it's the Russian idea I'm speaking of... Only to the Russian, even in our day, has been vouchsafed the capacity to become most of all Russian only when he is most European...' Bakhtin would signal this as the typical 'dialogic contrariness' that populates Dostoevsky's world. How does one understand it? An embrace of imported Westernised ideas or a clash of incompatibility with Russia's Eastern civilisation? Solzhenitsyn in his time will have experienced Russia's ruin by the wilfully executed collision of the two. He is in no doubt who to blame for the imposition on Russia of Bolshevik despotic 'Western style' Marxism. Lenin himself, not Stalin's 'errors' (denounced by Premier Nikita Khrushchev at the Twentieth Party Congress of the USSR in 1956), for establishing the Gulag system and the inquisitional Cheka security service (so like the Jacobins' ruthless Committee of Public Safety in 1793). Lenin is clear from the start to steer away from Nechayevite self-sacrificing terrorism (which got his elder brother Sasha hanged for plotting the Tsar's assassination in 1887) towards the iron-clad logic implemented by the Bolsheviks in power. 'The sow that eats her young' applies to Bolshevik autocratic digestion when in 1921 the party obeyed its one-system only rule and mercilessly suppressed the *soi-disant* anarchist Kronstadt sailors who rebelled in protest against the Soviet government in whose creation they had crucially participated for not delivering on promised constitutional reforms and fundamental civil liberties. It is sad to behold these sailors of mostly peasant stock ingenuously expecting the Bolshevik grandees to accede to their populist demands for basic freedoms so long awaited. Approved by Leon Trotsky and led by Felix Dzerzhinsky's Cheka, the insurrection was crushed. The last of what Solzhenitsyn deemed the *buntarstvo* – the old rural type of pre-industrial spontaneous uprisings – in this case signalled the Bolsheviks' repression of idealist libertarian socialism and a decisive turn to one-party totalitarianism.

I have a sense of conspicuous symmetry that allies Nechayev's vengeful slaying of his former comrade Ivanov to Verkhovensky's opportune murder of the idealist Shatov, both made the scapegoats of their adherence to antiquated Russian values, and the linkage of these marginal single purges as the eventuality – again that word of rehearsed predestination – of the mass purging of the peasant mariners as the first step en route to the betrayal of Communism itself. The itinerary thereafter is set for the revolutionary killing fields. To count the dead is a nauseating obscenity. The numbers glance meaningless off the mind: always uncertain figures trailed by the gallows shape of a question mark. Five million of famine due to Lenin's War Communism policy of 1921–1922; a conservative estimate of ten million, some calculate 4.2 pecent of the population, from the disasters of Stalin's mass collectivisation, purges and Gulag confinements; Mao Tse-tung's Great Leap Forward in 1958–1961 causing thirty-five to forty-five million dead and the Cultural Revolution another two or three million; the Khmer Rouge follows with the annihilation of some two million or 25 percent of the 7.8 million Cambodian population between 1975 and 1979.

Any one of these regimes is worse, far more debilitating to the human spirit, than Nazism and its programmatic genocide, not on comparative account of the numbers perished, not for the unimaginable assembly-line systematisation that mechanised Nazi death camp procedure and which has forever terminated any possible post-Holocaust negotiated recourse to the imagination – different not for these reasons, although they are all contiguous to our very skin, but because nothing of genuine lasting hope for humanity can be built on Nazi racialism, whereas Communism has been premised fundamentally on the principle of hope for the long-term betterment of universal humanity, like a demythologised Christianity that would sponsor paradisaic wellbeing on earth. Communism, in its guises of 'really existing Socialism', has been an unconscionable treason of that faith by drowning it in blood; a worse crime of the centuries, which bequeaths cynicism and despair in place of hope, the slurry of resignation to inhumanity, and whereby Communism and Nazi become parallels that meet on the horizon of an irrecuperable future.

Evil? No, I have not lost sight of evil, my quarry. This has been a head-on impact with evil on a colossal, global, historical scale. What is to be said about that? Banality or calamity? Genocide is the often-misapplied designation. It should be used cautiously. Doctrinaire ideology in the twentieth century – be it noted atheistic in all instances – has amassed the greatest number of killings in history but is not accountably genocidal. The dire American term for such excesses of unaccountability, 'collateral damage', only speaks worse of human beings in progress to collective Anthropocene suicide. The vitriolic Viennese satirist, Karl Kraus, early in the twentieth century, even before Hitlerite bad grammar got hold of the German mind, had assured his readers that a typographically misplaced comma would suffice to cause world catastrophe. Clear to him the neologistic masquerade of evil in our time.

It should be evident that I have not simply permitted a tumbleweed of extraneous details to roll on deviantly from my original concern for the gratuitous act of evil. The accumulation of these vagrant incidents should begin retrospectively to spread open like a fan in a panoply of sense. I seek no single unit of meaning but to visualise a clearing into the density of history. I follow the compass point of Gide's magnetic pull to the gratuitous act which leads on errantly.

I am convinced that Dostoevsky's social anxieties were rooted deeper still in a Doppelgänger split in his personality between his resurgent Orthodox Christian piety masquerading within Tsar-worship, like Ivanov or Shatov, and a secret attraction in him to the revolutionary exigency of Nechayev's spirit. I can offer no proof of this schizoid conflict in Dostoevsky except to insist that the ferocious and truly demon-possessed characterisations in his novel *The Possessed* could only result from the author's own unresolved psychical turmoil, not from a cool detached orchestration. Although I disapprove absolutely of biographical imputations which are indulgent anecdotage – an author cannot be known by the characters he invents – nonetheless, whether or not I succeed to strike the right vein of diffusion in Dostoevsky's previsionary complexity, one thing is sure, and Gide, as a morally contradicting writer himself, has not failed to note it. Through the kaleidoscopic variegations of Nechayev into fictional Verkhovensky, of one real murder into a fiction told of another, of one real cell of fanatic accomplices into a novelist's assemblage of beguiled conspirators, Dostoevsky's vision holds true of an axiomatic terrorist transformation that seeks to undermine the foundations of all hitherto existing traditional civilisations, no matter Christian or Islamic or Buddhist or Hindu.

Just as mercury was once used to treat syphilis, despite its poisonous toxicity, so too let us call it a 'mercurial temperament' that has been introduced inro the centrally social vein of conduit that weakens the nervous system of civilisation, and that Dostoevsky feared was spiritually imperilling him; against which his own nervous system rebelled with severe recurring attacks of epileptic shock. Epilepsy, from the Greek, 'to seize, get hold of', known in the past as the 'falling sickness' because in the fall to earth the sufferer is grabbed by pernicious underworld creatures; and in antiquity was also known as the 'sacred disease' inflicted by the gods; believed in medieval Europe caused by demonic spirits. Dostoevsky would know all this superstitious folklore, and yet, whatever medical science might tell him, he was also aware of Jesus thrice reported in the Gospels casting out the devils that possessed epileptics. Mark 9:17-29 tells of the man who brought his possessed son to Jesus: 'I spoke to thy disciples that they should cast him out; and they could not.' To which Jesus replies, 'O faithless generation, how long shall I be with you? how long shall I suffer you? bring him to me'. The son's fits are described with clinical fidelity. To the father's plea for help, Jesus says, 'all things are possible to him that believeth.' What the father cries out 'in tears' would profoundly speak to Dostoevsky's inner doubts: 'Lord, I believe; help thou my unbelief.'

The same story of cleansing in Luke 9: 37-43 is followed by a passage crucial to understanding Dostoevsky's fascination with childhood innocence and the perverse abuse to which it is subject. 'Then there arose a reasoning among [the disciples] which of them should be greatest. And Jesus perceiving the thought of their heart, took a child, and set him by him. And said unto them, Whosoever shall receive this child in my name receiveth me: and whosoever shall receive me receiveth him that sent me: for he that is least among you all, the same shall be great.' Gide fastens on this theme of regeneration by becoming 'as a child to enter into the Kingdom of Heaven' and refers it to the comment of the moral philosopher Jean de la Bruyère (1645–1696): 'little children have neither past nor future, for they live in the present'. He goes on to quote the child-like innocent Prince Myshkin who is liable to epileptic attacks as we read in Dostoevsky's novel *The Idiot*: 'At that moment I seem somehow to understand the extraordinary saying that *there shall be no more time*.' Gide's gloss on Myshkin's euphoria is that of undergoing what the Gospel teaches – direct participation, 'unwearying in its insistence upon these words, "*Et nunc*"… "*And now*". The perfect joy Christ means is not of the future, but of the immediate present'.

Epilepsy, child-like innocence, the eternal moment in the present – these are the motifs that Gide links to the pivotal character Kirillov in Dostoevsky's *The Possessed*. Let us first heed Kirillov's extolling his sense of eternity in the 'uncanny rapture' of the moment. 'There are seconds – they come five or six at a time – when you suddenly feel the presence of the eternal harmony perfectly attained. […] If it lasted more than five seconds, the soul could not endure it and must perish. In those five seconds I live through a lifetime, and I'd give my whole life for them, because they are worth it…' He is describing the sensation of the 'aura' that precedes an epileptic fit. His interlocutor, Stavrogin, warns him: 'be careful, Kirillov, that's how epilepsy starts'. 'It won't have time,' Kirillov smiled gently. No time, because Kirillov is shortly to carry out his pledge of committing suicide.

Alexei Nilych Kirillov (sometimes spelled Kirilov) is a young science-minded engineer (being European-educated and hence 'Westernised' is something suspect in Dostoevsky's eyes). He is the metaphysical hero at the heart of Dostoevsky's novel, who, in Gide's view 'carries on his shoulders the entire plot of *The Possessed*. We are aware that he intends to take his life, but not that his suicide is imminent: self-destruction is, however, certainly on his mind. Why? The motive is withheld almost till the very end of the book.' Verkhovensky's planned murder of Shatov will be attributed to Kirillov and provide a sideshow distraction from the enactment of the revolutionary conspiracy. Verkhovensky become jittery lest Kirillov change his mind. He thinks instead of using the suicidal engineer to kill Shatov. Kirillov replies dismissively to this: 'to kill someone else would be the lowest point of self-will, and you should show your whole soul in that. I am not you; I want the highest point, and I'll kill myself…'

Now, at last, he throws open the door of rapturous revelation to Verkhovensky:

> I can't understand how an atheist could know there is no God and not kill himself on the spot. To recognise that there is no God, and to recognise at the same instant that one is God oneself is an absurdity, else one would certainly kill oneself. If you recognise it, you are sovereign, and then you won't kill yourself, but live in the greatest glory. But one, the first, must kill himself, for who else will begin and prove it? … Now I am only a God against my will, and I am unhappy because I am bound to assert my will…But I will assert my will, I am bound to believe that I don't believe. I will begin and make an end of it and open the door, and save – mankind. For three years I've been seeking the attribute of my Godhead and I've found it; the attribute of my Godhead is self-will. That's all I can do to prove in the highest point my independence and my new terrible freedom. For it is very terrible, and I am killing myself to prove my independence and my new terrible freedom.

Kirillov offers his voluntary atheistic suicide in Christ-like salvation of humanity. More a metaphysical paradox than a blasphemy parodying the Divine Messiah. Gide can now identify the original pulse of his idea. 'Kirillov's suicide is absolutely gratuitous. I mean to say there is an absence of outward motivation…what absurdities are introduced into this world under cover of a *gratuitous act*.' But in the next paragraph he seems to contradict himself: …gratuitous, but *not* without a motive.' Gide is posing a 'motiveless motive', a voluntarist self-sacrifice 'for others', which bears a hazardously Russian idea that Dostoevsky must know at its core is the very essence of nihilistic terrorism. Dostoevsky indeed knows it and makes Kirillov in his clairvoyant seizure its true blazoning warning, the *inimitable* archetype; not Nechayev whose Catechism conducted the Narodnaya Volya and other diverse violent revolutionists up to their end in the Bolsheviks' ultimate reclamation of state terrorism. We have yet to realise that nihilism can act gratuitously *with or without God.*

I will add one more enlightening observation on the gratuitous suicide in the maze of absurdity. Albert Camus published his essay *The Myth of Sisyphus* in 1942 amid the darkness of France under Nazi Occupation. He became editor of the underground French Resistance newspaper *Combat* in 1944 and wrote critically in it of the unthinkable A-bombing of Hiroshima and Nagasaki that 'an average city can be wiped out by a bomb the size of a football'. '…our technical civilisation has just reached its greatest level of savagery. We will have to choose…between collective suicide and the intelligent use of our scientific conquests.' A time when nihilism could well be forefront in one's mind to occasion suicide. He begins his essay: 'There is but one truly serious philosophical problem, and that is suicide. Judging whether life is or is not worth living amounts to answering the fundamental question of philosophy. … you can appreciate the importance of that reply, for it will precede the definitive act.' Your answer could be your last.

He leafs through Dostoevsky's *Diary of a Writer* and finds him imagining in the instalments for December 1876 the reasoning of 'logical suicide'. 'Convinced that human existence is utter absurdity for anyone without faith in immortality. …since I consider this comedy perpetrated by nature altogether stupid, and since I even deem it humiliating for me to deign to play it…In my indisputable capacity of plaintiff and defendant, of judge and accused, I condemn that nature which, with such impudent nerve, brought me into being in order to suffer – I condemn it to be annihilated with me.' Camus remarks: 'This suicide kills himself because, on the metaphysical plane, he is *vexed*. In a certain sense he is taking revenge. This is his way of proving that he "will not be had".' There is sardonic humour in a suicide provoked by metaphysical vexation. Kirillov's logical suicide, however, is on another scale of extraordinary ambition, as Camus says: 'He wants to kill himself to become God.' To go further, I would say instead, not to become 'God' but to *replace* him. Kirillov does not harbour the idea of becoming a 'God-man'. On the contrary, he 'fancies for a moment that Jesus at his death *did not find himself in Paradise*. He found out that his torture had been useless.' 'The laws of nature,' says the engineer, 'made Christ live in the midst of falsehood and die for a falsehood'. Solely in this sense Jesus indeed personifies the whole human drama. He is the complete man, being the one who realised the most absurd condition. He is not the God-man but the man-god. And like him, each of us can be crucified and victimised – and is to a certain degree.' Therefore, when Kirillov logically premises that 'if God does not exist, I am God', he really means that god-like freedom on this earth is not to serve an immortal being, while being convinced of a death without a future. 'It is no longer a question of "vexed revenge" but of revolt: Kirillov's pistol shot will be the signal for the last revolution'. Revolution not of Verkhovensky's paltry terrorist kind that he despises; rather it is by way of his 'pedagogical suicide' that humanity will be set free from the empty threat of immortality. He must kill himself 'out of love for humanity,' Camus says, 'He must show his brothers a royal and difficult path on which he will be the first'.

Nietzsche assigns the 'death of God' to the decadent feeble-minded nihilism of modern man. Dostoevsky presents it differently, logically, as a killing enacted by Kirillov's bullet in the brain, where the man-god God must end, and also put an end to Dostoevsky's own complaint, his life-long thorn in the flesh, the uncertainty of God's existence. 'Before terminating in blood an indescribable spiritual adventure,' Camus adds, 'Kirillov makes a remark as old as human suffering: "All is well".'

Camus is aware of Gide's lectures on Dostoyevsky but concludes differently from him. Whereas Gide dwells on the obsessed Gospel-tormented Dostoevsky, Camus has another purpose for the Russian author. Which is the question of suicide in a universe of absurdity. His well-chosen emblematic myth of Sisyphus, the titan condemned by the god Zeus to suffer the punishment of futile labour by pushing a huge boulder uphill that must at once roll down, and to begin again, up and down eternally, the very essence of absurdity. Camus addresses the rarest cause of suicide, the one committed 'on reflection', and in that sense motiveless as the solution to the absurd. His steadfast position is clear: 'Even if one does not believe in God, suicide is not legitimate.' Existence is grounded on the absurd – Camus allows no exit – and the only final legitimate answer to it is not suicide but to go on living, fully aware of its absurdity in the shadowless noonday glare of Camus's favoured pagan Mediterranean light. Kirillov's pistol shot of universal liberation was pointless. It went unheard. We go on wandering lost as before in the desert of antinomy, in the inescapable paralogistic contrariness of beliefs. Dostoevsky, although familiar with the problem of absurdity, is not in Camus's opinion an absurdist but 'existentialist' writer. (Existentialist is not unalloyed praise in Camus's book: his close war-time friendship with the arch-Existentialist Jean-Paul Sartre ended in bitter feud over their divergent attitudes to Stalin, political violence and the question of French colonialism in Algeria.) What contradicts absurdism in Dostoevsky's writing is not its Christian character, surprisingly Camus avers, since it is possible to be at once Christian and not believe in the afterlife. He comes up with the ultimate prodigiously absurd idea that would cause Gide at first to gasp in sharp intake of breath, that is, to postulate 'the absurdity of the Gospels'. Camus bolsters that egregious notion with another more stunning affirmation: 'It throws light upon this idea, fertile in repercussions, that convictions do not prevent incredulity'. He imputes to Dostoevsky a familiarity 'with these paths' that he refuses and instead concludes thus for Kirillov and his entire dark palette of characters: *'existence is illusory and eternal'*. I would think this belief ought to recruit Dostoevsky for the supreme Absurdism.

I perceive the outlines of a vista almost too contentiously expansive to take in, from Gide's intuition of the gratuitous act in 1914, on the eve of the First World War's introduction to an incomparable scale of mechanised de-individualised carnage, to Camus some three decades later voicing an absurd freedom, while Europe sank its identity under Nazi blood-drenched domination. These two viewpoints between them look across a terrain of historical calamity – and my tumbleweed on its incidental travels over the killing fields of history has gleaned the charred remains of genocidal wars and revolutions. Dostoevsky benefited from a stylite platform of foresight from which he could preview a future world in fearsome upheaval that his Nechayev-inspired terrorist Verkhovensky anticipated with great exhilaration. And it came to be a twentieth-century reality in the abattoir of WWI, the Bolshevik revolution's long drawn-out Gulag repressions in the Stalinist era, the WWII Nazi atrocities, and A-bombing of Japan. The juggernaut of history rolled across the century and continues no less calamitous across ours to level out responsibility and de-personalise evil We can grasp as though in a single horrifically compressed interval the German army's first use of chlorine gas in 1915 to asphyxiate its enemies on the Ypres front and SS henchmen in the 1940s dropping Zyklon-B pellets through the roof vent of the Auschwitz extermination gas chambers – and hold that specimen interval on a Vernier scale calibration as an epitome model of the furthermore appalling evils of our time. Yet the greater the escalation of evil that occurs, the more it is absorbed and integrated, vanishing as if in a sort of social acculturation whereby evil undergoes the de-individualisation of banality and calamity.

Kirillov's man-god homicide, so to speak, is an aberrant anti-Christ suicide from one viewpoint, from another it succeeds to carve a hole of the gratuitous act in de-individualised evil. Better, more exactingly absurd, if Kirillov went on living, according to Camus's credo, hinged on his idea that 'convictions do not prevent incredulity'. This idea, 'fertile in repercussions', which it certainly is, while it might redeem personal responsibility, is also its potential erosion by cynicism. Camus seems unaware that a conviction without belief, though it may be properly absurd, risks being self-deceptively in bad faith, as Jean-Paul Sartre would argue existentially. That way lies the expediently amoral revolutionary's approval of mass killings. I recall Gide's sobering warning: 'what absurdities are introduced into this world under cover of the gratuitous act…'

Gide's scrutiny of the gratuitous act takes us afield to events in his own experience that would compose a novel in itself. To begin with, a disability secreted in Gide's life made him aware that Dostoevsky's story of possession is something else than fear of nihilist terrorism, something more than merely fiction, even something beyond his enchantment with the unique religiously-inspirited destiny of Russia. Rather, instead, imagine it as a prolonged state of the aura, the sudden clairvoyant bedazzlement of mind, like an annunciating angel, that is precursor to epileptic seizure. If I am deemed to exaggerate, then take it nonetheless as an expression of the chaos within Dostoevsky's soul which finds echo in Gide's cleaving to the gratuitous act of evil. What is that echo responding to a secret in Gide's life to which I have alluded?

Secretive would not seem appropriate to describe Gide's lifetime's career of autobiographical exposure, who openly confessed his pederasty and published his extensively maintained *Journal*. Confessional pride, one could say, if not exhibitionist arrogance. His most bewildering spectacle occurred in 1934 when this individualistic urbanist declared himself a Communist disciple of the Soviet Union, 'an unprecedented experiment capable of sweeping along the whole of humanity', for which he was willing to pay the price 'of my life were it necessary to assure the success of the Soviet Union, I would gladly give it immediately'.

His enthusiasm did not survive a visit to the Soviet Union in 1936. Adamantine dissidence of spirit prevented him falling victim to Lenin's cynical category of 'useful fools' reserved for foreign 'fellow travellers'. Neither was he duped by Stalin's sly charlatanism nor seduced into mouth-agape wonder at the marvels of the Soviet Union while touring under the strict guidance of Disneyland-like chaperones during his visit. He scandalised the left upon return by publishing his denunciation of the Soviet Union's 'homogenisation' of its citizens: happiness of all is only achieved by the de-individualisation of each [...] In order to be happy, conform.'

Gide died in 1951, at the end uttering *c'est bien, c'est bien* ('it's fine, it's fine') as though echoing Kirillov's last words. 'All is well.' François Mauriac, the Catholic writer expressed his unease at the way Gide, that 'evil pilot of souls', had taken leave of the world, apparently tranquil and wholly unrepentant. Mauriac was vindicated by the Vatican placing Gide's entire oeuvre on its Index of Forbidden Books in 1952. Nobody in the literary intelligentsia dared voice unambiguous tribute to this writer who despite his professed candour remained elegantly aloof and evasive. Jean-Paul Sartre unexpectedly stepped forward in homage to Gide, paying him the inestimable favour of enlistment to Existentialism, while having to overlook Gide's evident attitude of non-commitment. 'He could, like so many others,' Sartre writes, 'have relied on concepts, made up his mind when he was twenty on whether he was going to be a believer or an atheist, and stuck from then on to his decision. Instead of which, he made a point of *testing* his relationship to religion. Hence, the living dialectics that led him eventually to atheism is an itinerary that can be retraced after him, but it does not lend itself to an abstract definition... What makes Gide's example unique is the fact that he chose to *become* the truth he was sensing.'

Which truth is it that Sartre is stalking in Gide's life? The map is not the territory, it's said. The truth of the territory is what you set foot in, where in reality you can lose your way, and in which the map of intellect may not give helpful guidance. Fiction disintegrates into particles, as in random Brownian motion, and reassembles as compelling domestic history. So it is to tell Gide's true story. Only after his death in 1951, could the occulted truth emerge, finally confessed in his last book, *Et Nunc Manet in Te*, 'And Now She Remains in You', referring to the wife of Orpheus, Eurydice, lost to Hades and published in English translation as *Madeleine* in 1952. Gide's lost 'Eurydice' is his wife Madeliene Rondeaux, his cousin two years his senior, whom he married in 1895. He admits a passionately ideal love for her but within the bondage of a *marriage blanc*, that is, an unconsummated marriage that lasted forty-three years until her death in 1938. His asexual adoration of Madeleine, a pure love untainted by desire, all those years, while at the same time fully luxuriating in his pederastic affairs of which she was to her misfortune reluctantly aware. She retired early on in their pseudo-marriage to distance herself from Gide's frantic chase of the exotic to a life on her inherited Normandy estate in the eighteenth-century château of Cuverville, a three-storey manor with fourteen bedrooms in a seventeen-acre park surrounded by three hundred acres of farmland; splendid though it sounds, her true domain was willingly circumscribed to the rear pantry, the milk room, storeroom, and vast kitchen of gleaming copper ware in which she devoted herself to ascetic daily chores of domestic maintenance 'in a stifling odour of kerosene, wax and turpentine'. Gide witnessed her 'lovely hands gradually become ugly by dint of labouring like a 'skivvy housemaid', as though the cleanliness to which she religiously confined herself might sanitise her husband's sinfulness. She sacrificed herself to virtual anonymity – no letters from her, no diaries, few photographs, barely any evidence of her existence – apart from the frequent custodial references in Gide's *Journal* where she appears again incognito, not as Madeleine but under guise of 'Em', like a child intoning 'M', short for Emmanuèle, the pseudonym he devised for her.

He understood to his own self-punitive disquiet what the disfigurement of her hands, her seclusion and piety, signalled desperately to him. She existed forty-three years terrorised in the gilded captivity of his delusion. Here he is, too late, after her death, facing up to his unconscionable tyranny: 'but when, today, I reflect on our common past, the sufferings she endured seem to me...so cruel that I am unable to understand how, loving her as much as I did, I was unable to shelter her more. But this is in part because my love involved so much thoughtlessness and blindness'. 'Thoughtlessness' in Gide's apologetic use should alert us to Hannah Arendt's dismayingly similar terminology to verge on reprieve of Eichmann's banality of evil. He goes on:

> I am amazed today at that aberration which led me to think that the more ethereal my love was, the more worthy it was of her – for I was so naïve as never to wonder whether or not she would be satisfied with an utterly disincarnate love. That my carnal desires should be addressed to other objects scarcely worried me at all, therefore. And I even came to convince myself comfortably that it was better so. Desires, I thought, belonged to man; it reassured me not to admit that woman could experience similar ones unless she were a woman of "easy virtue". I must confess the outrageous fact that such was my heedlessness, which can be explained or excused only by ignorance which life had encouraged in me...

Again, we can pause on Gide's expedient sanctuary of 'heedlessness' and consider it in Arendt's suggested sense of banal atonement for the inexcusable. Evil is not the work of demons but of ordinary 'heedless' humans. The genius of Gide's writing, its imposing moral scope, forbids him the alibi of ordinary 'heedless' person.

Gide reiterated a series of unmindful acts of cruelty irremediably wounding to Madeleine. In 1916, at the age of fifty-seven, he absconded to England to begin a quasi-conjugal relationship with sixteen-year-old Marc Allegret that lasted until 1927. (She retaliated by burning all of his treasured correspondence.) He admits only to the 'remorse of having warped her destiny' by denying Madeleine any hope of motherhood, while allowing himself indulgence in the 'procreative act' by fathering a daughter, Catherine, in 1923 with thirty-three-year-old Elisabeth van Rysselberghe, his brief and only sexual liaison with a woman, though she stayed devoted to him and resided in the next door apartment to his on the rue Vavin in the Paris 6th Arrondissement. He ends his memoir on Madeleine's forty-three years of domestic Calvary resolutely insisting that his love for her was exerted upon him by her utter dissimilarity:

Yet however different from me she may have been, it was having known her that made me so often feel like a stranger on this earth, playing the game of life without too much believing in it, for having known through her a less tangible but more genuine reality. My intelligence might well negate that secret reality; with her, I felt it. *And in the absence of the pure sound that soul gave forth, it seems to me thenceforth that I had ceased to hear any but profane sounds, opaque, faint, and desperate.*

I overhear in those word the acuity of Stendhal's moral psychology. Totally sincere. And not. Madeliene vanishes in that glance over his shoulder, as Eurydice yanked back into Hades when Orpheus turns for a moment to glance at her; and apt choice of mythic allusion for his book title. However, I have italicised the last sentence in the preceding quote for reason of closer inspection. Something more can be overheard. Gide's transgression is better diagnosed in clinical germs as a form of dissociative narcissism. The image of the mythic Narcissus reflected in the pool of his self-regarding sexual preference deafens him to the nymph Echo's lovelorn predicament. Echo's futile laments to heedless Narcissus fade away to her namesake condition, an echo of herself. Such is the archetype of Madeleine and Gide in their distressingly misaligned stories – and Gide will too late, as though Narcissus were suddenly restored to hearing Echo, record 'the absence of the pure sound that soul gave forth'.

Three times, like the three knocks of the dramaturge's staff on the stage floor drawing the audience's attention to the curtain rise in classical French theatre; like the Gospel tells of Peter's three denials of Christ before the cock crows; we find Gide turning to the seductions of the gratuitous event, first by erasing the ethical line between 'honest man and the knave' in 1909, and then testing motiveless gratuity a second and third time in two novels in 1914 and 1925 in which hoax and deception are prominent features, as they are paralleled in his own life. Was he practising the gratuitous act of evil in reality by victimising his wife, and not simply theorising it in fiction? Foolish question. The answer seems redundantly obvious. And I have been proposing it all along indirectly by putting Gide himself under reflective Dostoevskian scrutiny of fiction. Dostoevsky endeavoured to disencumber himself of possession by several conflicting demons, and one most close to him, Kirillov, the metaphysical anti-hero, the blasphemous iconoclast who destroys the image of Christ in his soul by self-sacrificing himself. That is the key, self-sacrifice.

The gratuitous act is what Gide attributes to Kirillov; it is not something Dostoevsky assigns to his act of suicide. Self-sacrifice was an abysmal vertigo of attraction for Dostoevsky which had its background fascination in the underground Christian spiritualist sect, the Skoptsy, 'Eunuchs', originated in the eighteenth century, who engaged in the rite of castration of their male brethren and the mastectomy and vulvectomy of their women participants in order to eliminate lust. The seventeenth century established the flagellant sect, the Khlysts, and later other persecuted Christian movements, the Dukhobors and the Ikonobortsy, cults rooted in the soil of serfdom and the peasantry. Self-mutilation extinguishes evil. Dostoevsky was only too awake to Christ, the supposed gentle 'Lamb of God'. commanding self-mutilation in his Sermon on the Mount: 'And if thy right hand cause thee to fall, cut it off and cast it from thee; for it is profitable for thee that one of thy members should perish, and not that thy whole body should be cast into hell.' (Matthew, 5:30). Suicide in this light is a milder form of self-sacrifice; but it too is a tentacle of chastisement that issues as if from the *chernozem*, from the Russian black earth itself, in search of the final reckoning. And here too is the ancient gnarled and ingrown forestry of indignation prepared for the revolutionary conflagration that must come, the apocalypse that Dostoevsky awaits fearfully.

Gide seems far remote from that in his splendid Normandy château at Cuverville, and so too Madeleine, its prisoner chatelaine. But dissimilarity is Gide's fatal attraction, he confesses. He could ascribe to Kirillov's suicide what his previously gestated rationale of the gratuitous act seemed evidently to offer him as speculative explanation. However, there is more, a dreadful prospect to imagine, that Madeleine presented herself to Gide as a living experimental specimen of self-sacrifice, right there in the Cuverville laboratory in which she was wilfully incarcerated. No going back. No undoing of Madeleine's claustrophobic condition. She is like one those immured cataleptic brides in Edgar Allan Poe's gothic tales. Gide buries Madeleine a second time by withholding the secret of her concealment. He admits it in an entry to his unpublished intimate diary, dated 26 January 1938, in Marseille, in which he writes of finalising the proofs of the prestigious Pléiade edition of his *Journal* (1889–1939): 'upon rereading it, it seems to me that the systematic suppression (at least until my loss) of all the passages relative to Madeleine have, so to speak, *blinded* it. The few allusions to the secret drama of my life become incomprehensible through the absence of what would throw light on them; incomprehensible or inadmissible, the image of that mutilated me that I give there, which presents, in ardent place of the heart, a hole'. In his choice of words, 'absence', 'mutilated', 'hole', I hear the faraway muffled resonance of Kirillov's pistol shot.

Have I come at last to the *individual* discovered in the gratuitous act of evil? Or is it moral disablement of volition that again lapses into banality? Evil inflicted by inured self-indulgence. I am thrown back on Dostoevsky's insight that he assigns to Dmitri Karamazov's *interrogative* appalment as originally expressed in the novel: 'If there is no God, is everything permitted?' We have an answer. Dostoevsky goes further, much further, in Kirillov supposed 'logical suicide'. It may not be evident to readers of *The Possessed* that Dostoevsky has approached the creation of Kirillov by the back door of apophatic theology traditional in Russian Orthodox Christianity, a mystical form of negative theology, if my earlier definition of it is recalled, which denies any possible access of knowledge to God by the human intellect. The question is not of Dmitri's feared atheistic inexistence of God, or of Nietzsche's 'death of God' by nihilistic infidelity, but, for Kirillov, of a negative intuition of God only accessible by his *pure* gratuitous act of self-sacrificial annihilation. And, for Kirillov, it is the once-and-for-all individual gratuitousness of his act, the suicide of the man-god, that puts an end to evil which can only exist by purpose of divine dictate. Self-mutilation to eliminate evil – a terrifying idea that flashed on Dostoevsky's mind by example of Russia's primitive spiritualist self-harm movement, the Skoptsy. Possibly. But something more than 'possibly', and far darker in Dostoevsky's outlook, is steering gratuitousness into the metaphysical arena of theology. The inexistence or even death if god is merely sensationalist. What does decisively matter with grave theological outcome is the *end of transcendence* which results from modernity's enlightened progress.

I consult the text by the social philosopher Peter Sloterdijk, *God's Zeal*, in which he addresses 'seven aspects of the phenomenon of transcendence'. His seventh stage of transcendental meaning is particularly of interest to

me, on revelation, which is characterised as 'the belief that a higher power
beyond, usually known as "God", turns its attention to individual humans
in special moments – out of love, sympathy or outrage – and chooses them
as recipients of messages that, following certain criteria of authentication,
are interpreted as revelations....revelation means a message "from beyond"
that obliges its recipient to submit gracefully.' The story of Job's testing by
God in the light of Jung's analytical view can be seen to fit this frame of
revelatory transcendence. As Sloterdijk observes:

> the concept of revelation...sets up an analogy between the feudal relationship
> of lord and vassal and the cognitive relationship of object and subject, with a
> clear emphasis on the primacy of the lord and the object. According to this
> model, the receipt of a revelation corresponds to the extreme of vassalic pas-
> sivity. It marks a case in which listening and obeying coincide...It is immedi-
> ately clear why this model loses its plausibility, both social and
> epistemologically, in cultures characterised by devassalisation. The notion of
> purely receptive subjects transpires as logically and empirically untenable...
> The "turn towards the subject" not only makes revelation depassivise itself – it
> also enables it to free itself increasingly from narrower religious contexts: it
> can no longer be restricted exclusively to the unique declaration of a trans-
> cendent sender, as in the case of holy scripture... the facts of the science indus-
> try and artistic creation in modern times offer unambiguous proof that the era
> of merely received revelations has come to an end. The activist culture of
> rationality has seen the development of a strong antithesis to the passivism of
> ancient and medieval times that is waiting to be understood by the advocates
> of the older concept of revelation.

Sloterdijk has sentenced transcendence to the Jacobins' guillotine,
rendered it acephalous, literally without a head. Chaos, the utter chaos of
a reign of revolutionary terror, would be Dostoevsky imagining a
Westernised-style modernising loss of transcendence in Russia's highly
'vassalised' Tsarist culture. But it is the present fix of globally non-
transcendental society that Sloterdijk appeals to: 'the devotees of the old
ways are faced with the task of acknowledging how gravely they have
overestimated religious revelation as the key to the nature of all things, and
underestimated the illumination of the world through awareness in life,
science and art...without a certain convergence of the tenets of religious
revelation and non-religious worldly illumination, the thoughts of the

religious would be taken over by irrational arbitrariness.' Need I say, 'irrational religious arbitrariness' is upon us, and evil goes on wandering heedless and headless in the vague terrain of secular non-transcendence. Leading to genocides.

GENOCIDE DENIAL

Abdelwahab El-Affendi

In June this year, a ninety-six-year-old German grandmother was given a sixteen-month prison sentence by a Hamburg court for repeatedly claiming that Auschwitz-Birkenau camp was not a concentration camp. This was the last of many convictions the unrepentant Nazi elderly lady has received in recent years. German law makes it illegal to deny the Holocaust. So does a score of countries in Europe and around the world. In Austria the prominent sixty-eight-year old British right-wing activist and historian David Irving was given a three-year sentence by a Vienna court in 2006 for remarks he had made in Vienna seventeen years earlier. In a speech he delivered in 1989, he described the Holocaust as a fairytale. In April 2019, a French court sentenced the essayist Alain Soral to a year in prison, for Holocaust denial, after posting derisory images and remarks on a website he runs.

While a majority of European countries penalise Holocaust denials to certain degrees, the argument for this being an unjustifiable restriction on freedom of expression has been duly made. In fact the Spanish Constitutional Court struck down in 2007 as unconstitutional aspects of provision of the Criminal Code that penalized the denial and justification of the Nazi Holocaust, arguing that the mere expression of such views does not necessarily incite genocide.

These arguments notwithstanding, questioning episodes of massive suffering for which a considerable weight of evidence continues to pile up is usually linked to questionable motives. It at least suggests that the interlocutor does not value the lives of the victims enough. It certainly aims at undermining the claims of the victims' heirs and defenders, calling them more or less liars and fabricators. There is an element of malice here, an attitude that shows no care about the suffering and torment of the victims, of the loss of their kin. It matters little what cruelty they have been subjected to, or whether they lived or died. Usually, it is linked to the feeling that 'they deserved it,' or even the claim that those defending them may also deserve the same fate.

One may argue that episodes relating to the Holocaust, or to comparable instances of mass cruelty, such as the Stalinist purges, Chinese famines, Khmer Rouge Killing Fields, Bosnian massacres, Rwandan 100 days of slaughter, and others, have been shrouded in some mystery. The perpetrators took care to hide them behind well-constructed barriers, consign them to remote areas, or even cause the evidence to vanish into smoke. They usually did not boast daily about them in multimedia platforms. There was also that barrier of constant denial. It thus usually took a long time before evidence emerged, and much more before it became believable. The US War Office, as Samantha Power points out in *A Problem from Hell: America and the Age of Genocide,* refused to allow reports by escapees from Auschwitz to be published, arguing that the American public would not believe their stories.

The exception is of course the illegal immigrants who flooded from the early sixteenth century onwards, into the homelands of natives of the continents the illegal immigrants called America. Those armed illegals from England, Spain, and elsewhere in Europe, were so brazen in their abuse of the locals that they glorified their theft and genocide of the locals as great victories. They continue to do so more than five centuries on. But these are a special category of perpetrators.

What happens, however, if such massacres were public, broadcast live, around the clock, in painful detail? What do you call denial in this case? If someone was dismissing this as 'a fairy tale,' after seeing all of this, reading multiple reports by United Nations agencies, human rights organisations, health officials and aid workers, and survivors, on every form of media outlets? And if this sustained coverage went on and on for almost twelve months, they still continued to deny, belittle, and dismiss this televised torment, taking refuge in lies and self-deception? How long can their sanity be accepted, or sustained?

I am speaking of Gaza, of course, that narrow strip of seaside land, extending from the northern borders of Egypt to the South-East border of the rest of occupied Palestine. The enclave has become the world's most notorious killing fields after the 7 October attack by Hamas when a limited episode in the ongoing conflict between Israel and armed groups snowballed into a no-holds barred one sided assault on Gaza. The first act of denial started with calling this devastating one-sided attack on Gaza a war. From day one, the Israeli president described Gazans as 'human animals', while the minister of defence announced publicly that Gaza will not receive food, water, medicines, or electricity, absolutely none. American, German, British, French, and other allies poured limitless supplies of weapons, equipment, and cash into one of the world's strongest armies, to help it fight civilians. There has never been anything like this, with the powerful states of the world assisting the wanton murder of utterly defenceless captive civilians. All tried to 'reinterpret' the genocidal statements of Israeli leaders extremely charitably. All shouted in unison that Israel was 'defending itself', and has every right to do so. Although what we kept seeing on our screens is a one-sided onslaught on unarmed civilians, mass destruction of homes, hospitals, schools, universities and every structure in Gaza. What we did not see on our screens is that the defenceless civilians were there as refugees when they were driven out from their homes by the very state firing its mighty guns into their 'refugee camps'. They have been languishing there since 1947, and have been under a smothering siege since 2005.

Most interestingly, the 7 October attack in Gaza, which killed about 1,200 people and kidnapped over 200, was described as the resumption of the Holocaust, and a campaign to exterminate Jews. As I have explained in detail elsewhere, no matter how we describe the 7 October attack, it cannot qualify as a genocide. To start with, the bulk of genocide research theories concur that genocide is almost exclusively committed by states. More importantly, sub-state actors do not usually have the capacity to conduct genocide, which requires a capacity to identify, locate, separate, and imprison the target population so as to conduct systematic killings. In any case, Hamas could not conduct any systematic killings with the few hundred personnel it had sent into Israel, and the few hours it had there. Not against such a heavily armed garrison-state like Israel, backed unconditionally by the world's mightiest states.

In fact, Israel was doubly responsible for the high number of killings. First, because its so-called super-army failed to wake up from its slumber quickly enough when it received information about the attack. Most

Hamas attackers did not expect to survive for long, let alone conduct a number of trips into Israel and back, with hostages. The Israeli army has the capacity to thwart the attack and prevent Hamas fighters from returning home with hostages. But it did not use it. Second, it became clear within days that the bulk of the killings, including deaths at a nearby music festival, were the fault of an Israeli counterattack. The Israeli used attack helicopters and other devices to incinerate a large number of Israelis beyond recognition. Further evidence emerged when the Israeli military revised casualties from 1,400 to 1,200, admitting that 200 were in fact dead Palestinian attackers. This was a further revelation of the use of massive fire that Hamas did not have.

In any case, a besieged impoverished enclave like Gaza could not and cannot threaten Israel with destruction, even if it was fully armed with tanks and airpower, since Israel has defeated multiple Arab armies, usually within days, even without its present intensive arsenal of ultra-modern AI weapons. So, the widely accepted and disseminated propaganda that Israel needs to defend itself by conducting a genocide in Gaza cannot stand up.

What is intriguing, and very troubling, is that centres of commemoration of the Holocaust, like the Yad Vashem, were at the vanguard of denial. For example, Dani Dayan, the chairman of Yad Vashem, responded negatively to a letter sent from fifty-six leading holocaust and genocide scholars asking the Centre to condemn the genocidal rhetoric of Israeli leaders and society. According to one of the signatories, 'over 500 genocidal public statements have been made by [Israeli] leaders, senior military officers, lawmakers, journalists, and other shapers of public opinion'. He also cited an Israeli journalist that rhetoric supporting genocide is inescapable in Israel, whether on TV, social media, in cafes, or private conversations. However, the Yad Vashem response was to claim that such rhetoric was 'marginal', and referring to 'countless acts and statements' from Israel indicating desire to comply with 'proper moral norms', 'within the constraint Hamas imposes on us'. In other words, Israeli is beseeching Hamas to give it permission to be moral and relent from their genocidal rampage. 'Look what they make us do!', to cite a Nazi adage.

We are on uncharted territory here, with prominent scholars like German philosopher Jurgen Habermas indicating a Hegelian stance that Germany's moral commitment is to stand behind Israel, no matter what. In other words, if Israel thinks that genocide is good, then so be it. As Israel kept murdering children on live TV, that is what Germany in fact did, supplying the weapons and ammunition, and everything else necessary, including the arrest of protestors. Many other academics, intellectuals, religious leaders, heads of states, parliaments, media organisations, and substantial sections of public opinion, thought the same. A daily dose of televised genocide was most welcome, even if it goes on for months and years.

Apparently, the bulk of Muslim nations and Palestine's Arab neighbours, became part of the pack. Resigned to this unbearable brutality, or complicit in it. The result is a vicious genocide in which the bulk of the world is collaborative. A genocide about which the courageous dissenters who dared to point out the emperor's missing garment were shouted down, maligned, hounded out of their jobs or their school (if they were part of the many conscientious student protesters). Even wearing the signature Palestinian keffiyeh became a sinful display of antisemitism. According to the prominent French academic, Didier Fassin, self-censorship has reached up to 98 percent among junior academics in the US, and it is not that much lower among senior academics.

Public denial became *the* ritual. When Israeli Prime Minister Benjamin Netanyahu told a packed Congress Hall, on July 24, 2024, that a certain self-proclaimed historian of urban conflict told him that Israel's conduct in Gaza was the most restrained in the entire history of urban warfare, he received a standing ovation. He also told his credulous audience that the courageous and conscientious students and others protesting the Gaza genocide have been funded by Iran!

In this upside-down world, those who protest against genocide, are condemned and maligned, while those who rejoice in it become the heroes of the day. As Fassin perceptively points out, this upside-down world is based on a rhetorical repertoire that could be called the 'rhetoric of denial'. Its components include 'presentism', 'a radical de-historicization of recent events'. In this case, it imposes an assumption that the Palestinian-Israeli conflict started on 7 October, in total oblivion of the egregious crimes Israel has been committing against Palestinians for nearly eight decades,. It even overlooks the very visible phenomenon of 'refugees camps,' in which the bulk of Gazans are crammed, indicating that they have been uprooted from their homes to make room for 'Israel'. Thus, Israel has every right to defend itself against this totally unprovoked attack that came out of the blue!

Another tool in this discursive repertoire is 'hyperbole', as exaggeration: 7 October attack as a 'new Holocaust,' is launched by all those Palestinian 'Nazis'. Or as extrapolation, condemning settlements as 'illegal' reveals intention to destroy the State of Israel. Student protestors shouting 'intifada!' are in fact calling for genocide against Jews, and so on. Most effectively indicting any criticism of Israel as 'antisemitism'.

'Distortion' is another rhetorical figure used to cover the visible crimes of indiscriminate killing (plainly seen in actual scenes, or in statements by army spokespersons, or admissions of former military or intelligence officers). Instead, official spokespersons spread the propaganda that 'the most moral army in the world' does everything possible to spare civilians, giving prior warnings and directing civilians to 'safe zones' (where they are of course instantly bombed). Distortion includes explicit denial of genocide occurring in Gaza by using semantics, accusing Palestinians of being the problem and aggressors, or accusing anyone who cries 'genocide!' as having 'an unconscious desire to have a genocide perpetrated against the Jews'. Thus while actual televised genocide is brazenly denied using twisted rhetoric, slogans such as 'from the River to the Sea' are condemned as expressions of genocidal intentions.

This perceptive anatomy of the rhetorical tools of denial are crucial for discovering attempts to deny genocide and hide it within lies. There are troubling resemblances with strategies of Holocaust denial. In both cases, the denier sincerely believes the crimes have not been committed. They just do not care about the victims, and care more about the perpetrators. They in fact secretly relish the brutality meted to the victims, and believe that they deserve it.

There is another dimension to this, well-illustrated in an open letter by Habermas, considered by many as a major left-wing intellectual, and his three other colleagues, published widely on 13 November 2023. Like other deniers, their concern was indeed for the perpetrators. Their primary worries were for the rise of antisemitism in Germany, which could escalate if Israel was linked to genocide. The second, linked to this, was wishful thinking that Israel would hopefully not stoop that low. When the letter was published, this may have been marginally plausible, but only for true believers. There was a quasi-religious dimension to this partly wishful, partly precautionary assertion. It is evident in the key phrase in this open letter: 'despite all the concern for the fate of the Palestinian population, however, the standards of judgement slip completely when genocidal intentions are attributed to Israel's actions.' There is an element of sacralisation of the State of Israel, an entity that *could not have* such evil intention. Like Jesus Christ, it is not capable of sin. That is beyond wishful thinking for a state that has been based on property grabbing, ethnic cleansing, and mounting persecution of their victims. Unlike other genocidal states, such as post-War Germany, Israel failed to repent and cease its crimes. Rather, it continues the same sins of land and property theft, victimisation of the victims, and descending into its own style of fascism.

The rhetorical aspect of denial has another important dimension to it. Apart from justifying, and attempting to conceal or underplay genocide, the rhetoric is a significant aspect of the genocide process itself. Narratives are also crucial to instigating genocide in the first place. What my colleagues and I have called 'narratives of insecurity' and what Dirk Moses, Australian scholar of genocide, classifies as 'permanent security,' are central to bridging the gap between ordinary political strife and the descent into brutal one-sided violence against civilians. Moses takes as his starting point the German Nazi leadership's striving to annihilate the Jews, to the last child, as a political threat. This was necessary to achieve 'permanent security' for Germany, by eliminating present and future threat, and ensure that such threats would not re-emerge. Such themes were also present in treatment of Indians by European settlers in America, and other cases. Our perspective uses the broader concept of 'narratives of insecurities', that is stories in which certain groups or entities are embedded as existential threats. This can start from 'terrorist' threats to cultural threats to identity. In these cases, the mere presence of the Other poses a grave threat that has to countered. Like the rhetoric camouflaging and explaining away genocide, these narratives construct 'threats' (like Muslim, Communist, immigrant, Palestinian) which are cast as a deadly existential threat. In the latter case, the very existence and suffering of the 'Palestinian' is constructed and presented as a threat. This leads to more persecution and dispossession, ironically accentuating the threat. The

Palestinian is also constructed rhetorically, as an outside, and 'uncivilised intruder' in her own home, a perennial 'terrorist', 'backward savage', threatening the 'civilised' society of the 'advanced' Israeli.

Gaza is the typical case where the other is constructed narratively, using hyperbole, distortion, dissimulation, and pure lies. Here, a deliberately impoverished, besieged, wholly civilian population is brazenly presented as an existential threat to one of the most heavily and thoroughly armed settlements in the world. This 'threatened entity' can then receive tons and tons of ammunition and munitions, more sophisticated weapons, intelligence and financial assistance, to undertake saturation bombing of this enclave. Day after day, night after night, children are blown into smithereens, families are buried in rubble, hospitals and schools are turned into killing fields. But this evident barbarism is narrated as 'civilised' self-defence against the 'barbarians'.

These savage scenes, transmitted by social and unsocial media to every home around the globe, have stirred anger in many young and old hearts around the world, hearts that did not buy into the rhetoric of denial, and were not bought by the powers that be, or intimidated by bullying. This is an indication that morality and ethical integrity can survive even nuclear incinerations or equivalents. The narratives of dissimulation did not hide the naked savagery. Life is fighting death.

Speaking of narratives, there are of course limits to what narratives can distort, hide, or misrepresent. Especially in this case, where genocidal violence is graphically and painfully visible around the clock, around the world, the rhetoric of denial is too thin and lame to sustain the alternative narrative of invisible innocence, and inexistent humanity. It is interesting how evil generates its own antitheses: virtue, integrity, courage.

Movies and other forms of fiction are interesting versions of coherent and suggestive narratives. In most cases, they construct opposing contrasts of good and evil, in various shades. In each plot, there are usually heroes and villains. As the plot unfolds, the villains usually display their evil nature, and indulge in all sorts of wicked villainies and acts of depravity. The more their excesses progress, and the innocent suffer and endure, the more the audience is enraged and craves a reversal, where the innocent are saved, their injuries avenged, and their hero walks in triumphantly to vanquish evil and restore injustice. The more evil, ruthless, and wicked and wanton the villain has been, the more spectacular the ending must be.

We are approaching the finale of this action movie. The villains have shown so much depravity and bestiality that it is difficult for the scriptwriters to keep pace and imagine more evil. The innocent have suffered so much, they can barely endure more. Few of them might survive to reach the finale. A good scriptwriter would not wait too long before giving the paying audience what it is waiting for. That is always inevitable in movies like this one.

And we all know what is going to happen in the remaining minutes of this show. It is more likely to be the most spectacular finale ever.

CHAMPIONING BOSNIAN GENOCIDE

Sean Goodman

On the afternoon of Friday 15 March 2019, twenty-eight-year-old Brenton Tarrant stepped into his 2005 Subaru and headed for Al Noor Mosque in Christchurch, New Zealand. He livestreamed his car ride on Facebook and, as he drove, a song played from his car's speakers that primarily featured heavy use of the accordion and trumpet, a steady backbeat, and a man singing in a non-English language. He stepped out of his car when he arrived at the mosque, and as a worshiper at the front door greeted him with, 'Hello, brother,' Tarrant responded by firing his shotgun nine times into the building. He then dropped the gun, armed himself with an AR-15, entered the house of worship, and shot indiscriminately into a crowd of worshippers.

After his murderous rampage at the Al-Noor Mosque, Tarrant got back into his car and headed for the Linwood Islamic Center across town. His livestream cut out during this drive, and whether Tarrant knew this or not, it did not discourage him from wreaking more havoc once he arrived at his second destination. In total, Brenton Tarrant murdered fifty-one Muslims before he surrendered to local authorities.

Since that day, dozens of academics and journalists have analysed Tarrant's motive. It is considered by most, including the perpetrator himself, to be an act of anti-Islamic terror fueled by white power nationalism. The evidence is insurmountable and appears in various manifestations throughout Tarrant's livestream. Everything he wrote before, and everything he included on his livestream, seemed to have a second meaning, from the seventy-four-page manifesto he titled 'The Great Replacement' that he emailed to multiple addresses before he started shooting, to the various slogans he wrote on his AR-15, to the music he played in his car. One of the slogans he wrote on his assault rifle was, 'Remove Kebab,' an internet meme often circulated in far-right forums that is a reference to the Turbo-folk song he played for his audience. The song was originally titled: 'Karadžić, Lead Your Serbs,' and is a Serbian nationalist anthem released during the Yugoslav Wars, and contains anti-Muslim and anti-Croat lyrics.

Brenton Tarrant's decision to livestream his act of mass murder was unique, but his decision to invoke imagery stemming from the Yugoslav Wars, particularly of the anti-Muslim variety, was not. Indeed, the celebration, or trivialisation, of crimes committed against Bosnian and Albanian Muslims during Europe's most violent conflict since World War II, began almost as soon as reports of war crimes came out of the former Yugoslavia.

Various scholars from multiple disciplines contend that in the last decade of the twentieth century, western media outlets depicted the Yugoslav Wars as a series of conflicting narratives and fragile alliances. To the uninformed, this framework complicates a cohesive understanding of events. Nevertheless, some facts about the Yugoslav Wars remain indisputable: Slovenia and Croatia were the first two republics to declare independence from Yugoslavia in 1991, Serbs living in the Republic of Bosnia declared independence for Republika Srpska soon after, fighting lasted for roughly ten years, Serbian forces withdrew from Kosovo after NATO conducted a seventy-eight-day bombing campaign, between 130,000 and 140,000 civilians died, and over four million people experienced displacement. Another indisputable fact is that the International Criminal Tribunal for the former Yugoslavia (ICTFY) convicted the former president of Republika Srpska Radovan Karadžić and the leader of the Army of Republika Srpska Ratko Mladić of genocide. Moreover, the Serbian president of Yugoslavia, Slobodan Milošević, was indicted for war crimes and genocide but died in 2006 before the court reached a verdict.

Multiple sources, including eyewitness accounts and international NGOs, have recorded a litany of war crimes that occurred during the war in Bosnia. These crimes include rape, ethnic cleansing, and massacres that were perpetrated by Serbs, Croats, and Bosnian Muslims (Bosniaks). On the surface, Serbian war crimes inflicted upon the Bosniak population stand out for their brutality and scale. Some examples of these atrocities include establishing literal 'rape camps' in the towns of Foča and Pale and holding Bosniak fathers at gunpoint and forcing them to castrate their sons.

On a deeper level, these nightmarish war crimes stand out due to reports indicating that these were not random acts of violence, but rather, part of a larger deliberate genocidal policy orchestrated, approved, and upheld by Serbian leadership.

One piece of evidence that supports the claim that Serb forces were engaging in war crimes and genocide is a photo captured by the BBC journalist Matthew Price. In the centre of the image stands a young, shirtless, and emaciated man behind a barbed-wire fence with a dozen young men behind him. The man is Fikret Alić, a Bosniak prisoner of war detained in a Serb-held prison camp in the town of Trnopolje. TIME Magazine printed the image on the front page of its August 1992 issue. Despite the image creating public outrage, the Bosniaks received no help from the international community until 1995. That year in July, Ratko Mladić entered the newly captured town of Srebrenica and proclaimed, 'we give this town to the Serb people as a gift. Finally, the time has come to take revenge on the Turks [Muslims] in the region.' Soon after this proclamation, the Army of Republika Srpska, under his command, executed over 8,000 Bosniak men and boys outside the town. NATO and the United Nations Protection Force then launched a three-week bombing campaign targeting Serb military positions within Bosnia. Operation Deliberate Force occurred shortly after the Srebrenica massacre, but the official reasoning NATO and the UNPROFOR (UN Protection Force) provided for involvement was due to a separate massacre that occurred a month after Srebrenica in the city of Sarajevo. The campaign helped bring an end to the war in Bosnia, which concluded with a peace agreement signed by the warring parties in Dayton, Ohio in the US.

Like the earlier conflicts in the Yugoslav Wars, the Kosovo War consisted of multiple moving parts and conflicting historical accounts that are centuries old. In 1989, the Serbian president of Yugoslavia Slobodan Milošević took over the previously autonomous province, angering the ethnic Albanian majority and emboldening the ethnic Serbian minority. Milošević often utilised Serbian nationalism, and in June of that year, commemorated the 600 anniversary of the Battle of Kosovo with a speech at the Gazimestan monument. Despite acknowledging the multi-ethnic makeup of Yugoslavia, Milošević spoke specifically to the ethnic Serbs in the crowd of over one million:

> Six centuries later, now, we are being again engaged in battles and are facing
> battles. They are not armed battles, although such things cannot be excluded
> yet. However, regardless of what kind of battles they are, they cannot be won
> without resolve, bravery, and sacrifice, without the noble qualities that were
> present here in the field of Kosovo in the days past ... Six centuries ago, Serbia
> heroically defended itself in the field of Kosovo, but it also defended Europe.
> Serbia was at that time the bastion that defended the European culture, reli-
> gion, and European society in general.

Milošević proceeded to rule Kosovo in the 1990s as an authoritarian,
employing Serbian police to repress opposition. Such repression led to the
emergence of the Kosovo Liberation Army (KLA), which aimed to have
Kosovo secede from Yugoslavia. After the KLA coordinated successful
attacks against the Serbian police, the Yugoslav Army entered the province.
Initially, fighting between the KLA, Serbian security forces, and the
Yugoslav army resulted in over 3,000 deaths and the expulsion of over
300,000 inhabitants.

NATO leaders working with the Clinton administration pored over an
exhaustive list of options before deciding to conduct an airstrike, including
mediating a potential peace treaty between the two groups and working
with the Russian Federation to avoid military intervention. Advocates for
intervention posed legitimate concerns, such as the possibility of the
fighting sparking a wider regional conflict, and the possibility of another
Srebrenica-style massacre. The latter was legitimised after international
monitors confirmed that Serbian security forces executed forty-five ethnic
Albanian civilians in the village of Račak. Although the Serbian government
claimed that the forty-five killed were part of the KLA, independent
reports revealed that the dead included the elderly, a woman, and a child,
wore civilian clothing, and showed no indications of fighting. After NATO
forces conducted a seventy-eight-day airstrike against Yugoslavia, the
Yugoslav military surrendered and withdrew from Kosovo. The airstrikes
proved to be a military success for NATO, and likely averted another
genocide. Despite this, Operation Allied Force was and remains a
contentious issue.

Although NATO touted Operation Allied Force as a success, it was not
without serious miscalculations and unintended consequences. During the
campaign, ethnic cleansing against Albanians intensified, resulting in over

800,000 refugees. Human Rights Watch reported that the bombings resulted in 400–500 civilian deaths. Two notable instances of civilians killed by NATO bombs include seventy-three Albanian refugees and three Chinese diplomats. Moreover, after the Yugoslav army withdrew from Kosovo, there were reports of heinous crimes committed against the remaining Serbian population by Kosovo Albanians forces, including ethnic cleansing.

The white power movement in the United States and Europe negatively portrayed Bosnian Muslims and appealed to Serbian grievances as far back as 1995. In the July 1995 issue of the white supremacist magazine *American Renaissance,* one author alleges that US immigration policy will bring in 'boatloads of Rwandans, Liberians, and Bosnian Muslims.' In a June 1999 article of the magazine, the founding editor Jared Taylor writes that NATO's objective in Kosovo was to stop the removal of Albanians by removing ethnic Serbs. That same year, white power leader Louis Beam published an essay titled, 'Kosovo: The Alamo of Europe,' in which he writes, 'Sex offender Bill Clinton is supporting the Kosovo Liberation Army (KLA), a terrorist organisation … The KLA, for several years, has bombed, killed, and murdered innocent Serbian men, women, and children in an attempt to set up an independent Muslim government in the Christian Nation of Yugoslavia.' Echoing the rhetoric of Mladić and Milošević, Beam's essay reveals how Serbian nationalists envision themselves as both martyrs for and defenders of Christendom:

> 600 years ago Islamic hordes invaded Christian Europe. They destroyed every-thing in their path. Those who refused to convert to Mohammedism suffered horrible fates. The Serbian women were first raped and then sold along with their children into slavery. Serbian men not killed on the battle field were castrated and blinded to make them docile slaves for their Turkish masters. Whole cities became a single funeral pyre with their flames reaching toward heaven for the thousands who lived in them as they were burned by the invad-ers. At one point in their advance into Serbia the Turks nailed some 12,000 Serbians to crosses mocking the death of Christ and the Faith of the Serbs. The Turkish invasion of Europe seemed unstoppable as they swept over every-thing in their path with fire and sword. Until they reached the Kosovo Plain.

A Southern Poverty Law Center report on Beam's essay additionally alleged that Neo-Nazis across Europe were demonstrating against NATO intervention, while some were even travelling to Yugoslavia to fight alongside the Serbs.

Despite the Yugoslav military surrendering in 1999 and Kosovo becoming an independent nation in 2008, the transnational white power movement continues to champion Serbian nationalism. On the hate site Stormfront, a 2007 blog post by a user who identifies as an ethnic Serb denies the genocide in Srebrenica and writes, 'you will see how coalition between Jewish zog [Zionist occupied government] governments and Islamic fanatics make this whole story up!' More recently, a 2017 post titled 'History's Greatest Kebab Removers,' lists several European leaders who fought Islamic forces throughout the centuries, the last figure posted being none other than Ratko Mladić. Indeed, the 'Remove Kebab' meme remains popular in other far-right social media websites such as Gab, where several users have more recently posted 'Remove Kebab, Remove Banana, Remove Bagel,' the last two referring to the desire to inflict genocide upon Black Americans and Jews.

Adopting Serbian nationalism has transcended far beyond internet posts. Between 2016-2018, Tarrant reportedly visited multiple countries in the Balkans, including Croatia and Bosnia. In addition to the 'Remove Kebab' meme, Tarrant also alleges in his seventy-four-page manifesto that the US 'slaughtered Christian Europeans' by siding with 'Islamic occupiers' in Kosovo. He also writes that he was inspired by Anders Breivik, the white supremacist who murdered seventy-seven people in Oslo and Utøya, Norway, in 2011. Breivik also wrote and published a manifesto before his murder spree but was 1,420 pages longer than Tarrant's. The terms 'Bosnia,' 'Serbia,' and 'Kosovo' are cited hundreds of times throughout the text. In 2020, investigative journalists at Bellingcat reported that Robert Rundo, the founder of the American white supremacist street-fighting group the Rise Above Movement, was living in Serbia and networking with local white supremacist groups while attempting to recruit new members. A separate report on Rundo produced by *Balkan Insight* writes, 'Kosovo has become a case study for alt right believers in the Great Replacement theory that says Muslims are trying to displace white Christians'.

The 'Great Replacement' is a racist conspiracy theory that alleges social elites are orchestrating the replacement of white populations by non-white populations through migration, industrialisation, and secularism. Multiple adherents to the 'Great Replacement' have committed acts of terror. Such adherents include Robert Bowers (who murdered eleven people at the Tree of Life Synagogue in Pittsburgh, Pennsylvania, 2018), Patrick Crusius (who murdered twenty-two in a predominately Latinx community in El Paso, Texas, 2019), and Payton S. Gendron (who murdered ten Black Americans at a supermarket in Buffalo, New York, 2022). Gendron also published a manifesto and livestreamed his mass shooting, and according to an Anti-Defamation League report, copied large portions of Tarrant's manifesto. These specific acts also fit into the concept of 'leaderless resistance,' a popular idea within the white power movement. While he wrote an essay about Kosovo and Serbian nationalism, Louis Beam's most famous essay is on leaderless resistance. In the essay, Beam posits that destabilising governments is best achieved through non-hierarchical 'cells' consisting of small groups or individuals, rather than through top-down organisations. Instead of portraying these murderers as 'lone wolves' as they so often are in Western media, it is more appropriate to identify them as actors who are a part of a larger movement. Serbian nationalism did not cause Tarrant or Breivik to commit mass murder, rather, it perfectly aligns within a larger web of white supremacist terrorism that targets Muslim, Black, Jewish, Latinx, and other marginalised communities across the globe.

There is another sinister undercurrent in Tarrant's imagery and pertains to the graphic he used on the front page of his manifesto. The graphic shows eight slogans and simplistic artwork divided into a circle. From right to left the slogans read, 'worker's rights, anti-imperialism, environmentalism, responsible markets, addiction-free community, law & order, ethnic autonomy, and protection of heritage & culture'. In the centre of the circle is a *sonnenrad*, an ancient Germanic symbol used by various white supremacist groups. Above the circle are the words 'Towards a New Society' and below the circle are the words, 'We March Ever Forwards'. The image captures the essence of Third Position politics, which, according to the geographer Alexander Reid Ross, allows fascism to draw 'left-wing notions of solidarity and liberation into ultranationalist, right-wing ideology.' Previous examples of Third Position politics include white supremacist leader Tom Metzger promoting anti-capitalism and William Luther Pierce (author of *The Turner Diaries*) expressing the desire to sway young, white Marxists towards white nationalism. The Yugoslav

Wars is but one example out of many in which this left-right overlap exists.

The transnational white power movement openly champions the Bosnian genocide and Serbian aggression during the Kosovo War and is connected to a larger project of white supremacist murder. This would understandably lead one to assume that those who affiliate with the political left would aggressively oppose such a narrative. Unfortunately, many notable figures within the Western and international left have engaged in a different type of historical revisionism towards the Yugoslav Wars. Instead of championing genocide, they deny it outright.

In July 1992, *Living Marxism*, a British magazine launched by the Revolutionary Communist Party, published an article titled 'The Serbs: The "White Niggers" of the New World Order'. The author victimises the Serbian military as being 'subjected to the sort of propaganda treatment which Western imperialists have usually reserved for Arabs or blacks—or in the British case, for the Irish.' In a September 1992 article titled 'Bosnia: The Invention of a Holocaust', the author Joan Phillips engages in genocide denial by reasoning, 'If there were terrible atrocities taking place in Bosnia, I doubt we would be reading about them every day in the newspapers.' The legacy of *Living Marxism* lies in their denial of the Bosnian genocide, and it would ultimately bring about their demise: after accusing the production company ITN of falsifying the infamous image of Fikret Alic, ITN sued *Living Marxism* for libel in 2000 and won. To clarify, *Living Marxism* took a hard turn right a few years before engaging in genocide denial, but many 'true' Marxists and leftists are just as brazen in their denial. In the UK, genocide denial found its way to the former Labour Party leader Jeremy Corbyn. In 2004, Corbyn signed a motion supporting a 1999 *New Statesmen* article by the late Australian journalist John Pilger. In the article, Pilger writes that Serbian actions in Kosovo were a far cry from genocide. Years later, he continued this assertion, going so far as to say that the ICTFY exonerated Milošević and that 'there was no genocide. The NATO attack was both a fraud and a war crime'.

Prominent leftist academics and journalists in the United States are no less subtle in their genocide denial. In 1999, the distinguished American linguist Noam Chomsky published *The New Military Humanism: Lessons from Kosovo*. Readers of this short book could be forgiven for their ignorance regarding the brutality the Serbian military inflicted on the ethnic Albanians, considering Chomsky either purposefully or accidentally forgot to include them in his analysis. Instead, Chomsky frames Milošević as an individual acting in defiance against US imperialism and responding to 'Islamic' forces within the KLA. Chomsky's analysis also suggests that any Serb attack against ethnic Albanian civilians was rooted in their perceived alignment with the KLA. In a 2011 email correspondence with the journalist George Monbiot, Chomsky describes the Srebrenica massacre as a 'horror story, and a major crime' but refuses to acknowledge it as a genocide because it 'so cheapens the word.' Additionally, Edward Herman, who co-authored *Manufacturing Consent* with Chomsky in 1988, wrote a book denying the Bosnian genocide at Srebrenica in 2011, in which he said that the Srebrenica massacre was exaggerated. Adding to his record of genocide denial, Chomsky wrote the forward to the book.

Michael Parenti, a Marxist philosopher, published *To Kill a Nation: The Attack on Yugoslavia* in 2000. Parenti suggests that the reason Western media chose to 'demonise' the Serbs had less to do with genocidal acts and more to do with the fact that in 1989, the Yugoslav population elected former Communist party members over 'US-backed democrats.' In addition to discrediting the image of Fikret Alic and reports of mass rape committed by Serb forces, Parenti suggests that the number of victims in the Srebrenica massacre was less than one hundred. As to why the Serbs did not have a good public relations team, Parenti blames it on Western-imposed sanctions (forgetting to remind the reader that sanctions were also imposed on Croats and Bosniaks and ended up helping the Army of Republika Srpska). Regarding the Račak massacre in Kosovo, Parenti describes it as a 'well-timed well-engineered story' in which the bodies were 'placed in a ditch that night or early morning by the returning KLA unit to create the impression of a massacre'. Parenti appears to be parroting Yugoslav-state talking points, made obvious by the fact that Milošević wrote the preface for the Serbian edition of *To Kill a Nation* and that Parenti acted as Chairman of the US National Section of the International Committee to Defend Slobodan Milošević in 2003.

In 2006, the journalist and founding editor of *The Intercept* Jeremy Scahill wrote an opinion piece in the *Huffington Post* in which he portrays Milošević as a war criminal who just happened to be a victim of US imperialism.

Scahill adds to Beam's portrayal of Milošević as a defender of Christendom by writing:

> Little attention, therefore, has been paid to Milosevic's long-term efforts—which predated 9/11, the 1999 NATO bombing and his own trial—to expose the presence of al Qaeda in the Balkans—from Bosnia to Kosovo … To this day there are reports of training camps in Bosnia, which remains under occupation. It is also a likely training ground for future blowback.

The paragraph reads like it was written by a Bush-era neoconservative, rather than a man who has given scathing and rightful critiques of the US invasion of Iraq, Afghanistan, and its continuous aid to Israel. On the other hand, this portrayal is almost expected, given the fact that the same year Scahill published this article he described Bosniaks as 'white Al-Qaeda' in a talk in New York City. Although he introduces the phrase as racist, it is essentially a non-apology, since he follows up by validating the term by saying there is 'a small minority, but not insignificant minority of people in Bosnia who really are in sync with this sort of Islamic militant agenda.' Almost annually, Scahill reminds his thousands of followers on X (formerly Twitter) the anniversary of NATO's bombing of Belgrade. Unsurprisingly, a quick search for 'Srebrenica' or 'Račak' on his profile reveals 'No results.'

More recent manifestations of Bosnian genocide denial and the minimisation of Serbian atrocities from the left have appeared on X. For example, when Russia launched its full-scale invasion of Ukraine in February 2022, multiple accounts ranging from organisations to individuals legitimised Russia's concern over 'NATO expansion' by providing a list of NATO operations that have resulted in the major destruction of lives and property, such as its involvement in Afghanistan and Libya. Included in that list is NATO's involvement in the Yugoslav Wars, but no further context is provided (including Russia's role in the Yugoslav Wars). Another user with over ten thousand followers shared the photo of Fikret Alic on 13 August 2024, and wrote:

> In '92 the US used a single staged photo to persuade the world that Serbia was committing 'genocide'. In Palestine today photographic evidence of US-supported genocide is ubiquitous, unavoidable, and horrific, while human rights orgs whistle. You can't overestimate the cynicism.

Who needs the likes of Louis Beam and Jared Taylor endorsing your cause when well-respected individuals like Chomsky and Parenti can do it in their stead? Karaždić, Milošević, Mladić, who could not ask for better spokespeople?

To be sure, criticising US military action is almost always warranted, given its abysmal record. In her book, *A Problem from Hell: America in the Age of Genocide*, Samantha Power criticises the US and its inaction during the Bosnian genocide. She alleges that the Bush administration was well aware of Serbian war crimes and made the decision to not intervene as early as 1992, despite the fact that 'no other atrocity campaign in the twentieth century was better monitored and understood by the US government'. While another academic, Dale C Tatum, writes 'the war in Kosovo was a war that should not have occurred, but it occurred due to the indifference of the US and its Western European allies.' Most credible and academic accounts of the Bosnian genocide and Kosovo critique inaction by the international community. They also underscore critique is possible without minimising lived experiences of survivors. If there is going to be criticism towards Western powers during the Yugoslav wars, it should be for their unwillingness to prevent genocide.

The issue of genocide denial and the trivialisation of war crimes within the left is not reserved for Bosnia and Kosovo. Activists and researchers have seen this play out in other regions where war crimes and genocide have occurred. Whether regarding Syria, with prominent leftists denying atrocities committed by the Assad regime, or justifying China's self-ascribed 'People's War on Terror' against the Muslim Uyghur population in Xinjiang, to accepting Putin's ludicrous 'de-Nazification' justification for invading Ukraine. The language surrounding these populations sounds eerily similar to language used by those who so many on the left claim to abhor. If one were to replace the accusation that jihadists were operating among the civilian population in Bosnia and Kosovo with jihadists were operating among the civilian population in Gaza, then one would have a typical talking point that is being used to justify Israel's genocide against the Palestinian population in Gaza.

By denying genocide and omitting war crimes perpetrated by Serbs, and instead opting to portray them as victims of Western imperialism, leftists create an opportunity for future Tarrants to justify white supremacist murder. It also legitimises genocide denial at the state level, which, in some cases, enforces denial through violence. Regardless of time or place, genocide denial usually comes in the form of four phases. 1. Denial: 'Nothing happened.' 2. Reluctant Acceptance: 'Okay, we admit that something happened, but it was not as bad as you are saying it is.' 3. Victim Blaming: 'Okay, fine. We admit that something happened, and it was bad, but it was the victims who started it. If the victims didn't start this, then there would have been peace.' And, 4. Prideful Acceptance: 'Yes. Something did happen, and it was bad, but we are happy to do it again if you don't shut up about it.'

For those of us with a moral backbone, it should be obvious to disengage from this framework altogether. Instead, we should see it as a duty to educate those who are ignorant that genocide is the crime of crimes. If we deny or minimise genocide, then we are just as culpable in enacting harm as those who champion it.

SYSTEMS OF CATASTROPHE

Liam Mayo

The first time I heard of Bassem Youssef was in 2011 when a colleague of mine from Egypt showed me videos of *The B+ Show* on YouTube. 'This guy is amazing – he is really sticking it to the government!' Shamim announced to me, as a small group of us gathered around his laptop to watch the videos. We'd all been watching what had transpired in the Middle East since the Arab Spring. For many of my workmates, these events had very real implications for the places they used to call home, places where most of their families still lived.

The video plays for a few moments and then our small group breaks into a loud roar of laughter. Not me though, I don't speak Arabic. 'He's very good, Liam. Trust me. He's a very smart guy.' Shamim chortles at me.

It is almost fourteen years before I come across Bassem Youseef again. I remember him because of his striking green eyes and handsome jawline. His hair is greyer now. This time he has popped up on my incessant social media feed; that thing from which I seem unable to divorce myself. It is a clip from an interview with Piers Morgan that has gone viral. Bassem is speaking English. He is also an American citizen now.

Referring to the Hamas-Israel war, Youssef jokes about killing his Palestinian wife – 'they're very difficult people to kill … I try to get to her every time, but she uses our kids as human shields'.

Piers shifts uncomfortably. 'Dark humour there, and I understand why. Because no…'

'It's not dark humour. I really try to get her every time, but she uses our kids as human shields. I can never take her out.'

Piers tries to correct trajectory. '… Again, I understand the humour, but to be serious, Bassem, about this tonight, there is…'

At one-point Bassem pulls out a graph, comparing the number of Palestinian deaths to Israeli deaths. He points to the 2014 ratio of twenty-seven Palestinians killed for every Israeli. He calls this 'a very good exchange rate'. Dark and deadpan, it is gripping and terribly entertaining to watch.

'What I'm saying' Bassem continues, 'is what is the exchange rate for today? So you guys will be happy, that's my question. I want to know.'

Piers fires back – 'Well, it's not me, it's not me, guys. I'm not on either side here.'

The two go back and forward, Piers attempting to pin Bassem down to a statement he deems earnest enough to befit the subject matter, Bassem's biting retorts continually evade Piers' agenda.

Throughout the interview, neither use the word genocide.

The Holocaust does come up though. Piers asks '… It's about… It's about the way Hamas behaved on October the 7th was, like savages, like a pack of savages. It was the worst atrocity against Jewish people since the Holocaust. There has to be a response. And my question, be… My question for you is, what is the proportionate response?'

And thus, we arrive at the nub of Piers's position – indeed the position that has haunted the international discourse surrounding the war in Gaza since October 2023 – the notion of a proportionate response.

Let's assume Piers is not deliberately conflating the term 'proportionate'. Proportionality does have a place in what is often described as the 'laws of war'. It is a principle of international humanitarian law that restricts attacks on lawful military targets near civilians and civilian structures, prohibiting those expected to cause excessive incidental harm relative to the anticipated military advantage. It mandates a pre-attack analysis to assess potential civilian casualties and requires planners to choose weapons that minimise collateral damage. If it becomes clear that an attack will result in disproportionate harm or the target is not a military objective, the operation must be suspended or cancelled.

What Piers is doing here, like many in the West who are observing the war in Gaza have been doing, is seeking to use the parameters of agreed upon principles of war to reasonably and rationally ground and position the discourse. What Baseem demonstrates with his dark humour and exchange rate allegory is that to contextualise the issue in this way leaves the conversation entirely bereft of nuance and indeed humanity. What Piers is doing is prioritising one set of principles at the expense of others, he is seeking a straightforward answer to an extremely complex question: can the means justify the ends? Bassem is emphasising the fact that there are massive problems with the notions 'means', 'justify', and 'ends'.

This may not necessarily be a flaw in reasoning, rather a flaw in the structures that we call upon to formulate our reasoning.

The Means

On 1 November 1755, a massive earthquake devastated Lisbon, killing about a quarter of its population.

At the time, Lisbon was a prosperous, cosmopolitan city at the heart of the Portuguese Empire and one of Europe's wealthiest cities. The earthquake triggered a tsunami that struck the city's harbour, and buildings not constructed to withstand the huge tremors collapsed almost instantly. With 1 November being All Saints' Day, many of the homes and churches had candles lit, that when knocked over sparked widespread fires that amplified the destruction. This was an earthquake of immense magnitude, whose tremors reverberated across modernising Europe, stirring deep anxieties among Enlightenment optimists.

Prior to the Lisbon earthquake, European thinkers had indirectly explored the relationship between nature and society through the lens of the problem of evil; how to reconcile the existence of evil with an omnipotent, omnibenevolent, and omniscient God. The disaster in Lisbon brought to the fore the notion that the force of nature is indifferent to the piety of humanity and will unleash destruction without warning, rhyme, or reason. The Lisbon earthquake, it appeared, was not a divine punishment for earthy misdeeds, but an example of nature acting according to its own laws. This was a new type of catastrophe that required a new type of reconciliation.

The philosopher and social theorist Theodor Adorno noted that the Lisbon earthquake reached far enough to cure Voltaire of Leibniz's theodicy. He argued that the visibly comprehensible catastrophe of the natural world was insignificant compared to the social catastrophe, which defies human imagination as it created a real hell from human evil. How could humanity have failed to protect itself from such horrors. Adorno points out that the earthquake challenged Gottfried Wilhelm Leibniz's optimistic philosophy that we live in 'the best of all possible worlds'. The devastation inspired the French writer and satirist Voltaire to critique Leibniz's view in his work *Candide*, where he proposed that such profound suffering could not be reconciled with the idea of a benevolent, all-powerful God. Thus, humanity needed to equip itself with better tools to understand the world around them.

For the philosopher Immanuel Kant, living in the aftermath of the earthquake in the Prussian city of Königsberg, the disaster highlighted the profound impact of natural threats on civilisation. Initially, Kant's work, like many of his peers, was grounded in speculative and theological ideas, emphasising a divine order in nature. However, the earthquake prompted a shift towards empirical and material explanations, leading Kant to focus on human freedom and responsibility rather than divine teleology. He formulated a detailed theory to explain seismic activity, drawing on scientific literature, reports from Königsberg about the Lisbon earthquake and related events, and his overarching theory on the formation of the Earth's crust.

The focus after the Lisbon earthquake shifted toward bringing nature under human stewardship. This change aimed to control and manage nature, not only to protect the innocent from its merciless wrath, but to ensure that nature did not hinder the progress of a thriving human society again. This turn was pivotal in shaping European thought in science, philosophy, and ethics, laying the foundation for Enlightenment thinking. The goal was to reshape the world through scientific reason, viewing it as an external and measurable reality. These tools and methods were designed and treated as value-neutral, providing data to predict and control future events. This opened the path for humanity to break free from theological constraints, positioning humans as the ultimate arbiters of truth and destiny.

Shortly after the catastrophic Lisbon earthquake, Sebastião José de Carvalho e Melo, who would later become known as the Marquis de Pombal, navigated the city's ruins to reach King Dom José I. The king, having narrowly avoided the disaster because he was staying at his country palace, was unsure how to restore his ravaged kingdom. Dom José relied on Pombal, who was his secretary of state, to take charge of recovery efforts and rebuild the ravaged city. The king gave his chief bureaucrat full endorsement and delegation of authority.

During his twenty-two-year tenure, Pombal seized the earthquake as an opportunity to modernise Portugal, infusing emerging Enlightenment principles with bureaucratic systems, to rebuild Lisbon. He introduced a new building code featuring innovations such as the Pombaline cage - a masonry building that incorporates a wooden structure for anti-seismic reinforcement – and firewalls and oversaw the creation of a gridiron street plan in the Baixa district. Pombal's focus on scientific observation and empirical evidence, as opposed to viewing the disaster as divine retribution, facilitated significant research on the earthquake and ensuing tsunami. His commitment to reasoned and rational planning modernised Portugal and established new standards in urban planning and disaster resilience that continue to shape Western bureaucratic perspectives today.

The transition from the Enlightenment to the modern world saw an expanded scope for reshaping the world through human effort. With the natural world now under our control, rationality was used to impose order and reason for the subjugation of the non-West, women, the marginalised, maligned, vulnerable, and disabled. The philosopher and cultural critic Walter Benjamin was particularly intrigued by the ways in which the Lisbon Earthquake ushered in a new worldview that would eventually mature into the myth of modernity. He famously portrayed history as a continuous catastrophe, describing the 'angel of history', who gazes upon the wreckage of the past while being relentlessly pushed into the future by a violent storm. This storm, he claimed, is what we call progress; and reminds us that progress is often accompanied by destruction and human suffering.

The political theorist and philosopher Hannah Arendt argued that wars and revolutions determined the physiognomy of the twentieth century, because their justification was the total domination over individuals and societies through the complete subjugation and control of all aspects of life. She identified the First World War as the start of 'total war,' characterised by new, highly technical weapons and tactics that targeted entire populations, not just military forces. In total war, the line between soldier and civilian blurs, and the scale of violence and destruction destabilises societies and provokes radical change.

'Total war' points to the warfare of modernity, where rapid technological advancements, industrialisation, and the rise of nation-states enabled destruction on a much larger and more devastating scale. This form of war demands total commitment from the population and legitimises extreme measures in pursuit of national or ideological goals. Thus, what emerges with modernity is the complete subjugation and control of all aspects of life, eliminating individual spontaneity and moral agency (the means), to achieve total domination of a society (the justification), to achieve the ends.

But what ends does total war seek to achieve? Well, as Benjamin observed, quite simply put, the ends is always about progress.

The Ends

Across Europe, the idea that progress is inherent to human nature began to take hold more firmly in the decades following the Lisbon earthquake. The Industrial Revolution, which transformed economies, cities, and societies, was underpinned by the belief that human beings had the capacity to continually improve their conditions through innovation, industry, and science. This belief in progress as a natural extension of human capabilities extended beyond Europe as nations around the globe, especially through colonialism, assumed European models of development and industrialisation.

This worldview, grounded in the mythological belief that time equates to progress, assumes that history is a natural progression towards improvement, enshrined by the conventions of strong and functional bureaucracy. Modernity's progress is often celebrated for its social advancements in justice, ethics, and morality, all of which are enshrined in strong bureaucratic systems. However, as the philosopher of modernity Marshall Berman notes, whilst modernity brought with it a sense of exhilaration at the possibilities of progress, it is also tinged with a recognition of the constant destruction and upheaval that this progress entails. The purpose of strong bureaucratic systems, he notes, is to ensure that this destruction and reconstruction is undertaken through reasoned and rational processes.

This type of progress, what Benjamin calls the piling of catastrophe upon catastrophe, implies that progress is a narrative shaped by the victors and transmitted from one ruler to another. History becomes a battleground where societal memories are contested, divided between what is deemed true and the influence of those in power. Thus, by the time we reach the Holocaust, the paradox of catastrophe and progress has become an entirely normal part of modern society. We need only look at the British endeavours against the Boer in South Africa between 1899 – 1902. Or those of the Spanish against Cuban rebels in 1896. As the Polish-British sociologist Zygmunt Bauman observes, the Holocaust was not an anomaly but a manifestation of modernity's darker potentials.

Bauman reminds us that modern systems, built on efficiency, rationality, and bureaucracy, can easily be co-opted for horrific ends. In *Modernity and the Holocaust*, Bauman views the Holocaust as a lens to examine the dangers embedded within modern societal structures, rather than as an isolated event neatly set apart from the rest of history. He calls for vigilance against the ethical risks within these systems and invites deeper reflection on how societal structures can be manipulated for destructive purposes. The bureaucratic efficiency, technological advancements, and rational planning that are hallmarks of progress are also instrumental in the execution of genocide.

This challenges the tendency to see the Holocaust – indeed genocide more broadly – as a unique aberration and instead integrates it into the broader narrative of human history. It also calls into question the conditions that allow such catastrophic events to arise within the frameworks of modernity and rationality. How can a just, moral, and ethical society allow such horrific human catastrophe to take place?

In 1943, after witnessing the horrors of the Holocaust, the Jewish-Polish lawyer Raphael Lemkin devised the term genocide. 'Genos' is the Greek word for race or tribe, and 'cide' is 'to kill' in Latin. His campaign to have genocide recognised as a crime under international law came to fruition in 1948 when the United Nations Genocide Convention was adopted. Raphael Lemkin's effort to criminalise genocide reflects, what we would commonly understand as, a form of moral and legal progress. By establishing genocide as an international crime, the international community sought to prevent future atrocities and further advance human rights. This is demonstrative of a notion of progress where societies strive to create systems and frameworks that promote justice and prevent inhumane practices.

After the establishment of the Genocide Convention, bureaucratic systems within international organisations, such as the United Nations, play a crucial role in monitoring, enforcing, and promoting human rights. The bureaucratic structures involved in the implementation of international laws and conventions reflect a commitment to progress in protecting human dignity and preventing genocide. What we have here, in essence, is the use of bureaucratic instruments, to enshrine into bureaucracy mechanisms to prevent and protect against actions that have historically been deployed and enacted by similar bureaucracies. Thus, for Lemkin and the United Nation, progress is not achieved through Benjamin's piling of catastrophe upon catastrophe, rather by piling bureaucracy upon bureaucracy.

So, we may ask, does this piling of bureaucracy upon bureaucracy achieve our goal of progress?

Well, applying a bureaucratic lens to the matter, the most apparent measure of the effectiveness of this approach would be its ability to prevent or mitigate the actual occurrences of genocide in real time. Have we made progress? How many genocides have there been? And, more significantly, how many have been prevented?

In recent years, the term 'genocide' has been applied to numerous historical and contemporary events, each carrying substantial implications. Notable cases include the 1995 Srebrenica massacre in Bosnia, ruled as genocide by the International Criminal Tribunal for the former Yugoslavia (ICTY), and the 1932–1933 Soviet-engineered famine in Ukraine. The Indonesian invasion of East Timor (1975) and the atrocities committed by the Khmer Rouge in Cambodia, which resulted in 1.7 million deaths, are often debated under the label of genocide. While these acts were catastrophic, the Khmer Rouge's political motives fall outside the UN's specific definition of genocide. More recently, the International Criminal Court (ICC) issued an arrest warrant in 2010 for Sudanese President Omar al-Bashir on genocide charges in Darfur, and in 2016, the US accused the Islamic State of genocide against minorities in Iraq and Syria.

In 2017, The Gambia filed a case with the International Court of Justice (ICJ) accusing Myanmar of genocide against the Rohingya people, leading to mass displacement and deaths. By 2021, the US, Canada, and the Netherlands officially accused China of committing genocide against the Uighur population, citing forced sterilisation, mass detention, and forced labour, though China denies the allegations. Historically, at least three genocides are widely recognised as meeting the 1948 UN Convention's definition: the Armenian genocide (1915-1920), which Turkey denies, the Holocaust, where over six million Jews were murdered, and the 1994 Rwandan genocide, which claimed around 800,000 lives.

Bill Clinton, US President during the 1990s, has publicly expressed profound remorse over the international community's failure to act during the Rwandan genocide. He has described this inaction as one of the biggest regrets of his presidency, reflecting that intervention might have saved hundreds of thousands of lives. He remarked, 'I think we could have saved at least a third of the lives that were lost… if we had done what we could have done'.

The reluctance of UN member states to intervene in such crises arises from a complex blend of factors. Central to this is the principle of state sovereignty, which grants each nation authority over its internal affairs and views external interference as a violation of that sovereignty—a foundational element in the narrative of modernity. This principle fosters a cautious stance, where countries are hesitant to criticise or act against one another, even in the face of grave human rights abuses. Additionally, the fear of escalation plays a crucial role, as intervening in a state's internal conflict could exacerbate the situation or trigger a larger regional or global crisis. Political alliances and economic interests add further layers of complexity, as states may be unwilling to oppose or intervene against nations with whom they share significant relationships.

Historical precedents and legal constraints also influence the UN's approach. Past interventions shape contemporary responses, and legal hurdles, such as the need for Security Council approval, can delay or prevent action. In the case of Rwanda, these factors combined to result in a tragic failure by the international community to prevent genocide, illustrating the profound challenges and limitations faced by the UN in responding to crises.

So, if we observe here that the means – genocide – justifies the ends – progress – how are we to rationalise the incoherence between progress as the piling of catastrophe upon catastrophe, the ongoing destruction and reconstruction, and the notion of progress as the creation of systems and frameworks that promote justice and human rights. Thus, to contradiction of modernity. As Bauman said, bureaucratic structures are indifferent to the human suffering they might cause and in its pursuit of efficiency, the bureaucracy is always blind to the ethical implications of its actions.

Just as the early Enlightenment thinkers attempted to reconcile how the existence of evil with an omnipotent, omnibenevolent, and omniscient God, are we able to reconcile the evil that exists within modernity?

I am reminded of Bassem's exchange rate allegory: 'what I'm saying is, what is the exchange rate for today? So you guys will be happy, that's my question. I want to know.'

Wisdom

You may recall Benjamin's angel of history, overlooking the wreckage of history, thrust into the future by the winds of progress. Benjamin was a German Jew, who attempted to flee Nazi persecution during World War II. When he was denied entry to Spain, he took his own life. His suicide in 1940, at the age of forty-eight, is often attributed to his despair over the rise of social nationalism and leaves us with one key question unanswered: what was it that the angel of history saw from its purview?

What we are clear on is that Benjamin was distrustful of the promises of modernity. *The Storyteller* is his lament of the rise of commodified print media and the profession of journalism. He was deeply concerned about what he saw as the decline of storytelling as the conduit of wisdom. Long before the internet of things, Benjamin foresaw the ways in which the modern printing press would lead to the notion of information as a universal natural category. He viewed information as the promise of a quick and easy solution to immediate problems. However, he argued, information cannot convey wisdom because it presents experience in an abstracted form, already detached from its original context and 'shot through with explanation.' Information's 'prime requirement is that it appear 'understandable in itself.'' This is contrasted to storytelling which serves as the true vehicle of wisdom, precisely because it avoids explanation. Unlike information, which must always sound plausible, the storyteller embraces 'marvels'—things that defy explanation. In fact, half the art of storytelling is to preserve the story from explanation as it is retold; wisdom lies within waiting to be discovered. Stories, therefore, remain open to reinterpretation across changing contexts, passed down from one generation to the next.

In the 1930s, during the shadow of the rise of the Nazi party in Germany, Benjamin explored the potential of radio as a democratic medium through a series of broadcasts for children. These broadcasts focused on natural and industrial disasters such as floods, fires, volcanic eruptions, earthquakes, and train wrecks. Benjamin saw radio as a tool to reconcile the gap between science and public interest, believing it could foster a more democratic approach to knowledge by making complex events more accessible and relevant to everyday life. Through these broadcasts, Benjamin sought to promote an epistemological shift toward a more inclusive and participatory form of communication. And in doing so, he aimed to harness the potential of radio as a tool for promoting popular enlightenment.

Observers interpret Benjamin's broadcasts as allegorical warnings about the looming disaster of National Socialism. Yet, they may also be understood within the broader context of post-World War I intellectual efforts to theorise human behaviour in response to catastrophe. These lectures not only highlight Benjamin's acute political foresight but also reflect a deeper engagement with how societies make sense of crisis amid rapid technological change and industrialisation. His concern extended beyond the immediate dangers of fascism to the broader erosion of wisdom in a world increasingly dominated by technological advancements and the commodification of information, where deep, contextual understanding is replaced by superficial, abstract knowledge. His attempt here was to reintroduce the art of storytelling to the medium of information.

With his account of the Lisbon earthquake Benjamin's primary concern was to narrate catastrophe, particularly for a young audience, by entertaining without sensationalising the event. He experimented with various narrative strategies, shifting from a scientific explanation of seismology to journalistic reporting on the destruction and then to a first-person account of an Englishman who survived the earthquake. While some of his scientific facts were outdated or incorrect, Benjamin's focus was on the transition from objective reporting to the more subjective and morally charged eyewitness narrative. The Englishman's testimony, deeply personal and evocative, served as a counterpoint to the detached tone of science and journalism, emphasising the human experience of disaster and hinting at the broader social and political vulnerabilities exposed by the earthquake.

As Benjamin explored the moral weight of personal testimony, he simultaneously acknowledged the competing authority of scientific knowledge, interrupting the Englishman's account to verify geophysical data from other sources. Yet, he concluded on a note of scepticism, that while science might one day predict earthquakes, for now, human understanding lags behind the instincts of animals like dogs. This final reversal underscores Benjamin's ambivalence toward modern technological advancements and information-centric narratives, subtly critiquing their limitations in capturing the complexity and wisdom embedded in human experience. Benjamins ultimate message is that information alone cannot convey wisdom because it presents experience in a detached, overly explained form that must appear self-contained and plausible, whereas storytelling, by avoiding explanation and embracing marvels, keeps narratives open to reinterpretation across audiences and across generations.

We may never know what Benjamin's angel of history foresaw. Just as we may never get an answer to Bassem's human exchange rate question. And we may never know what the angel made of humanity's yearning to pile catastrophe upon catastrophe as a means to progress. Just as we may never know why Benjamin felt suicide was his best avenue.

But what we may derive from these is that the catastrophe of war is fundamentally unrepresentable. Not simply because of the human suffering, but also because human suffering is inadvertently acknowledged, enshrined and/or facilitated by the very systems that espouse contradictory objectives. And that, we cannot truly discuss that which we cannot comprehend. That perhaps the wisdom we may garner is that the tragic silence of suicide, and the leaving of questions unanswered, is the most poignant retort to the flagrant contradictions of modernity.

Knowledge

Postmodernism was an attempt to expose or, more accurately, to deconstruct the contradictions that exist within the systems of modernity.

I am reminded of the 1979 Vietnam War epic, *Apocalypse Now*, directed by Francis Ford Coppola. Like a surreal fever dream, the film delves into the horrors of war and the darkness within the human psyche, drawing inspiration from Joseph Conrad's novella *Heart of Darkness*. The film follows Captain Willard – who is our angel of history - on a secret mission to assassinate Colonel Kurtz, a rogue officer who has set himself up as a god among a local tribe.

Like the angel of history, Captain Willard is caught in a relentless forward motion of progress through destruction, witnessing the suffering left in its wake. Willard's journey up the river mirrors the angel's backward gaze at history, where progress is marked by ruin and catastrophe. This is vividly illustrated in the beach landing scene where American soldiers, led by Lieutenant Colonel Kilgore, demolish a Vietnamese village to the sound of Wagner's 'Ride of the Valkyries'. The juxtaposition of classical music with brutal destruction creates a nightmarish, operatic spectacle, highlighting the absurdity and mechanised nature of the war.

Willard, narrating his journey upriver, describes the military as a corporation in the industry of war, where human lives are reduced to mere assets and liabilities, dehumanising the conflict into a coldly calculated enterprise. The strange presence of film crews and journalists amidst the scenes of chaos adds another layer of absurdity, showing how the war is fought not just on the battlefield but also in the media, turning real-life horrors into consumable content. Willard, like Benjamin's angel, is powerless to alter the course of history, embodying a tragic awareness of the cyclical nature of violence and destruction.

Not by coincidence, the literary critic and philosopher Fredric Jameson called the Vietnam War 'the first terrible postmodernist war,' suggesting that it embodied the sensibilities of an emerging historical epoch. In postmodernism, knowledge is seen as fragmented, subjective, and deeply influenced by social, cultural, and historical contexts. The Vietnam War was marked by immense complexity and ambiguity, with a lack of clear moral or ideological frameworks, which is consistent with postmodernism's rejection of grand narratives. Unlike earlier conflicts that were often justified by appeals to nationalism, freedom, or democracy as absolute values, the Vietnam War revealed the fragmentation of these ideals, with competing narratives from different actors—governments, media, protesters, and soldiers—each presenting different versions of truth.

This contrasts sharply with modernity's faith in progress, objectivity, and universal truths. Postmodernists reject grand narratives—comprehensive explanations like scientific rationalism or Enlightenment ideals—arguing that knowledge is intertwined with power structures and historical contexts, making any claim to objective truth inherently suspect. This shift is evident in how the Vietnam War was mediated and experienced. The extensive media coverage of the war shaped public perception, exposing the disconnect between the US government's official narratives and the brutal realities on the ground. The Vietnam War became a symbol of how knowledge and information, even when widely disseminated, often fail to catalyse meaningful change, with power systems resisting both moral and factual challenges.

The social theorist and cultural critic Ziauddin Sardar's critique of postmodernism, particularly in *Postmodernism and the Other,* highlights its limitations in addressing non-Western perspectives. Sardar argues that postmodernism operates from a Eurocentric lens, marginalising non-Western voices and failing to engage the complexities of the 'Other,' especially in the contexts of colonialism and globalisation. He warns that postmodernism's relativism risks leading to nihilism, where rejecting all meta-narratives paralyses action in the name of justice, ethics, and morality. Thus postmodernism, like the bureaucratic structures of modernity, is simply another system or process enabling subjugation in the name of progress.

Sardar advocates for a more constructive engagement with modernity's tools, recognising the ethical responsibility to engage with marginalised voices while acknowledging power dynamics and historical injustices. In this way, Sardar critiques the passivity inherent in postmodern thought, particularly its failure to account for the lived experiences of those outside the Western paradigm. This critique resonates with what played out with the Vietnam War, where the data was present, the atrocities were undeniable yet entrenched political power systems prevented meaningful action.

The fragmented, postmodern understanding of the Vietnam conflict reveals that knowledge, no matter how abundant, can be rendered irrelevant in the face of entrenched structures that prioritise control, profit, and dominance over human life. This tragic irony—where the more we knew, the less it seemed to change—underscores the disconnect between information and accountability. Despite detailed reports of atrocities, such as the estimated two to three million total deaths across Vietnam, Laos, and Cambodia, which included as many as 627,000 Vietnamese civilians, those responsible for the devastation were never prosecuted for genocide or war crimes under international law.

Indeed, despite clear violations of human rights by the US, including bombings and massacres that devastated Vietnamese society, the United Nations' Genocide Convention was never invoked against any state actors involved. The evidence of atrocities was overwhelming yet entrenched political interests and global power dynamics blocked meaningful intervention. In this sense, Captain Willard's journey in *Apocalypse Now* reflects the futility of knowledge in a modern world where awareness does not lead to salvation, but rather to the ongoing cycle of violence, unchecked by reason or justice.

And today, with knowledge of the past and the clarity of foresight, the structures we rely on are either too fragmented or entrenched in maintaining the status quo, meaning the collective international community cannot align action with what we understand to be true.

Information

The philosopher and media theorist Marshall McLuhan highlights this paralysis with his idea that 'the medium is the message', describing how the overwhelming flow of information and the mediums through which it is delivered shapes our perception and engagement, making it difficult to distinguish signal from noise and effectively act on the knowledge we already possess.

Writing in the early 1960s, McLuhan was interested in the form of communication itself, particularly through new technologies, and the way they shaped human perception more profoundly than the content delivered. As society transitioned into the age of television, advertising, and digital screens, McLuhan observed that images became the dominant mode of communication, replacing written and spoken language as the primary carriers of meaning. In the postmodern world, images are not just representations; they create reality, dissolving the boundary between what is true and what is simply portrayed. The image, detached from any original or deeper truth, becomes an empty signifier, capable of being manipulated to evoke any reaction or belief, with no inherent obligation to represent reality.

McLuhan's ideas echo and extend Benjamin's warnings about the detachment of information from its original context. While Benjamin saw mechanical media stripping wisdom from stories, McLuhan saw the rise of mass media images as dissolving the very concept of authenticity altogether. In postmodernity, information is no longer merely abstracted but is replaced by the spectacle—a world where images bombard individuals to the point that they become passive consumers rather than active interpreters of meaning. The image becomes hyperreal, offering a simulacrum (an effigy) of reality, where distinctions between truth and fiction are indistinguishable.

Thus postmodernism, with its dissolution of authenticity and the rise of hyperreal imagery, has paved the way for catastrophe itself to be commodified and transformed into an industry. As the boundaries between reality and representation blur, the spectacle of disaster becomes not just an event to respond to, but a phenomenon to be managed, packaged, and consumed across various sectors. This shift marks a profound evolution where the response to catastrophe is no longer just about addressing immediate needs but about orchestrating a complex, multi-disciplinary system that capitalises on crisis.

What has emerged with late-stage modernity is catastrophe as a spectacle, consumed and mediated through global attention. The spectacle of catastrophe is not limited to the event itself but extends to the industries that emerge around preparing for, responding to, and recovering from such disasters—whether natural or human-made. These industries span sectors such as emergency management, insurance, construction, technology, healthcare, NGOs, education, and government agencies. Disciplines like risk assessment, environmental science, public health, law, and psychology all converge to create an intricate system aimed at navigating disaster. Catastrophe is no longer just an occurrence; it becomes a focal point of attention, shaping economies, technologies, and political responses.

This spectacle-driven ecosystem seeks not only to mitigate the impact of catastrophe for the good of society but also to reinforce the narrative of progress. It moves beyond merely understanding the devastation, addressing the human actions that have caused or worsened disasters. As such, catastrophe itself becomes a driver of progress—an industry that sustains and advances society by confronting destruction while simultaneously capitalising on it. In this way, the spectacle of catastrophe both reveals the fragility of human systems and serves as a tool for their continuous fortification and evolution. This is the professionalisation of the relativism of information. And this is the professionalisation of progress.

In this sense, McLuhan's view of media intertwines with Benjamin's view of the printing press, as both thinkers suggest that modernity's progress, particularly through its media and communication technologies, not only erodes our capacity to engage with truth but reshapes what truth even means. As postmodern theorists have argued, in an age dominated by screens and symbols, reality itself is mediated through fragmented and constructed images, leaving individuals adrift in a world where meaning is perpetually deferred, never fully graspable. This shift in communication patterns not only devalues the wisdom that Benjamin found in storytelling but also transforms the very fabric of how we perceive and interact with the world.

Thus, Benjamin and McLuhan both illustrate the paradox of modernity: while it promises enlightenment, reason, and progress, it simultaneously obscures deeper truths by prioritising surface-level information and spectacular images over complexity and authenticity. This erosion of the capacity to discern truth, combined with the saturation of media-driven images, leaves society in a precarious position—one where the ability to truly comprehend reality is constantly slipping away amidst the noise of the modern world.

Brazilian philosopher and writer, Vilém Flusser, a media theorist whose work has gained increasing relevance in the West, argued that our relationship with 'technical images'—images produced and mediated by technology—has fundamentally altered our experience of reality. According to Flusser, we no longer exist solely in the tangible world but inhabit multiple realities simultaneously, mediated by emergent technologies. These abstracted realities shape our perceptions, values, and behaviour, influencing how we engage with the world and construct our sense of self.

Flusser's concept of the 'Ladder of Abstraction' highlights how our efforts to understand the world through increasingly abstract forms, like technical images, have distanced us from the concrete reality of material existence. Technical images, which do not require human intervention to be produced, are generated by automated, hermetic systems—'black boxes' that obscure the processes behind them. This abstraction, Flusser suggests, has transformed how we perceive and interact with the world, shifting our understanding of reality itself.

In today's world, this process is most evident through our use of smartphones and other digital devices, which serve as the primary tools of abstraction. These devices reshape how we experience and express the self. No longer confined to a single, embodied existence, we now present ourselves simultaneously as both physical beings and as digital profiles—fragmented, disembodied representations in the virtual realm. Our identities become scattered across these multiple realities, as we exchange the solidity of the physical body for the digital fluidity of pixels and data points.

This shift, according to Flusser, is the result of an unspoken cultural agreement, a 'pact of disintegration,' in which we willingly fragment ourselves in exchange for the benefits of digital connectivity. The physical self becomes intertwined with the digital self, blurring the boundaries between the two. As a result, we not only live in a tangible, molecular world but also inhabit a digital world that deeply influences our identity and behaviour.

For Flusser our immersion in and dependence on digital realities has far-reaching implications for how we understand and construct the self, and indeed how that self-interacts with the world. As our interaction with technology deepens, it transforms not only our communication and interaction but also our fundamental sense of existence. Just as the bureaucratic structures of modernity and the knowledge systems of postmodernity enable subjugation in the name of progress, our interaction with the world through digital realities both abstracts our experience of the world and subjugates the essence of the self.

Data

When I read Flusser, I think of the writer William Gibson who, in *Pattern Recognition*, reflects on the idea that space—whether physical, virtual, or conceptual—has become an infinite repository of abstracted data, derived from the vast networks of computers within human systems. In this view, data no longer exists simply as information in its original, tangible form but as layered abstractions, filtered through digital interfaces and computational processes, detached from their real-world contexts. These abstractions are constantly generated, stored, and manipulated across the global matrix of interconnected systems, turning space itself into a vast field of disembodied information.

Sardar offers a compelling critique of how contemporary society engages with data, information, knowledge, and wisdom. He argues that the overwhelming abundance of data does not lead to greater understanding but rather to confusion and fragmentation. For Sardar, data is nothing more than raw, unprocessed facts and figures, collected from a variety of sources—be it social media, scientific experiments, or corporate analytics. On its own, data holds no inherent meaning. It is merely a collection of detached points, devoid of context or interpretation.

In today's world, we are engulfed by what Sardar calls an 'information smog'—a dense fog of disconnected data that obscures our ability to make sense of the world. Paradoxically, the more data we accumulate, the harder it becomes to derive true knowledge or wisdom from it. Information, without interpretation or connection to broader systems of understanding, does not bring clarity. Instead, it deepens our ignorance. Sardar suggests that this data deluge leads us not toward enlightenment but toward confusion, leaving us disconnected from the truth.

This fragmented data does not contribute to the construction of knowledge but rather to its dismantling. Thus, information exists as isolated snippets that fail to come together into coherent narratives or meaningful frameworks. As society increasingly relies on data and algorithms, we risk losing the essential interpretive work needed to transform data into human understanding. Wisdom—defined as the highest form of knowledge, combining facts with ethical insight and long-term thinking—becomes even more elusive in this fragmented, data-saturated environment.

Sardar's critique echoes a broader disillusionment with the limits of rationalism and the inadequacy of knowledge systems born of modernity. He draws parallels to earlier critiques of modern warfare, where the accumulation of information did little to prevent destruction or foster understanding. Similarly, today's raw data—without proper cultural, ethical, and historical frameworks—cannot lead to genuine insight or meaningful action. Instead, we are caught in a perpetual state of information overload, where true knowledge and wisdom slip further out of reach.

Compounding this problem is the role of algorithms and the corporate systems that control our digital environment. Algorithms, embedded in the software of websites, search engines, and social networks, perpetually monitor online behaviour and determine which content gains visibility. These algorithms are designed to feed users more of what they already want, creating a feedback loop that reinforces existing beliefs and preferences. This system is not neutral. Corporate interests, eager to exploit big data, use algorithms to manipulate what we see and consume, selling our behaviour as a commodity.

The rise of digital influencers and social commentators further complicates the relationship between lived and virtual realities. Retail companies, interest groups, and ideologues acquire data to target vulnerable individuals, infiltrate social networks, and use algorithms to create echo chambers. These influencers, normalised by digital culture, shift our perception of truth, knowledge, and expertise. In the digital age, the lines between truth and propaganda blur, and the marketplace of ideas becomes just that—a marketplace, driven by profit rather than wisdom.

Platforms like Twitter (now X) have democratised truth, making all truths relative. The power to create and disseminate truth has shifted from traditional institutions—governments, media, science—to individuals who hold devices. In this new reality, each user can learn from others in a reciprocal cycle of influence. When an opinion or idea resonates, its influence grows rapidly, and those who espouse these new 'truths' become influencers, supported by followers who propagate their message. This is how algorithms and data now control the flow of information, shaping our perceptions and realities.

The American author Eli Pariser coined the concept the 'filter bubble' reveals how algorithms selectively guess what information we would like to see, based on our tastes, locations, and browsing history. While the internet may seem like an open public space, it is in fact a commercial space driven by the laws of the market. Our culture has created technology to meet its needs, but now this technology defines our culture. What we consume online shapes our truths, colonising our minds and our ways of being.

Thus, in our digital age, data has replaced wisdom, and truth has become fragmented. The contemporary use of data, driven by algorithms and corporate interests, has clouded our ability to maintain coherent narratives and discern truth. We are left with an ever-increasing amount of information but without the ethical or interpretive frameworks needed to transform it into knowledge and wisdom. In this new reality, ignorance flourishes, and the very systems that promised to bring us closer to truth may, in fact, be driving us further away from it.

A viral video of Bassem Youseff using his dark humour to neutralise the sensationalist media juggernaut that is Piers Morgan is only as effective as our ethical and interpretive frameworks to transform the knowledge we are being delivered into wisdom. And as we have discovered, the further we subjugate the self through our interaction with this form of media technology, the more bereft we are to attain that wisdom.

The Justification

So, let's return to Bassem Youseff's viral interview with Piers Morgan. And, particularly, to this lingering query: do the means justify the ends? Piers is our medium, in the McLuhan sense: the medium is the message. His role here is to maintain the grand narrative of progress and does so through the power structure of sensational journalism. Bassem is our storyteller, in the Benjamin sense: the art of the story is to preserve the story from explanation as it is retold. This is a stalemate.

Enter Jeremy Boreing the managing director of *The Daily Wire*, a conservative American news and media company founded in 2015 by Boreing and the conservative political commentator Ben Shapiro. *The Daily Wire* is known for promoting conservative viewpoints on a wide range of political, social, and cultural issues, often taking a stance against liberal or progressive ideas. It has gained a significant following, particularly among audiences who lean right on the political spectrum, and its content often focuses on free speech, limited government, traditional values, and criticisms of mainstream media and 'cancel culture.'

Boreing is fairly matter of fact about what he sees as being the thrust of the debate: 'First of all, the question of how many sons of b*tch have to be killed in order to end this conflict. I suppose that the answer is, as many of them as it takes. That doesn't mean that I, or Ben, or any decent person in their right mind, is happy with the killing of civilians. Uh, I posted at the very beginning of this conflict that a woman or a child blown apart in Gaza is just as tragic as a Jewish baby killed in one of the settlements. That doesn't mean that Israel's actions and the actions of Hamas are morally equivalent. You know, the tragedy is the tragedy, but the moral equivalency is nonsense.'

Piers is more comfortable with an interviewee who is at least earnestly speaking directly to the matter, rather that esoterically using humour. 'Let me ask you though, Jeremy, what, I mean, the question which I think is the big question, what is a proportionate response to that outrage on October the 7th, which is the worst attack on Jewish people since the Holocaust? What is proportionate?'

Jeremy goes on. 'Certainly, well, first of all, I don't know what a proportionate response is or why we would want it. I suppose a proportionate response would be for 3,000 Israelis to go through the fence, gun down innocent Palestinian women and children, burn their bodies, burn them alive, take hostages, rape their women. No one wants a proportionate response. No, no moral person could possibly call for a proportionate response. The purpose of war is to defeat your enemy. The West has, in my lifetime, forgotten the purpose of war because the true cost of war is so terrible. The last time the West engaged in war and won it was World War II, and they did it through incredible brutality. They did it by bringing their enemies to heel.'

You can sense Jeremy building to his crescendo, and here it comes. 'I would say that the only way to morally justify a war is to win it. Otherwise, your argument, the very argument that brought you into the war, "this enemy must be defeated", ends up being proven a lie.'

And there we have it. As simple as that. Boreing remains steadfast to the myth of progress. And in one simple statement demonstrates the continuing relevance of the words of the German politician and chief propogandist of the Nazi Party Joseph Goebells: 'a lie told once remains a lie. But a lie told a thousand times becomes the truth'.

And all I am left feeling is that there is wisdom in the words of the Irish poet William Butler Yeats. 'Too long a sacrifice. Can make a stone of the heart.'

NOKHCHI-CHUO

Marat Iliyasov

Nokhchi-chuo is a small place on the northern slopes of the Caucasian mountains, where the Nokhchi have dwelt for centuries. *Nokhchi* means 'people', an endonym implying a collective, united people who exist. This *chuo*, or place, is now known to the world as Chechnya, an imperialist term the Russians gave to the region. They also named the Nokhchi, 'Chechens'. The Russian term 'Chechnya' has no place in the Nokhchi worldview, therefore it has neither meaning nor effect. Prior to the Russian Empire's instrumentalisation of the term, it was just a way that their neighbours referred to them. For approximately three centuries this term has slowly taken its effect on the land, collective memory, and the very physical existence of Nokhchi as the international community got used to the new term the Russians had given to Nokhchi-chuo. 'Chechnya' to the Nokhchi is not only pejorative, suggesting a tone that diminishes the value of the place, but due to the long-lasting confrontation with Nokhchi, became almost a synonym for the Other – the opposite, the uncivilised, the enemy, the terrorist. After many decades, Chechnya has become a foundational tenet of contemporary Russian identity itself.

Indeed, Russia would not be what it is today without Chechnya – its villainised historical other that fought the longest for its own freedom. Ironically, this struggle actually fostered Russian imperialism and fed a depreciating attitude toward all of the conquered and incorporated ethnic groups. The first Nokhchi president and the founder of the modern Nokhchi-chuo, the late General Dzhokhar Dudayev, described this attitude as 'Ruscism', arguing that it is a 'heavy form of fascism'. Dudayev died defending his homeland from Russian invasion in 1996, but this definition of Russia remained in the memory of those colonised by Russia. Since Russia's full-scale invasion of Ukraine in 2022, a campaign of social media posts and shares demonstrates that a search is underway for more of Dudayev's analysis which offered deep insight into the Russian mind while also predicting further conflicts and wars – including the present Russian-Ukrainian War. The internet has made it possible for the wider public to realise what the people colonised by the Russians have known for centuries: Russian imperialism has been changing its form but not its content or its attitude towards the smaller nations in its periphery.

A quarter century after Dudayev, the question remains and is appropriately asked in the title of a 2021 book from the prominent French American scholar Marlène Laruelle: *Is Russia Fascist?* Relying on a robust methodology and scholarly research, Laruelle argues that Russia is not fascist. The book had almost one good year before it was confined to irrelevancy by the Russian invasion of Ukraine. The war has invigorated the unpopular assessment of Dudayev and various non-mainstream scholars such as the Polish-American diplomat and political scientists Zbigniew Brzezinski, the Russian political theorist and activist Ilya Budraitskis, and the Russian economist Vladislav Inozemtsev: Russia is indeed fascist. Before this reality could surface, the world witnessed two Russian invasions in the Nokhchi-chuo, occupation of Georgian territories, and bombardments of Syria. To appreciate this fact, we must go back to the early days of Russian imperialism.

Before the Caucasian War (1801–1864), the relationship between the Nokhchi and the Russian Empire included both peaceful trade and military clashes. After the annexation of the South Caucasus state, Georgia, in 1801, Russia could no longer tolerate the independence of the North Caucasian tribes. The Empire needed control over the land and routes that lead to the South Caucasus and the local tribes were an obstacle. The orders from the Tsar were clear – to subdue the locals or exterminate them. The Russian historian Rostislav Fadeev called this war 'the longest and the costliest' out of all the wars that the empire ever waged.

At the end of that war, when the local tribes had already exhausted their human resources, Russian victory could not be secured without placing a 300,000-strong army in the region. The ratio was approximately one soldier to every ten natives, many of whom were children, elderly, or women. For the sake of a more organised resistance, many Nokhchi sacrificed some of their freedoms and established a theocratic Islamic state known to history as the Imamate. Imam Shamil, a Dagestani imam, led the

Imamate from Nokhchi-chuo, which provided him with the bulk of his military force and economic power. After twenty years of upholding a very costly resistance to the Russian military, Shamil surrendered. At that point the Nokhchi-chuo was in complete ruin. The Nokhchi started the war with a population size of approximately 200,000 people. Only half of that saw the end of the war. How many people died remains unclear.

Indeed, Russians massacred entire towns, sparing no lives. The Nokhchi preferred it this way too. It was better to die than to surrender and end up as Russian captives. In 1819, a genocidal massacre took place, the Dadi-yurt Massacre where the village of Dadi-yurt was completely destroyed by Russian forces under the orders of General Alexei Yermolov. We only know about the Dadi-yurt Massacre thanks to the famous Nokhchi artist Piotr Zakharov. He was the only survivor of the massacre. At the age of two years old, he was recovered from the ruins of the village, adopted, and raised by the family of the man who ordered the massacre, General Yermolov.

Neither this war in its entirety nor individual episodes of it (such as the Dadi-yurt Massacre) were recognised as genocide. The subsequent expulsion of the Nokhchi from their lands to the Ottoman Empire, that resulted in loss of many lives, also remained unacknowledged. The only episode of the Caucasian War that garnered the attention of the international community was the expulsion of the Circassians to the Ottoman Empire. In 2014 it was recognised as genocide, but only by the Georgian Parliament. The decision to recognise the genocide was made in a context of Georgian confrontation with Russia, when Tbilisi was looking for support from the North Caucasians.

After the conquest, the Nokhchi were forced to undergo a severe change in identity. The Russian Empire could no longer justify mass killings, resorting instead to an attempt of turning the Nokhchi into loyal citizens. The Russian administration forced alien practices upon the Nokhchi. They changed their traditional system of law into a system foreign to the natives. People neither understood the new rules nor considered them just. Following the classic customs of colonialism, the Russian Empire started extracting the oil that Nokhchi-chuo had in abundance. A Russian fortress was built on the ruins of a decimated Nokhchi settlement and given the name the *Groznaya* – the Russian word for menacing. As oil extraction picked up, a town grew around the Groznaya, becoming a major centre for oil production. Further resource extraction was accompanied by appropriation of the land from the Nokhchi, to be distributed amongst the Cossacks – the age-old enemies of the Nokhchi. Restrictions on learning and practising religion further stunted the development of the Nokhchi, severely limiting the potential to have a traditional intelligentsia. Russia offered instead a career pathway in the military. The only upward-bound path was to serve the empire by suppressing freedom and colonising others. Some educational opportunities were offered to native boys, that is of course if they assimilated to the Russian curriculum. The Nokhchi, in their traditional ways, were doomed to starve, to die as criminals, or to assimilate into the 'new' culture. Even though it is clearly genocide by all definitions, there is a continued denial of this genocide.

Colonial rule in the Nokhchi-chuo continued after the revolution in Russia and subsequent coup by the Bolsheviks in 1917. The collapse of the empire presented the Nokhchi with an opportunity, which they could not waste. However, the attempt to regain their freedom was unsuccessful. The Soviets reconquered the Nokhchi-chuo by 1925. Before that, the Reds, as the Bolsheviks were commonly known at that time, were killing everyone who were actively fighting against them. Later, they limited their targets to certain groups: the *kulaks* (rich farmers), the clerics, intelligentsia. This is well described by the late famous Nokhchi scholar Abdurakhman Avtorkhanov in his book *The Killing of the Chechen and Ingush People*. Avtorkhanov, who himself was a part of the Bolshevik elite, personally observed what was happening on the territory of Nokhchi-chuo. According to him, the Soviets specifically targeted the existing as well as up and coming leaders, many of those who were well respected by the people. The scale of the repressions was so big even the native Nokhchi communists were infuriated and led their own rebellions. Most of these rebellions were regional, but even when forces were united, they were not capable of challenging Soviet power.

Taking place throughout the 1940s, these rebellions were a sign to the Soviet dictator Josef Stalin that the Nokhchi were not assimilated. Thus, they were potential nonconformists. Stalin ordered their forceful removal from their homeland. To justify this act, which became known as the Deportation – *Ardakhar* in Nokhchi – the Nokhchi were accused of collaboration with the Nazis. A very strange accusation considering that the Soviets themselves also collaborated with the Nazis and that the Nazis never entered Nokhchi-chuo. The Nokhchi were transported thousands of miles away to face starvation and death in the cold Steppes of Central Asia.

The Ardakhar resulted in the death of approximately half of the Nokhchi population, who succumbed to disease and hunger during and right after the three-week long journey. This loss and injustice reinforced the hatred that the Nokhchi felt toward the Soviet state – just another form of the Russian Empire, which conquered their land, colonised it, and then deprived it of its people and resources. The Nokhchi sentiments toward the Soviet Union is vividly described by the famous Russian writer Alexander Solzhenitsyn in his *Gulag Archipelago*. He writes that the Chechens 'they are a nation that refused to accept the psychology of submission ... I never saw a Chechen seek to serve the authorities, or even to please them'.

The open resistance to the many attempts to assimilate them is critical to understanding the Nokhchi psyche. The French historian Nicolas Werth, in his study of the history of Chechnya under Soviet rule, cites Soviet archives describing Nokhchi behaviour in Central Asia. Rather than submitting and following the regulations imposed by the Soviets, the deported Nokhchi disregarded them. Eight years after deportation, the Deputy Minister of Interior Affairs Bogdan Kobulov reported 'the attempt to eliminate the Chechens, their culture, way of life, history and, most of all, their group consciousness by deporting and dispersing them, has failed'.

The cultural genocide of the Nokhchi during the Ardakhar was not entirely unsuccessful. Many Nokhchi lost hope of ever returning to their homes. Out of desperation and to secure their future, many Nokhchi began using Russian and Soviet names for their newborns, such as Nataliya, Sergey, Mels (an abbreviation of Marx, Engels, Lenin, Stalin), or Raikom (shortened from *Raionnyi Komitet*, Russian for 'The District Committee', which was the highest Soviet ruling organ at the district level).

The deportation has remained the biggest traumatic experience in Nokhchi collective memory. As the Nokhchi historian Mairbek Vachagaev recalled during a public lecture in Bern, Switzerland in 2023, even the cruelty of the last wars did not overshadow this experience, which became hallowed as a chosen trauma for the Nokhchi. The pain experienced extended beyond the massive death toll and declining population. Their homeland was lost. At the whim of Moscow, an entire ethnic group was turned into homeless orphans. In 1957, when some Nokhchi were finally allowed to return to their homeland they had a new challenge to face. Russian settlers had received 'free' houses after the Ardakhar and refused to give them back to their Nokhchi owners. Their hatred for the Russians and continued insistence on living in accordance to their traditional customs had the Russians living in Nokhchi-chuo complaining to the authorities and asking them to deport the Nokhchi again.

In the 1980s, the USSR was an economically stagnant and politically bankrupt state. The changes, which the Politburo adopted to refresh it, were rather cosmetic. But they were sufficient to start a chain reaction, which turned into an unstoppable process of rapid collapse for the Soviet political, economic, and societal structures. The elite failed to control reforms, lost the lead, and had to follow the masses. Moreover, the ruling Communist political party fractured into smaller groups that started fighting for power. The main struggle for leadership happened between the two top figures at that time Mikhail Gorbachev and Boris Yeltsin. The former held the chair of the General Secretary of the Communist Party since 1985. In line with the cosmetic reforms, he changed the name of his own position and became the first President of the Soviet Union. Yeltsin at that time was a popular politician and was considered a 'real' democrat and liberal. He quit his membership in the communist party and opposed Mikhail Gorbachev campaigning for the Russian Federation to be an independent state. Legally, Yeltsin relied on the Soviet constitution, which asserted that the country was a union of fifteen sovereign states with the same rights. With the reforms initiated by Gorbachev in the late 1980s, which are known as *perestroika* and *glasnost* (restructuring and transparency), real sovereignty became possible, and Yeltsin used it for political ascendency. His populist fight against the elites and use of public transport enchanted the world.

To wrestle power out of Gorbachev, it was not enough to ride the horse of liberalism. Becoming the president of the Russian Federation, which still was a part of the Soviet Union did not serve the goal either. Therefore, Yeltsin went all the way down by dissolving the Soviet Union and turning Russia into an independent state with no authority over it. Yeltsin propagated this move encouraging others to claim their sovereignty. This claim of sovereignty was not only for the fifteen republics of the Soviet Union, but Yeltsin even went so far as to say that even the various ethnic minorities who have demanded their own states should 'take as much of sovereignty as they can swallow'. It is unclear whether or not Yeltsin thought that the people of the ethnic republics of the Russian Federation would take his words seriously. However, the words were uttered and heard by the colonised peoples. Soon after, Yeltsin headed a Russian delegation to Belovezha, where together with the representative of Ukraine, who would become Ukraine's first president, Leonid Kravchuk, and of Belarus, political scientist Stanislav Shushkevich, he signed the act of disbanding the Union of the Soviet Socialist Republics. Yeltsin became a new leader. Gorbachev and the Soviet Union became history.

Now on its own, Moscow faced not only an erosion in their economic power and rising criminal activities, but the unexpected challenge born of Yeltsin's campaign words. People of the autonomous republics within the Russian Federation, Checheno-Ingushetia and Tatarstan in particular, also wanted to build their own states. They wanted a possibility for their children to learn their native languages and speak it in public. They wanted to foster local cultures and to practice their religious beliefs. They were tired of being forced to follow foreign rules and regulations imposed by the foreign administrators. They considered Russian culture, as it was, an attack on local customs and culture. They were annoyed with the Russian attitude toward them, casting them as inferior, savage, second-hand citizens.

Mutual hatred dominated Nokhchi and Russian relations up until the collapse of the Soviet Union. However, once the Nokhchi declared independence of their republic, they finally felt that they again were the owners of their own land and became welcoming hosts to the others. Overall this led to a more positive attitude and dynamic with Russians in Nokhchi-chuo. The Russians themselves did not like their new status as 'guests' and started leaving the republic. They were so used to the idea that they owned the republic that it was unacceptable to most of them to try to integrate into the Nokhchi society. Similar processes and sentiments dominated the relationship between the natives and Russians in other former Soviet Union republics.

The desire to live independently expressed by the Nokhchi and Tatars did not imply a real threat to the unity of Russia, as the other ethnic groups did not want to follow them. However, this imagined threat became the official justification of the First Russo-Chechen War from 1994 until 1996. By that time, the Tatars traded their claim for independence in exchange for more devolved powers, which were gradually taken back later anyway. Out of all ethnic groups of the Russian Federation, only the Nokhchi were really determined to go all the way to achieve their full political independence, refusing to make any deals to compromise on this. This triggered yet another episode of physical extermination by the Russian state.

The so-called Russian 'liberal democrat' Boris Yeltsin launched the Russian invasion into the Nokhchi-chuo in December of 1994. Yeltsin had instantly turned imperialist, determined to use military power to reconquer Russia's previous colonies. Thus, the attempt to democratise Russia died very shortly after it was born. Ever since, Russia continued in this vein.

The first post-Soviet Russian war against the Nokhchi-chuo lasted for almost two years. The entire territory of 11,000 square miles was turned into a polygon of the Russian military machine. Out of one million population, up to 100,000 civilians died during twenty months of war. Many were mutilated. Many disappeared. Many had their lives ruined irreparably. Horrible crimes that the Russian military committed were uncovered later in the form of mass graves, records of the witnesses, and photographs taken by natives and human right activists. These records confirmed that on many occasions Nokhchi civilians were purposefully targeted and killed by the Russian soldiers. However, the international community did not intervene to stop it, nor did it recognise that genocidal cleansings took place in the Nokhchi-chuo. The world's politicians, at the time, looked at what was going on through a very pragmatic prism: a necessary sacrifice for the sake of keeping Russia on the democratic track. The same mistake made in the 1930s, appeasing the Nazi appetite by sacrificing territory after territory. As occupation of Sudetenland followed by anschluss of Austria, Nokhchi-chuo was followed by the attack on Georgia in 2008, the annexation of Crimea in 2014, and finally the full-scale invasion in Ukraine in 2022.

Regardless the stacking of the board, the Nokhchi did not surrender. Faced with a probability of humiliating defeat, Russian military and politicians agreed for a truce and started negotiations. The result was the withdrawal of Russian forces from the Nokhchi-chuo, a victory for the Nokhchi. The Nokhchi celebrated for about two months. The population was singing and dancing on the ruins of their destroyed republic. Soon after the Nokhchi held presidential and parliamentary elections, which were recognised as democratic and free by the independent observers. The newly elected president Aslan Maskhadov soon negotiated a peace treaty with the re-elected Russian president Boris Yeltsin in 1997. At last, it declared, the '300-year confrontation' between Russia and the Nokhchi had ended. Yet, the independence of the Nokhchi-chuo was not recognised. The question was agreed to be addressed within the next five years. This never happened.

The victory of the Nokhchi shattered an already suffering image of Russia as a strong country and could have become a turning point for the Russians to embark on real democratic changes and the West to support these changes by helping the Russians and the Nokhchi to build their own respective states. Instead, after Yeltsin won his second term and the war was over, the West forgot about the Nokhchi-chuo. What mattered was that Russian 'democracy' was preserved and not allowed to backslide into communism. As for the Nokhchi and their attempt to rebuild and establish their independent state, it was left to Russia to deal with. In the eyes of the international community it was, after all, Russia's problem. Russia saw the situation differently. The question of why to invest into the lost territory was in the head of some Russian politicians. The restoration ended a few months after it began. Most of the allocated funds were conventionally embezzled along the way, leaving the Nokhchi with nothing.

It is debatable whether or not Kremlin strategists already had an idea of a 'revenge' war in mind, but the Russian population demanded strong leadership to sort out their post-Soviet woes. This need for a strongman required a demonstration, and, indirectly, the Russian people demanded a second war in Nokhchi-chuo. Strong voter support for Yeltsin's opponent in 1996, leader of the communist party, Gennady Ziuganov, sent a clear signal. Yeltsin's narrow win demanded a demonstration to secure his support. A Second Russo-Chechen War would do the trick, but required justification. Russian special services started creating an image of the Nokhchi-chuo as a hub for criminal activity and international drug dealing. Indeed, during the interwar period of 1996-1999, the republic was flooded with drugs and submerged into chaos. A new business of taking hostages and demanding ransom flourished in the fledgling republic. The idea was introduced by the Russian military, which had perfected the trade of abducted Nokhchi hostages, even the corpses of those killed during the war. Russian media keenly reported the criminal activities stirring up the population's support for military action.

To the world, the reputation of the Nokhchi was irreparably damaged after the brutal killing of six Red Cross medical practitioners was followed up by the beheading of four British engineers in the late 1990s. Only after the beginning of the second war was it revealed that Russian security services were, in reality, behind many of such crimes. During the interwar period, the Russian media worked hard to create the image of the republic as a territory out of control. The message that the media tried to convey to the Russian population was that independent Nokhchi-chuo endangers the security of Russia. The height of this propaganda effort witnessed a series of apartment building explosions that shattered Russia in the summer of 1999. Russian media suggested, and the Russian public believed, that the Nokhchi were behind these terrorist attacks. This belief remained unchallenged even after two FSB (Federal Security Services), the main successor of the KGB, officers were caught by the watchful citizens placing explosives in the basement of an apartment building in Ryazan city, six days after an explosion in Volgodonsk killed dozens. The explosions of 1999 killed more than 300 people and wounded around 1,700. These events are often seen as Russia's 9/11. Whoever was behind these terrorist attacks, paved the way for both the Russian people and the international community to support a new genocidal attack on the Nokhchi.

The atrocities one could witness during the second war in the Nokhchi-chuo surpassed those of the first war, but the world remained largely silent again. Vladimir Putin, who succeeded 'the throne' from the drunk and ailing Boris Yeltsin, was fully committed to reconquer the Nokhchi-chuo at all costs. This genocidal war was given the official name of 'Counter-Terrorist Operations', as it continued on for ten years, given further legitimacy by the subsequent US 'War on Terrorism'. Putin was welcome in international forums. It took twenty years and the aggression against Ukraine for the world to eventually recognise Putin as a 'war criminal'. The International Criminal Court even issued an order to arrest Putin in 2023, but only for the war crimes committed in Ukraine. The crimes committed in Nokhchi-chuo seem to have again been forgotten.

Today, Nokhchi-chuo is occupied. Left by itself against Russia, with no foreign support or supply, Nokhchi resists without resources or hope. Russia transformed Nokhchi-chuo into Chechnya again and worked hard to transform the Nokhchi into the loyal Chechens through local administration, establishing yet another colonial regime. To the Nokhchi, it means forcible change of cultural identity, in other words, cultural genocide.

This genocidal process is sweetened by the narrative that emphasises that Chechnya is ruled by the Nokhchi and that Russia, as a tolerant country, unlike the Soviet Union or Russian Empire allows the practice of Islam. Of course this fulfils the two most important elements of Nokhchi identity, ethnicity and religion. The problem is that the Nokhchi put in charge of Chechnya are Russian-appointed loyal puppets and the Islam permitted is a centrally-controlled, institutionalised, and reduced form of Islam. An imperialist narrative sees this as the only Islam possible, and other forms are deemed extremist.

Russian media contributes to the creation of the illusion that the Nokhchi achieved what they have long dreamt of, claiming that today's Chechnya is more independent than it was in the 1990s. In truth, the administration is completely unaccountable for its unlawful actions against its own people. Russian academics and the liberal opposition add to this chorus.

Naming the land of Nokhchi within the Russian Federation as Chechnya and its citizens as Chechen is recognising the fact of the colonisation of the Nokhchi people and erasure of the Nokhchi-chuo. Reclaiming the term Chechen as a category and Chechnya as a lived experience is recognising atrocities committed by Russia against the Nokhchi people. As long as Chechnya exists, the Nokhchi are diminished, but resistance continues.

GOD'S SHADOW ON EARTH

Robert Zayd KiaNouri-Zigmund

The Qur'an commands Muslims to stand for justice and resist oppression. Throughout Islamic history, we have witnessed the struggle between those representing temporal power, mainly the sultan or caliph, and those who represented ethical and religious power, mainly the scholars and saints. Despite the fact that Muslims number nearly two billion in population and have inherited a tradition primarily focused on equity and justice, the vast majority of states in the Islamic world are despotic regimes which use brute force to suppress their own populations. The countries that claim to be more Islamic than all others – Saudi Arabia and Iran – are the obvious examples. Saudi Arabia began its modern history with the destruction and desecration of the majority of Islam's sacred sites and at the same time the massacre of thousands of Muslims, primarily Sufi and Shi'a. The Islamic Republic of Iran used extreme force and executed hundreds to suppress the protests that took place after the death of Mahsa Amini while in the custody of the 'morality police'. The contemporary period, for all of its claims to progress, has brought with it some of the most violent, brutal, and despotic regimes and movements in recorded history. From the millions of civilians who were unjustly murdered by the United States and its allies in Iraq and Afghanistan, to the numerous dictatorial states across the Middle East and Africa, and the ongoing expansion of military occupations and conflicts across the world, we are witness to an unprecedented scale of oppression across the Islamic world and beyond. Yet, when the prospect of struggling for change is brought up in many Islamic circles today, we immediately find ourselves inundated with a rapid torrent of narrations in which the Prophet supposedly forbade resisting oppression and affirmed despotism. In a startling paradox, the same tradition which began by challenging the ruling powers of its time in the name of justice is now often weaponised to suppress dissent by those interested in keeping the powerful in power. There are a number of questions raised by this phenomenon and the obstacles it creates for meaningful change. What are the theological and legal justifications for political repression? What are the historical roots of the contemporary regimes? And, how do we chart a path out of the current situation?

In the Way of God

The Islamic period begins with the Prophet Muhammad's earliest revelations in Makkah in 610, with the first verses of the Qur'an confirming that he is a Prophet and that his role is to 'arise and warn'. (74:3). The Quraish, the dominant tribe of the city of Makkah, were extremely hostile to the teachings of the Prophet, especially with the verses which had commanded the protection of orphans, the freeing of slaves, and the rights of the poor and weak. A boycott was imposed upon the Prophet and his early followers, and ultimately the Quraish conspired to murder him. Fleeing to the city of Yathrib (later known as Medina), to the North, the Prophet and his companions established a fledgling society that would work to bring the Qur'anic model to life as a community of ethics and ideals. This new society was composed not only of the Muslim refugees, but also of the tribes that had invited the Prophet to come, who were predominantly Jewish. The Constitution which was drafted for the community included all of the tribes and did not establish the Prophet as an infallible ruler, but rather as an arbiter. The Constitution united Muslims, Jewish tribes, and several Arab tribes who were still involved in polytheism. Interestingly, the Constitution states that the Jewish tribes, Muslims, and Arab tribes 'constitute a single community' (*umma wahida*) and that the non-Muslim tribes have 'equal rights'. As the community grew and faced increased threats from the authorities in Makkah, they had to work to not only enact the reforms that were put forth by the Qur'an, which meant resisting internal oppressive structures, but also actively resist oppression from the outside. In many of these circumstances, the Quraish were exercising superior military and political authority and would have been seen as the dominant political force in the land. The Muslims only had the promise of divine support and their rigorous ethical framework. In other words, this was a matter of a moral movement opposed to a fundamentally tyrannical power structure. It is within this context that we can examine several passages of the Qur'an that speak of resisting oppression and the duty of believers to put aside their material concerns for a moral and ethical cause.

We can first look at the story of Moses recounted in the Qur'anic narrative, in which God instructs Moses to go with his brother Aaron and confront the Pharaoh. 'Go to Pharaoh, for he has truly become a tyrant (*tagha*)' (20:24). The word used here for tyrant is *tagha*, whose root connotes transgression, injustice, extreme wickedness, and cruelty. It is important to note that Pharaoh viewed himself as the supreme authority of his domain, and he truly believed that his will was the will of God. To make this point clear in a later passage of the Qur'an, Pharaoh announces that he *is* God and should be worshipped. 'Pharaoh said, 'Counsellors, you have no other god that I know of except me'. Moses is thus sent to confront Pharaoh because he believes himself to be beyond accountability and he continually oppresses and inflicts harm upon people. Pharaoh is enraged by the presence of Moses not simply because of his focus on worshipping one God, but primarily because the worldview and framework that Moses brings would remove Pharaoh from his high stature and remind people that they have inherent dignity and that God is with the oppressed. In other words, it would re-introduce divine morality and let the people know that if they resist Pharaoh's oppression, God will support them. The Qur'anic narrative continues, with Pharaoh promising to kill Moses to prevent such a threat from coming to pass. 'Pharaoh said, "leave me to kill Moses – let him call upon his Lord! – for I fear he may cause you to change your religion, or spread disorder in the land". Moses said, "I seek refuge with my Lord and yours from every tyrant who refuses to believe in the Day of Reckoning"' (40: 26-27)

In *The Study Qur'an* the commentary on this verse notes that 'change your religion' signifies that Pharaoh was afraid that Moses' message would cause people to turn away from worshipping him, thus ultimately leading them to consider rebelling in order to stop his injustice. The term used for corruption, *fasad*, belies its English translation, for it is far more potent a term. The commentary of the *The Study Qur'an* notes, *fasad* 'implies all manner of decadence and injustice, in regard to both rebelling against God and oppressing others, thus failing to recognise the rights of all…[it] can be linked to all manner of iniquity, such as arrogance, oppression, and failing to honour family relations…it is implicitly or explicitly connected to physical violence in several verses'.

Having established that Pharaoh's self-idolatry had led him to act as an oppressive tyrant, we can readily understand Moses' fear and hesitation when he is first tasked to confront him. Upon realising that they will be challenging him and recognising his military and political power, Moses and Aaron cry out to God: 'They said, "Lord, we fear he will do us great harm or exceed all bounds"' (20:45). If we picture the brutal regimes and forces of oppression that we witness today, this sort of concern will appear quite reasonable. With an oppressor who has no ethical framework, especially one whose soul no longer recognises good and evil, Moses and Aaron have a justified concern that they will be killed or tortured for speaking the truth. The reply they receive from God is immediate, and firmly announces that God is with those who resist oppression. 'He said, "Do not be afraid, I am with you both, hearing and seeing everything"' (20:46). While those who confront oppression today do not feel the security of a promise of divine protection from physical harm, the ethical message and the promise of divine proximity holds true.

Jumping forward to the lifetime of the Prophet, the *ummah* was facing active and ongoing oppression by the Quraish and their allies, and many of the people became afraid that if they were to assist in the struggle, they could lose their lives, wealth, or social status. The Qur'an reminds them that they must devote themselves to God and to the principle of justice and liberation more than anything else in life. 'If your fathers, sons, brothers, wives, tribes, the wealth you have acquired, the trade which you fear will decline, and the dwellings you love are dearer to you than God and His Messenger and the struggle in His cause, then wait until God brings about His punishment. God does not guide those who break away' (9:24). Here, the Prophet is told to chastise those individuals who are more attached to their worldly life and possessions than God's cause and call, warning them that they will be considered complicit in the transgressions that they failed to resist. This is compounded further in *Surah Al-Nisa*, in which the Qur'an reminds Muslims that they are not fighting and struggling for some aimless goal, or for some ideology, rather they are literally working to save lives from oppression and suffering: 'And what ails you that you fight not in the way of God, and for the weak and oppressed—men, women, and children—who cry out, 'Our Lord! Bring us forth from this town whose people are oppressors, and appoint for us from Thee a protector, and appoint for us from Thee a helper' (4:75).

In this passage, the believers are told that there are many people crying out to God for help, and they are in a position to answer that call and use their resources and lives to shatter the shackles of oppression. There is a very humanising component to this narrative, rather than just reminding the community that they have a duty to uphold moral principles, they are reminded that if they do not act, there are real people facing cruelty and violence that will continue to languish. The Qur'anic narrative created a paradigm in which in it is not merely sufficient to not commit oppression by oneself, but rather it is also obligatory to struggle against oppression wherever you find it, whether it be against your own community or a completely different one. This ethos is echoed throughout the formation of the early Muslim community. There is a well known hadith in An-Nawawi's Forty Hadith that emphasises the importance of challenging *fasad* (oppression and corruption) dependent on one's capacity in a particular situation. 'Whosoever of you sees an evil, let them change it with their hand, and if they are not able to do so, then with their tongue, and if they are not able to do so then [hate it] with their heart—and that is the weakest of faith'.

There are clear injunctions present in the Qur'anic and Prophetic model for creating a system based on justice and equity and working to destroy and deconstruct systems of oppression and injustice. This framework, which the Prophet sought to put in practice in Medina, lived on after his death despite the overwhelming forces that sought to crush the Islamic call for a continuous *jihad* (struggle) against oppression. In a narration attributed to Imam Ali, he is reported to have said 'the Kingdom can survive *kufr* (disbelief), but it cannot survive *zulm* (injustice)'. With this in mind, we begin to see the duelling forces between those who remembered and worked to uphold the Qur'anic model and those who sought to return the world to a state of *fasad* (corruption). An event that showcased this duality and forever darkened Islamic history occurred less than five decades after the death of the Prophet. The Prophet's grandsons, Hassan and Hussain had each been entreated to submit to the newly formed government led by Mu'awiya and his son, Yazid. Hasan tried to form an agreement with Mu'awiya to reduce the threat of oppression non-violently, by relinquishing any claim to political authority in exchange for Mu'awiya promising not to create a dynasty by appointing his son as successor. After poisoning Hassan, Mu'awiya broke the agreement and appointed his son. Yazid sent his military forces to Medina to try to receive legitimacy by compelling the companions and *ahlul bayt* (household of the Prophet) to take *bay'ah* (allegiance) to him. Hussain refused, recognising that if he, as the descendant of the Prophet and spiritual leader of the community, were to take such a pledge, even out of duress, it would allow the religion to lose its revolutionary nature and become forever submissive to the will of the powerful. He fled to Kufa, where he had received word that the population of that town wanted to join him. He never reached the destination, for he was cornered by Yazid's fighting force in a barren land known as Karbala (in modern day Iraq). Here, after entreating for multiple days to let him pass peacefully and spare the innocent, Hussain was brutally murdered by the army. This event shocked the consciousness of the nascent Muslim community, and was also the pivotal moment that established the ethical and spiritual state of the Umayyad dynasty, which began under Yazid's reign. This event not only split the community into what would later become known as Sunni and Shi'a, but it also shook the foundations of the entire community. Within the Shi'ia community, the response of most was to follow the leadership of the *ahlul bayt*, which meant identifying and clinging to the next *Imam* in line, Imam Zayn Al-Abidin, the son of Imam Hussain. Within Twelver Shi'ism, which is the largest branch in practice today, the Imams taught the importance of standing up to oppression, avoiding aiding despots, and supporting the weak and vulnerable against the forces that would seek to do them harm. The following tradition is attributed to the Imam Ja'far al-Sadiq, the sixth Shi'a Imam: 'the oppressor, the one who helps an oppressor and the one who is satisfied with it, are all partners in oppression'.

The tradition presents a framework in which the one committing the oppression, the one assisting them in carrying it out, and the one who is pleased with that person or praises them for their commitment to maintaining law and order, are all guilty of the crime of oppression and corruption. The moral lesson from this is clear, and raises an additional question, namely is it sufficient to merely *not assist* an oppressor, or do Muslims have an obligation to resist? In other words, is being complicit or not speaking out akin to assisting? Another saying, attributed to the fifth Shi'a Imam, Muhammad al-Baqir, clarifies this point, 'none of you should go to a place where a tyrant ruler is oppressing, and killing innocent people, if you are not capable of helping the oppressed. Because in the event of a believer being present in such a place it would be their religious duty to help their believing siblings'.

Here, we are told that if a believer goes to a land in which oppression is being carried out, they must be capable and ready to assist the oppressed. To go to such a place and not offer assistance would be as if one is passing tacit approval of the system while benefitting from the hospitality of the land. The next question raised by this framework is what does it mean to help the oppressed? Is it sufficient to provide them food and shelter? A tradition attributed to the Prophet enumerates this point: 'it is necessary to help a believer whether he is an oppressor or an oppressed one. If he is an oppressor he should be restrained from oppression and if he is oppressed he should be helped in obtaining his rights. He should not be deserted and left on his own'.

This hadith instructs Muslims that they must assist the oppressed in obtaining their rights and they must stop the oppressor from committing the injustices. In this way, we can put the Qur'anic framework in conversation with these hadith and find a very clear moral message that enjoins all believers to work to defend the needs of all who are oppressed, regardless of who they are. Within Sunni Islam, we find numerous traditions upholding the importance of the martyrdom of Hussain and the legacy of those that killed him. A well-known tradition attributed to Ibn 'Umar, a companion of the Prophet, makes the point. He was mourning the death of Hussain when a man came to him and said he had a very important question to ask him. The man then proceeded to ask a question about the ritual minutiae of whether it was permissible to kill flies while in the state of *Ihram* at Hajj. Ibn 'Umar became so infuriated by this question that he replied: 'the Prophet's grandson has just been killed in our midst, and you are asking me about killing flies?' Khaled Abou El Fadl comments on this narration, noting that the moral message of the story is meant to illustrate a serious defect in the priorities of the man who came to ask the question. It is important to make this note because while it is true that the Sunni tradition often claims the Umayyad and Abbasid dynasties as part of its theological and legal legacy, there still remained a deep understanding within much of the scholarship and the Sunni community about the need to uphold the principles that Hussain and the *ahlul bayt* stood for. With this in mind, we can now turn to the rise of the Umayyad dynasty, built from the same line as Mu'awiya and Yazid, and examine the way in which the tension between political power and religious teachings began to unfold.

Ummayad Propaganda

The Umayyad dynasty committed itself to challenging the Qur'anic and Prophetic models of justice and equity, recognising that it would unravel their political power and threaten their ability to govern and commit *fasad*. They realised that they needed to fundamentally challenge and deconstruct the system of ethics that the Islamic tradition carried with it. They could not alter the Qur'an, too many people already knew it by heart and the records had been set. However, they could introduce numerous fabricated hadith (narrations attributed to the Prophet) into the Islamic tradition. By injecting ideas into the *Sunnah* (tradition) of the Prophet that focused on blind obedience and submission to tyranny and oppression, they could co-opt and suffocate the moral teachings of the Qur'an. If nothing else, they could at least confuse enough people to prevent a united resistance from taking place.

Commenting on the Umayyad structural assault on the moral underpinnings of the tradition, Abou El Fadl describes a systematic effort:

> The Umayyad dynasty that murdered the grandson of the Prophet understood very well that this is a dangerous Islam. So they got to work. They invented an enormous number of hadith about the duty of obedience that is owed to a ruler even if the ruler is unjust...people simply need to say the *Shahadah* to be Muslim; people need only perform ritual acts; they do not need to think about what the Prophet himself did.

The construction and mass-fabrication of hadith required enormous funding and support. The Umayyads and Abbasids mobilised the construction and funding of schools and the patronage of scholars. While we can clearly not say that their sole goal was this redesign of the tradition, we can see there was an intense focus on reinterpreting and reforming the tradition to be friendlier towards those in power. Abou El Fadl continues his analysis, noting:

> Umayyad Islam put into service generation after generation of corrupt scholars who invented, narrated and collected hadiths, all to silence the Qur'an. What upheld the Islamic civilisation, however, is that there was always a sufficient percentage of people—not a majority, but a significant percentage—who committed their lives to studying principles, comprehending principles, and implementing principles.

The seizure of political power through military might allowed for the Umayyad and Abbasid dynasties to exert significant influence on the scholarship that they sponsored. It should thus be of little surprise that we find, for example, numerous hadith opposing rebellion in *Sahih Bukhari*, when he lived and relied on the political and financial support of the Abbasid state to complete his work. Ahmed Rasim al-Nafis, an Egyptian scholar, writes in *Bayt al-'Anqabat* that Bukhari's hadith regarding political leadership demonstrate a clear bias towards the Umayyad and Abbasid caliphate and their opposition to the *ahlul bayt* in particular as symbols of resistance to despotism. Another clear example is the statement of Al-Ghazzali that the Abbasid government had achieved its power through brute force and that it must be obeyed completely in order to prevent social discord. Two examples of clearly fabricated hadith which favour the ruler include one in which Abu Dharr reportedly being told that God would want him to submit to being forced out of his home and made a refugee by a tyrant because the ruler is to be obeyed (which occurred after the prophet's death) and another, now widespread narration which says that the sultan is 'God's shadow on earth'.

It is important to recognise that, though the dynasties and caliphates of the Classical period drew the Muslim community together around a common, symbolic leadership, the sultan or caliph themselves were not actually considered on par with the Prophet or the prophet's family, nor even the companions of the Prophet. In *The Routledge Companion to the Qur'an*, Paul L. Heck expands on the political theology of the early community:

> Conversely, the claim that scholars and saints, not sultans, are heirs to the Prophet suggests that sovereignty in Islam lies beyond worldly power (imperium), giving such religious figures authority to contest the pretensions of rulers to decide the community's laws apart from consultation.

In this section, Heck explains that sultans and leaders were never truly 'free' to adjudicate or determine religious rulings or issue decrees to the community without the consultation of local religious leaders, who themselves were meant to reflect the real, material concerns of the communities that they represented. This is an important note to make because we can see that the Umayyads and Abbasids, despite their best efforts, were unable to completely 'cleanse' the tradition of its ethos. Indeed, even the most well-known scholars are known for having disparate views on the right of the people to rebel against a state. As such, a counter-tradition developed that focused on hadith that favoured the right to rebel.

It is a fairly recent phenomenon in modern scholarship to challenge the predominant notion that rebellion was a black and white issue within Islamic legal and theological circles in the classical period. Despite the notion that the jurists and scholars were all in agreement that the tradition prohibited rebellion out of some sort of principle, we find this is a work of fiction. The reality is that within the juristic tradition, we see remarkable diversity. Ibn Taymiyya, known for his tendencies towards despotic governments (with the only condition being the mandate of his particular school of thought) criticised the jurists of his time and those that preceded him for allowing and even encouraging rebellion against injustice. In his *Majmu' al-Fatawa*, he takes them to task as having purposefully misunderstood and minsterpreted the Islamic tradition as part of some sort of ideological adherence towards 'Ali. The way he saw it, people should only be fighting against hypocrites and nonbelievers, not tyrants. The Sunni jurists Abu Hanifa and Malik, in particular, were said to have been actively involved in encouraging people to support a rebellion against the Abbasids in their own lifetimes.

Within Shi'a circles, we see several trends emerge. The first trend focuses on acquiring freedom from oppression, was characterised by fleeing from oppressive lands and political quietism, that is avoiding political power and association with it. The second trend is characterised by working within the government to support the oppressed while in a state of *taqiyya* (dissimulation). The last trend is marked by political activism and insurrection, which can be seen in the cases of several uprisings, including that of Zayd ibn 'Ali (who is followed by the *Zaydiyyah* sect of Shi'ism). It is important to make a distinction between Shi'ia traditions which emphasised quietism during this period. Unlike most of the Sunni hadith of the same type, these were focused on reducing the physical threat to the community, rather than lauding the ruler as being rightly guided or God-appointed. Indeed, a core concept of Shi'ism is that the proper leadership of the community only lies in the hands of the Prophet and Imams. Another key concern was that by associating with political power, one would inevitably become tied into political dealings and then corrupt the religious teachings and sciences. In essence, the concern of quietist Shi'a scholars was far more focused on maintaining the teachings of the *ahlul bayt* than it was on upholding the oppressive state.

The scholars maintained their role as a check to the institutions of political power, but as time went on, the rulers began to realise that they needed to find a way not just to reduce the potential threat of religious authority, but also try to have a close relationship with the religious scholars and jurists. As part of the importation of Greek and Persian ideas of politics and the state, we also see the association of the ruler with God's authority. We begin to witness duelling notions of Islam as a religious force that is capable of transforming society on the one hand and a means of suppressing dissent through assigning the ruler a quasi-divine status on the other. In particular, we see that through the Abbasid period, the ruler acquires a revolutionary character (for having overthrown the previous ruler) on the one hand and totalitarian, God-given command on the other. In *The Persian Prince*, Hamid Dabashi argues that this is an expansion of the archetype of the Persian monarch, carried over from Sassanid and Achaemenid times. Dabashi conceptualies this 'tension between the Persian Prince as royal authority and his alter ego as a Prophetic voice' and contends that:

The universal significance of the figure of the Persian Prince...is woven into the global map of Muslim empires and their histories...where the Iranian archetypal figure becomes definitive to the projected legitimacy of the whole political apparatus...No Muslim dynasty predicated exclusively on the Prophet's Qur'anic legacy came anywhere near that [Sassanid] longevity unless and until they actively began to incorporate Iranian, Byzantine, Turkic...cultural traits.

In essence, we begin to see the formation of the ruler as not only having received the community's implicit approval, but also that of the Prophet and ultimately God. Through weaving cultural and mystical narratives of kingship and patrimonial state building, the dynasties in the Islamic world began to find the symbolisms that were most capable of sustaining their political and temporal authority. This sort of mindset, once restrained to the political classes as a means of cementing their rulership, did not extend (with the exception of those like Ibn Taymiyya) to the generally independent scholarly, juristic, and theological classes. It is crucial to remember that, at this time, Islamic civil society was quite strong, and remained that way up until the colonial period. It is in our modern period, then, that we find a new revival of this sort of archetypal sovereign power that cannot be defied.

The Stain of Colonisation

In the contemporary period, we are met by what is arguably the ugliest chapter in Islamic political history. Across the Islamic world, and indeed in the land of the Prophet, brutal military regimes thrive, most with the financial and political backing of the United States and its allies. Perhaps one of the clearest examples of the ways in which the Umayyad doctrines of blind obedience and total authority have been revived is in the modern Saudi state. Through binding political and religious authority and leadership together, Saudi Arabia exerts internal and external influence on the Muslim consciousness and interpretations of political leadership and the right (or lack thereof) to resist oppression. Saudi clerics report to the authority of the de facto leader of the nation, producing fatwa after fatwa that emphasise the importance of doing what a ruler says, no matter what, and disagreeing only in private. Far from standing for dissent, even these clerics posit that even peaceful mass demonstrations are completely *haram* (forbidden). At most, they say that a person can 'advise' a ruler in private. The council of senior 'scholars' of Saudi Arabia issued a fatwa at the height of the so-called 'Arab Spring' stating that: 'the Council of Senior Clerics affirms that demonstrations are forbidden in this country. The correct way in sharia (Islamic law) of realising common interest is by advising, which is what the Prophet Mohammad established'.

The same statement claims that it is illegal under the shariah to 'issue statements and collect signatures' because they may be intimidating and create social discord. This council was given its authority by the Saudi King in 2010, with a legal decree stating that it is the sole organisation authorised to issue Islamic rulings. This provides a contemporary mirror to the Umayyad practice of appointing a cleric to issue edicts that form a state-sponsored version of the religion, with the added components of a surveillance state with access to more military and police power than any state in Islamic history. Such a state is capable of enforcing its whims in a way that is completely unprecedented. It is even a break from the Umayyad tradition when Saudi Arabia claims to be the sole interpreter of the Islamic tradition and denies the plurality of thought. It should thus be of little surprise that many clerics who disagree with the ruling authority, such as Shaykh Hassan Farhan Al-Maliki Maliki and Salman al-Ouda, languish in Saudi prisons or are executed for simply trying to preserve the authentic Islamic tradition. In one fatwa by the Grand Mufti of Saudi Arabia, in a patently bizarre fashion, the full force archetype alluded to earlier can be felt. In this fatwa, it is asserted that not only can the believing Muslim not rise up against the ruler, not only can they not protest against the ruler, and not only must they focus on their personal, private lives; rather, they must 'love the ruler' and 'defend the ruler'. This level of adherence to a despot is unprecedented, even in the works of someone like Ibn Taymiyya, who still upheld the right of the individual to have private contempt for the acts of the ruler. Such a practice of brutal authoritarianism, couched in religious dogma, can surely be seen in the recent claim by Mohammad Bin Salman that he is going to undertake a project to re-authenticate all of the hadith collections. A perfect example of this is the Saudi imposition of banning women from driving, and then subsequently lifting it – perhaps, to appeal to Western funds and weapons companies. While Saudi Arabia carries out a genocide in Yemen, along with the United Arab Emirates, and suppresses dissent in its own borders, it still leverages enormous religious and cultural power across the globe for the Muslim community. While pretending to combat the Wahhabi movement at home, it is actively exporting a specific version of puritanical Islam through its Global Center for Combatting Extremism (Etidal). This centre exports textbooks, Qur'an translations, and other Islamic sources across the Islamic world and into the West. The content produced by this centre identical in symbolisms and motivations to that of the Umayyads, with the added clarification that this is a joint project with the United States. In the UAE, which claims to be a place of tolerance, we again find brutal crackdowns against civilians and one of the most fervent countries in terms of normalising relations with the Israeli government while it is actively carrying out a genocide in Gaza. One of the UAE's most outspoken supporters, Hamza Yusuf of Zaytuna College, faced backlash for blaming Syrian people for their own suffering. In 2015, as part of a lecture, he said that God was humiliating the Syrian people for their attempt to disobey Bashar al-Assad, and that they are being punished for rebelling. He cites the hadith we discussed in the previous section that referred to the sultan as 'God's shadow on earth'. Yusuf also claimed that Donald Trump was a 'servant of God' in a speech, and then accepted a position in a commission in the government, all while actively working with Shaykh bin Bayyah of the United Arab Emirates.

This phenomenon is not exclusive to the Sunni world. The archetype of the *Persian Prince* (a lost hero coming to the throne to exercise his divinely appointed will) is clearly present and pivotal in maintaining legitimacy in Iran, which carried out a brutal crackdown on women's rights protests last year, and continues to engage in torture and suppression of protest movements. Except in Iran, the Prince comes in the shape of religious scholar. Indeed, it is crucial to note that Iran has continually been equally repressive and despotic in its blending of religious and political despotism as its Sunni-majority neighbours, if not more in certain cases. This is despite Iran's claim to represent Shi'ism on a global scale. Shi'ism has developed as a minority sect for over a millennia, with a specific focus on two key points: 1) avoiding political and worldly power at all costs and 2) resisting oppression and the despotic powers of rulers. In response to the

2022 killing of Mahsa Amini, who opposed mandatory hijab, the world watched the largest mass protests in Iran since the 1979 revolution. Reports from numerous human rights organisations suggest that her death came at the hands of the 'morality police', a police force dedicated to enforcing the Iranian government's interpretation of shariah law. Many protestors were injured or killed, and many more were imprisoned for their objections. Over 500 young men and women were executed for their protest activity following her death.

The Iranian government has carried out systematic and massive campaign of imprisonment, torture, and executions of dissidents. The Iranian government also has seized almost complete control of the traditional seminaries. Jurists who have expressed opinions counter to the government doctrine, military intervention, and domestic policies, even in private classes, face reprisal. Ayatollah Kamal Haydari, who expressed that it is possible to imagine a society in which the veil might not be needed is reportedly on house arrest. Likewise, under the guise of 'exporting the revolution', Iran has, among other efforts, financially, politically, and militarily supported the brutal Assad regime in Syria, which has carried out some of the most brutal massacres and torture campaigns in recent history. In a way, it seems that through Hamza Yusuf's mocking of Syrian protestors and Iran's backing of the Syrian regime, the clearest and saddest example of Sunni-Shi'a unity has been on the abandonment of the moral and ethical precepts of Islam in favour of political expediency, propping up whatever despotic rulers happen to be in place at any given time.

This new approach to Islam that formed under Ayatollah Khomeini's government can be characterised as a shariah of fear: fear of the West, fear of destruction of the state, fear of the uprising of Iranian dissidents, fear of other clergy and interpretations, fear of women's movements, fear of the young and dynamic who yearn for freedom. Critics of this new approach point to the lack of the sacred idealism and the presence of human fear as a determining factor. Many contemporary Shi'a jurists are of the belief that it threatens to destroy the foundations of the Ja'fari school if left unchecked. It is said that Allamah Tabataba'i, one of the most important Shi'a theologians and philosophers of the contemporary period, was informed of the death of his former student and friend, Murtadha Mutahhari during the revolution, and that Mutahhari was referred to as a

Shaheed (Martyr). In response, it is narrated that he replied 'in this revolution (1979 Iranian Revolution), there was one true martyr that was killed, and that martyr was killed unfairly and unjustly. That martyr was Islam itself'. Such a statement can only be understood if we recognise that the bedrock of Islam and Shi'ism is the centrality of justice and a rigorous set of moral priorities that, by their very nature, do not pay attention to political interests, geopolitics, or ideology, but rather to fundamental religious principles.

In all of these cases, an appeal to the religious heritage and the mythos of the ruler as God's representative is a consistent and unrelenting theme. It is telling that these nations only change their policies when it would be favourable to their political interests: namely, that they will receive more money and military support from the United States and its allies or from Russia and its allies, depending on orientation. The puritans themselves often are imprisoned for becoming so extremist that they end up turning against the very state that funded and supported them, as can be seen in the case of the Saudi Ikhwan, which was ultimately massacred by British forces when they tried to rebel against the Saudi state. Despite this repression, puritans across the world provide ample ideological and financial support to the Saudi state and dictatorships like it, such as Egypt. In *The Great Theft*, Abou El Fadl explains:

> Puritans would give the state powers that, in reality, are unprecedented in Islamic history. The state in the modern age is capable of mobilising enormous powers and intruding upon people's lives in ways that were unimaginable in the premodern period. Puritans use these exceptional powers to enforce what they believe to be the Divine Will. For instance, puritans believe that the state should force men to go to the mosque for prayers, and also force women to wear the veil.

Indeed, so long as their particular strain of Islamic thought is enforced against other Muslims, they do not care what the state does. We are truly witnessing a period of the revival and expansion of 'Umayyad Islam', a formulation of the tradition that pays little to no attention to beauty, ethics, and justice, and entirely focuses on individual ritual responsibility and the importance of law and order. If history is any indicator, the way to confront the co-opting of power is to exercise the revival of the ethical and moral teachings of the Islamic tradition. Such a possibility cannot happen through state funding or political leadership, it must occur through a systemic intellectual and ethical effort to rebuild and frame the role of the Islamic tradition in the contemporary period. The Prophet, the *ahlul bayt,* as well as many companions, scholars, jurists, and mystics, were well acquainted with the heart of the Islamic tradition as one that emphasises justice, equity, and the importance of fighting oppression. It is crucial that we work to build institutions and communities that foster creative thinking and moral integrity. We can take inspiration from a passage in the Qur'an that reminds us that we are responsible not only for engaging with and creating sources of knowledge and understanding, but for acting upon it: 'those who have been charged to obey the Torah, but do not do so, are like donkeys carrying books: how base such people are who disobey God's revelations! God does not guide people who do wrong' (62:5).

It is important that we pick apart this verse to understand its warning. God is telling Muslims the donkey analogy for an important reason. To inherit the revelation, and pride oneself on the cultural, ethnic, or ritualistic aspects of a religious community, especially while neglecting the ethical principles of the faith, is to disrespect the revelation and the One who sent it. It makes a mockery of the religion, and causes people to drift from the original message. The early community of Islam would not have converted to Islam if the message was as it is presented today. They understood Islam as a message of beauty and liberation. They also understood what it was not: a message of blind ritual, of obeying whatever ruler happens to be in power, of the oppression of women and minority groups. The work to change these structures is enormous, but it is not impossible. The Islamic world has faced calamities in the past, and there have always been a group who preserved the principles and ideals of the Qur'anic model. Education is the first step, and it is important that Muslims investigate who and where they get their knowledge of their own tradition from. While this is not something that can be corrected overnight, I think that it is clear that such a project of revival and beautification is the only way that the Islamic world will find its way out of this dark age. Indeed, as the Qur'an announces: 'God is the ally of those who believe: He brings them out of the depths of darkness and into the light' (2:257).

BIRTH OF BANGLADESH

Ali Nobil Ahmad

I

One overcast morning mid-way through South Asia's bloody monsoon of 1971, two pilots of the Pakistan Airforce made eye contact on the tarmac of Masroor Airbase. A large installation near Karachi in Sindh, Masroor was inherited by Pakistan from the Royal Indian Airforce at Partition, and renamed in honour of an ill-fated Air Commodore whose Martin B-57 bomber crashed after colliding with a vulture. Six months into *Muktijuddho* – Bangladesh's long, brutal war of liberation – the atmosphere at this hub of strategic importance in the south was tense.

Amidst acute suspicion toward Bengali servicemen among West Pakistan's mostly Punjabi ruling military elite, Flight Lieutenant Matiur Rahman, twenty-nine years old, had been grounded. As a suspected fifth columnist, he was confined to maintenance and safety duties on the ground. Nevertheless, as a veteran of the 1965 India-Pakistan war and flight instructor, Rahman commanded a certain respect. He was senior to Pilot Officer Rashid Minhas, a recently commissioned twenty-year-old Punjabi, on only his second solo flight, in a Lockheed T-33 training jet with its canopy open. Minhas taxied toward take-off. What happened next, what precisely was said and done by these two compatriots as their paths fatefully crossed on 20 August 1971, has been the subject of much speculation in both Pakistan and Bangladesh for decades.

We know for sure Rahman stepped onto the wing, forced his way into the instructor's seat, and hijacked the plane. Within minutes, it was airborne and on its way towards Indian Gujarat. A replica gun later found on Rahman's person may have been used to threaten the young pilot not to resist. Minhas's radio messages to Air Traffic Control at 11:28 am ('Bluebird 166 is hijacked!') convey something of the panic he must have felt as the plane took off under Rahman's control.

Fifteen minutes later, forty miles short of the Indian border, the plane crashed in such a way that led investigators to believe a struggle had taken place. Minhas appears to have jettisoned the canopy to eject Rahman from the cockpit but was unable to gain control over the aircraft. It stalled and plummeted to earth near a soft, muddy stretch of wetland near the Indus river delta, close to where it meets the Arabian Sea. The remains of both men were discovered in the wreckage.

Posthumously, Minhas became the first air pilot and youngest ever recipient of Pakistan's highest gallantry award, *Nishan-i-Haider* ('emblem of Haider' – an epithet of the Muslim Caliph Ali connoting bravery). Rahman, in turn, was awarded *Bir Sreshtho* – 'Most Valiant Hero' – the highest military award in Bangladesh, soon after it came into being four months later.

Both men were lionised in the countries that replaced the one they shared. The fratricidal drama of their final minutes – told and retold in countless documentaries, teledramas, and other narrations - has made for compelling legends of martyrdom.

A rare instance of symmetry in a conflict otherwise defined by dissonance and grossly unequal power.

II

There was nothing symmetrical about the Pakistan that perished with Flight Lieutenant Matiur Rahman and Pilot Officer Minhas, a nation of two wings separated by 1000 miles of Indian territory. West ruled East as an internal colony; a ruthlessly exploited, callously neglected hinterland stripped of resources and denied a fair share of the foreign exchange generated by its chief agricultural export, jute.

The background to secession is well known: Pakistan's first free and fair elections, which took place in December 1970, saw the East Bengali nationalist *Awami League* (AL) party win 160 of the 162 seats in East Pakistan, an absolute majority that gave it a democratic mandate to govern the whole country. Neither the Pakistan People's Party (PPP) led by Sindhi politician Zulfiqar Ali Bhutto, which came second at the polls with 81 seats in West Pakistan, nor the predominantly Punjabi military, which had ruled since seizing power in a coup in 1958, were willing to accept being led by a government of darker skinned East Pakistanis they regarded as inferior.

The army in particular had internalised colonial ideas about its origins in North India's martial races, whose purported fitness to govern was defined in opposition to the unworthiness of 'effeminate' Bengalis, maligned by the British for their prominence in anti-colonial subversion since 1857. This ethnic divide broadly overlapped with Cold War fault lines: West Pakistan's oligarchy of Muslim League politicians, military officers and landed families aligned itself to the Western capitalist block led by the United States in the 1950s, and drifted towards the ultra-right-wing religious orthodoxy of *Jamaat-e-Islami* as the sixties wore on. Populist forces associated with the AL, in contrast, veered closer to socialism, non-aligned India, and a pluralistic vision of Islam that incorporated Bengali language and identity.

Despite the PPP's socialist leanings, Bhutto ruled out sitting in a parliament led by the AL, a boycott that resulted in political deadlock. Events came to a head on 1 March when General Yahya Khan, then President of Pakistan, indefinitely postponed the opening of the National Assembly, cementing perceptions of electoral theft among Bengalis, who backed Mujib's call for a province-wide *hartal* – general strike.

On 15 March Yahya flew to Dhaka for emergency talks to find the city awash with Bangladesh flags and ringing with chants of 'Joi Bangla'. Feelings ran high, with club-wielding AL cadres and militant elements of the student movement expressing symbolic intent to fight for their freedom. A week later, Bhutto joined talks that proved to be a distraction from the military's intentions, reflected in a build-up of thousands of troops and weapons arriving from the West.

Early on 25 March, Yahya left Dhaka for his throne in the West. That same day, he ordered the launch of *Operation Searchlight*.

As night fell, Mujib was arrested by commandos and detained in West Pakistan where thousands of other Bengalis (with and without links to the nationalist movement) were interned for the rest of 1971. At around 10 pm, three battalions of troops rumbled out of their barracks in a massive convoy of tanks, trucks, and jeeps and headed towards Dhaka University. By the time they arrived on campus with orders to eradicate the intellectual headquarters of East Bengal's nationalist movement, some of those about to be 'sent to Bangladesh', to use the macabre terminology of their executioners, lay fast asleep, perhaps dreaming of a homeland they would never see. Without warning, hostels came under direct fire from heavy mortars, tank shells, grenades, and incendiary rounds. Those who resisted or attempted to flee burning and demolished buildings were gunned down. Troops stormed dormitories, firing indiscriminately at students and staff in hallways and bedrooms. Terrified congregations huddling in canteens were shot where they stood or dragged outside and finished off with bayonet thrusts. Professors were hauled from apartments and executed in cold blood. Their assassins, guided by lists of names and addresses of AL sympathisers compiled beforehand, murdered a number of their spouses and children alongside them, spraying entire families with bullets in their homes. Service staff and their families were also slaughtered, their quarters torched.

As the sun rose, firing slowed. Bullet riddled and charred remains of students and staff lay scattered in blood drenched corridors and grounds. A small number were kept temporarily alive to transport friends' and comrades' lifeless corpses to hastily bulldozed mass graves before being shot, bayoneted and shoved in themselves. All the while, soldiers looted the dead's belongings, physically and verbally abusing those forced into macabre processions.

While all this was happening, another column of troops set about decimating the Rajabagh headquarters of the East Pakistan police, believed to be sympathetic to the nationalist cause. Here too elimination began without warning when tanks opened fire on the sleeping quarters of over a thousand men, burning many alive before finishing off many of the rest in a duck shoot against resistors armed with ancient 303 Bolt action Lee–Enfield rifles.

Offices of East Pakistan's two leading newspapers, *The People*, an English language daily, and *Ittefaq*, a Bengali language publication, were also destroyed, their staff massacred. *Ittefaq's* premises were gutted by a fire that killed 400 people taking refuge, punishment for having openly supported Mujib.

Around noon the next day, columns of troops poured into Dhaka's Old Town. Guided by local informers who identified *Awami League* supporters' homes, tanks, and recoilless rifles demolished private dwellings and commercial properties along English Road, French Road, Nayer Bazaar, City Bazaar, and others. Cans of gasoline were carried by troops who razed entire neighbourhoods, shooting those who fled homes, burning alive those who could not. Hundreds of men, women, and children were massacred in each cluster of streets and bazaars, a pattern repeated across the old city until late in the evening.

By 11 pm, troops bellowing 'Pakistan Zindabad' and 'Nara-e-Takpir' began withdrawing to their barracks amidst plumes of black smoke, red horizons, the stench of death, and feasting vultures. Within twenty-four hours of *Operation Searchlight's* commencement, thousands of defenceless civilians and public servants had been massacred, countless public and private buildings obliterated, and large parts of the city set ablaze. The next morning, Saturday 27 March, curfew was lifted between 7 am and 4 pm. By noon, tens of thousands were leaving town with possessions, mostly on foot, the beginning of a vast and miserable forced migration that drove millions of refugees into India during the next nine months, and uprooted many internally. Amidst roadblocks and checkpoints choking exits, many had their paths blocked and found themselves stranded after curfew.

When killing resumed it spread to the outskirts of Dhaka. All the while, planes flew overhead on bombing missions.

From its earliest hours, *Operation Searchlight* combined a messy mixture of three overlapping drivers of extermination. The first was politicide: eradication of political opponents, intelligentsia, and any part of the state's coercive apparatus that might offer armed resistance.

The second was religious hatred against East Bengal's Hindu population. Even where 'political' targets were attacked, such as at the university, Professors were asked their religion before being shot. As the operation wore on, Hindus were killed without hesitation, irrespective of political affiliation, with men murdered after their genitalia were checked for circumcision.

'Why kill him?' asked Anthony Mascarenhas, a Pakistani journalist observing a certain Major Rathore, as he readied himself to execute a villager twenty miles south of Comilla. 'Because he might be a Hindu or he might be a rebel, perhaps a student or an Awami Leaguer'. In this reply, published in the opening paragraph of an article that exposed the scale of the genocide in June 1971, the interchangeability of religious and political identity in the minds of army personnel was already guiding their murderous conduct.

War memoirs such as those of Major Iftikhar-Ud-Din Ahmad are replete with remorseless confessions of having summarily executed 'non-Muslims'. As he saw, killing and expelling Hindus from their homes and the territory of East Pakistan was part of the soldier's duty to protect the nation. As a form of spiritual cleansing, it was enacted in gestures of ritual purification. In Comilla, he set time aside to enter the homes of displaced citizens and destroy sacred objects of worship:

> We saw their gods still lying around in different sizes and shapes. We had some shovels in our jeeps and with passion and vigor I began attacking the idols... As we were breaking [them] I felt deeply satisfied... I was experiencing spiritual calmness simply by demolishing the gods of... the real instigators of the current situation in my country.

Little wonder 80 to 90 percent of the refugees who fled East Bengal were Hindu, despite comprising between 10 and 20 percent of East Pakistan's population.

The third layer of murderous intent, distinct and separable from the aforementioned political and religious dimensions, was clearly evident in the generalised will toward extermination of Bengalis as an ethnic group identified through phenotype and/or articulations and expressions of language, culture, and attire. This ethno-racial impulse, which clearly fits legal definitions of genocide, was derived in part from the British colonial discourse adopted by West Pakistani elites throughout the 1950s and 1960s, in which Bengali inferiority was rooted in the environmental biology of a 'downtrodden race' whose emotions and mindset were products of its exotic climate and physiognomy.

Ethnic hatred toward 'Bingos', as they were referred to by West Pakistanis, was clear in the frenzied bayoneting of nationalists, but it also took coldblooded forms. For instance, when senior West Pakistani military men assessed the risk of defection by Bengali military personnel, they placed remarkably little value on Bengali life. Consider the eradication of over a thousand East Pakistan Rifles recounted by Brigadier Karrar Ali Agha, who describes one Lt Colonel's method of solving 'the problem of the enemy within':

> the Bengali officers and men being held in custody were brought to a ground near the Brigade Headquarters. Colonel Yaqub placed a heavy firing squad in

the spectators' gallery of a nearby squash court. The poor victims were
brought in batches in the court below and shot down... the next batch of
hapless victims were made to pick up the bodies of the previous batch and to
throw them in a collective grave, hurriedly dug by a dozer of the Engineers
Company... In all, 17 officers and 1325 soldiers were murdered in cold blood
that day...

As the army's assault got underway, it bred counter-violence by some
Bengali nationalist militants against East Pakistan's non-Bengali, Urdu-
speaking North Indian Bihari minority populations. The latter were
perceived by nationalists as having aligned with West Pakistan and thus
subjected to attacks by semi-organised gangs, some of whose collective
punishments degenerated into chauvinism and criminal atrocities. With
such incidents, the notion that the entire population of East Pakistan had
somehow to be replaced or subjugated by an alliance of Biharis and Punjabi
colonists became firmly entrenched.

Biharis, enlisted to rule through local 'peace committees' and loyalist
'*Razakar*' militias, were rewarded for their loyalty with lands, properties,
and possessions of the ethnically cleansed. In Ashuganj, a town in the
Meghna River delta, Major Ahmad proudly recounts looting cash,
jewellry, and dry food from expelled populations as a form of
redistribution: 'I always felt a deep spiritual satisfaction after distributing
their valuables among Biharis'.

Colonial racism melded with another, rather sad idea of race rooted in
the notion of authentic Islam of the (Saudi) Arabs. Being a true Muslim, in
the aspirational logic of this self-loathing discourse, required identification
with foreignness from the Indian Subcontinent and the gene pool of its
native peoples. East Pakistan's attachment to Bengali, in this Arab-centred
ideology, melded with colonial perceptions of physiognomic difference.
With darker skin connoting proximity to Hinduism, Bengali-ness was
viewed as a liminal condition.

A monstrous campaign of sexual violence was enacted to purify
bloodlines and 'make Muslims' of a degenerate race. In an abomination
with few parallels in history, women's minds and bodies were subjected
to indescribable suffering, injury, illness, and death. Extreme violence –
punching, kicking, throttling, biting, bayoneting of genitalia, mutilation
of breasts, and other manifestations of pathological, racialised misogyny

were reported from the very first night of *Operation Searchlight* at Ruqaya hall in the university of Dhaka.

Also well documented are countless instances of abduction, in which women and girls were taken to cantonments where they were raped by dozens of troops for days, nights, weeks on end. Tied naked to railings, starved and dehydrated in appalling, filthy conditions, many died having suffered in ways that are barely comprehensible. Some had already witnessed the murder of their menfolk and offspring in raids on their villages and towns, compounding the sense of despair and oblivion as they drifted in and out of consciousness.

Nur Begam, a woman whose parents and in-laws had already been killed by the army, recounted one such ordeal to the historian Yasmin Saikia in Rangpur, northern Bangladesh. Three weeks prior to liberation, her husband, a resistance fighter in the *Muhkti Bahini*, was tortured and shot in front of her before she was abducted. Confined to a hellish prison amidst acts of ghoulish depravity, she and many other women were subjected to extreme cruelty and relentless abuse by countless numbers of military personnel who raped them day and night:

> I did not have any clothes on. They had tied me to a chair with my hair. I could not speak, my lips were swollen, my face was puffed up and my entire body had bite marks. They cut my arms with blades because I was shouting... I was tortured until independence... one after the other. I saw two dead girls, they tortured even their dead bodies... I saw many girls in the bunker. There were 50 or 60 of us. My sister-in-law was there also, she died because of torture... The Pakistanis came in group after group...They did it in front of everyone... the girls ranged in age from 14 to 22... Their arms were smashed, so they could not raise their arms, my arm was also smashed... They tied me down... They had stretched my hands and legs wide apart... so they could use me. They kept me in that position.

Geoffrey Davis, an Australian doctor, spent six months supporting rape victims in Bangladesh from March 1972. A medical graduate who worked under the auspices of the WHO, UNFPA, and International Planned Parenthood Federation, Davis performed around 100 abortions a day in Dhaka, and variable numbers in other towns such as Dhanmondi. The women and girls he encountered, he told scholar and rights activist Bina D'Costa, 'all had venereal diseases of one kind or another', and 'such a degree of

malnutrition that a term foetus of forty weeks was about the same size as
eighteen weeks anywhere else.' 'When they got sick,' he told D'Costa, 'they
received no treatment', so 'a lot of them died in those camps'.

III

'I don't need people, just the soil.' General Tikka Khan's words to his
own men early on in Pakistan's disastrous campaign of 1971 neatly sum up
the thinking of Yahya's senior generals and military advisers – architects
of the genocide in East Pakistan. In the end, West Pakistan kept neither, a
measure of their catastrophic hubris and Bengali fortitude.

Like so many imperialist military campaigns of the Cold War – from the
US war on Vietnam to the Soviet invasion of Afghanistan – West Pakistan's
ended in humiliating defeat at the hands of a peasant population backed by
external forces, in this case India, which supported the Mukhti Bahini
insurgency with weapons and training before entering the conflict itself in
December 1971.

Within less than a fortnight of India's formal entry into the war, the
Pakistan army's campaign ended, as it began, with a depraved massacre
targeting the brain of Bengali nationalism just two days before it would
surrender: 200 doctors, journalists, academics, and other gentle souls
were vindictively denied a role in shaping the future of a nation whose
birth was now certain. It is a measure of how thoroughly the Pakistan
army was defeated that it lost in spite of political, diplomatic, and material
support from the United States and China, which backed it on account of
India's strategic alliance with the Soviet Union. On 16 December 1971, a
vanquished nation roused from a nine-month slumber, truncated and
denuded of the majority of its people. The 'fall of Dhaka', as this event
came to be described in the annals of West Pakistan's historical record,
was accompanied by the humiliating capture of over 90,000 Pakistani
prisoners of war: the largest surrender of modern times.

Even so, we (West) Pakistanis never really woke up.

To this day, the 'war' of 1971 is something of a taboo in polite company.
If at all, it is remembered by Pakistanis as a disastrous encounter with
India's military. Any reference to internal civil conflict involving Bengalis
is secondary to the only issue that matters: enmity with *Bharat*. In a
condescending narrative of 'treachery' and 'betrayal' that centres Indian

villainy, peoples of the former East wing are reduced to conduits of external influence and denied any agency of their own.

After the war, a steady stream of self-pitying memoirs by former officers made clear none would take responsibility for their role in defeat let alone perpetration of atrocities. Bhutto, who was handed the reigns of government for what proved to be Pakistan's first democratic interlude, found it convenient to blame Yahya. Over the years, 'the drunkard' has come to be despised not for the monumental suffering he caused Bengalis but for having lost the East wing, and lost face before the only audience that matters in Delhi.

Bengal's emancipation was thus framed as the breaching of a fortress that must be continually reinforced. To this end, Tikka Khan, the Butcher of Bengal, was rehabilitated and tasked with quelling insurgencies in the Northwest. Thanks to which, he is also known as The Butcher of Baluchistan. As for the army's crimes, these were buried with the dead.

Such was the scale of killing that outright denial is rare; instead Pakistanis downplay the numbers of civilians killed and raped. As early as April of 1972, Prime Minister Bhutto told an Italian interviewer Bengali estimates of three million dead were 'mad', suggesting instead 'there must have been something like fifty thousand'. As for 'the other story: the women raped and killed', he added simply: 'I don't believe it'. Most 'independent' estimates of deaths range somewhere between Bangladeshi and Pakistani figures. US officials, for instance, privately estimated around 200,000 dead around midway through 1971. Given the number of refugees and others who died of disease and hunger amidst displacement and collapse of the food system, and the countless disappeared whose corpses were tossed into mass graves or left to rot, the actual body count is unknowable, as is the vast number of rapes, most of which were never recorded let alone reported for obvious reasons.

In Pakistan, talking quantitatively is a way to avert qualitative confrontation of our role in a war of annihilation. Minimising numbers is not just a mode of attenuating horror; it allows the framing of atrocities as isolated acts of excess within an otherwise honourable campaign that faltered due to tactical errors. As the predictable pivot from numbers to apologia in Bhutto's interview illustrates, underlying all this is a deeper delusion: our objective to override East Bengali nationalism was not wrong, rather, the way in which it was pursued.

Other modes of genocide denial include obfuscation through distraction. Atrocities committed against Biharis are often used to draw false equivalences between the actions of the Pakistani state and armed gangs. Boosted by one particularly idiotic Indian historian whose shoddy scholarship vindicated the claims of apologists who tell us 'it was complicated', such comparisons are made despite the fact that the massacres perpetrated by Bengalis were on an altogether different scale and carried out without the kind of institutionalised backing accorded to Pakistan's national military.

Incidentally, when it came to population transfers in post-conflict negotiations, Biharis were swiftly abandoned, with Pakistan refusing to accept them as citizens or migrants.

Over time, as it became strategic to change tone, Pakistani officials have made concessions in their position, expressing regret in vague terms whilst emphasising the need for all to move forward. In 2002, Gen Musharraf visited a war memorial at Savar near Dhaka, leaving the following note in the visitors' booth. 'Your brothers and sisters in Pakistan share the pain of the events in 1971. The excesses committed during the unfortunate period are regretted.' Stopping short of an apology in the way that is typical of colonial powers keen to evade true reckoning with historical crimes, he urged his hosts to move on. 'Let us bury the past in the spirit of magnanimity. Let not the light of the future be dimmed.'

The real test of 'regret' is whether it is accompanied by sincere efforts at reform. Here Musharraf's position was unequivocal. Rather than address intra-regional tensions to prevent a repeat of 1971, he assassinated Baluch tribal leader Akbar Bugti for daring to ask for a greater share of the province's gas revenues. Two decades of insurgency, killings, tortures and disappearances later, Pakistan remains a paranoiac nation-state trapped in permanent fear of its own ethnic diversity. Unwilling to heed calls for rights and recognition from its own citizens, it sees India behind growing separatist sentiment in its distant peripheries, reinforcing the same cycle of bitterness that led East Bengal to go its own way.

IV

Pilot Officer Rashid Minhas was my mother's brother.

I know him as a face in photos and fragments of a life remembered fondly by our family. Also, as a character in projections and imaginings that occupy the void left by East Pakistan in our national memory. The cult of his martyrdom, like that of other *Nishan-e-Haider* recipients, is ubiquitous in Pakistan. I've seen his image everywhere, in every province I've visited: on walls, billboards, and children's textbooks across the country, including remote areas where the state's presence feels otherwise minimal. Sometimes I catch a glimpse when I'm investigating hardships and oppressions faced by the ordinary people of Pakistan in their everyday lives. I love my uncle, as I love all my family, but the sight of his presence in such settings invariably makes me wince.

A widely viewed telefilm told the story of Rashid Minhas's life, which countless strangers seemed to know minute details about. Growing up in the 1980s, I was repeatedly told about his heroics in thwarting a Bengali traitor; about the significance of his noble sacrifice in service of our beloved nation. Patriotic fans of his legend would visit the house, or express heartfelt admiration after learning of our blood relation in some other scenario.

One such admirer, in the immediate aftermath of his death, authored an Urdu quatrain inscribed on his gravestone:

> Though they both fly through the same skies,
> The flight of a true believer is distinct from that of a pretender.
> On Rashid's martyrdom Iqbal has proclaimed:
> The world of an eagle is distinct from that of a vulture.

In death, as in life, every effort was made to emphasise the distinction between the two men who perished in the wreckage of Bluebird-166 on 20 August 1971 – one, symbolised in this poem by an eagle, the other a vulture. Minhas was made a hero; Rahman branded a traitor and denied an honourable burial until his body was returned to Bangladesh in 2006 after decades of negotiations. Pakistani admirers of Minhas take little interest in the details of Matiur Rahman's life – just enough to sketch the outlines of a dark-skinned villain in a tale of Punjabi masculine courage.

Nationalists in Bangladesh portray him as destined to give his life for Bangladesh from a young age. Yet, there must have been a time when he felt unsure of what to do. What must Matiur have gone through in the days, hours, minutes leading up to the moment he would become an enemy of state in a country he fought for? Lying awake nights, did he ponder the plight of his wife and children if he made it safely through the hijacking and they not? Did he visualise the kinds of interrogation he would be subjected to if apprehended in the act of 'treason'? Did he fear the operation itself: speeding toward enemy lines at tree top level to evade detection by radars, without a helmet and parachute? Perhaps, as he contemplated such questions, some small part of him wondered whether he had it in him to go through with it. Perhaps, in difficult moments, some part of him gave into the idea that Bengalis were somehow inferior – less strong, manly, brave than their Punjabi brothers in arms – a lie he would almost certainly have had to contend with on a daily basis in an institution built on colonial myths.

Imagine too what his wife Milly must have felt, and his children as he kissed them goodbye for the last time. What did they go through when they were informed Matiur was dead; that he had been a traitor and would be remembered as such in the only country he knew?

In a world where aerial bombardment has brought endless horror in so many places – from Japan to Vietnam, Iraq to Gaza – decorating fighter pilots with medals denoting supreme courage seems nonsensical. What could possibly be less daring than detonating explosives from safe distance in the sky?

I take comfort from the fact my uncle was spared further participation in a military campaign that caused immeasurable suffering. For what it's worth, I'm told he was privately critical of West Pakistan's refusal to respect the results of the election of 1970, and disliked our people's arrogance towards the East wing. He was deeply uncomfortable with the grounding of his Bengali colleagues, and invited one – a personal mentor - home for tea as a gesture of solidarity. This doesn't change his allegiance, or our family's privileged ties to the Pakistani military.

In a society lacking in historical consciousness, however, perhaps it can contribute to a more informed discourse of remembrance, in which perpetrators finally reckon with our ignoble part in the genocide of 1971.

ROHINGYA

Kaamil Ahmed

Nur Alam was ten years old the first time he was forced from his home in Myanmar's Rakhine state. Soldiers had expelled him and thousands of other minority Rohingya from their villages and across the border into a town called Gundum. A fortnight later, soldiers on the other side rounded them up and sent them back to Myanmar.

Nur Alam would spend his whole life being forced back and forth across this border between Myanmar and Bangladesh. When I met him in 2018, he was in his fourth exile. Sat with him at the time, on a plastic stool outside a refugee community centre, was his grandson Mamoon who had arrived in Bangladesh less than a year earlier, the same age his grandfather was the first time he settled into a life in a tent.

Their family were among 700,000 who left after Myanmar's military launched a series of genocidal massacres against the Rohingya, which wrung the majority of the mostly-Muslim ethnic group from their ancestral homeland in western Myanmar. The intensity of the violence against them – including mass executions, arson and rape – alerted many in the world to the Rohingya for the first time.

But the reality is that Rohingya persecution has been experienced through decades and over multiple generations, not only during that extreme spike in violence that began in August 2017. I was well aware of this already – being in the midst of researching my book on the Rohingya refugee experience, *I Feel No Peace* – but my encounter with Nur Alam alerted me to a history of persecution that stretched back even further than I had realised. While I had come across Rohingya who in 2017 had become refugees for the third time – having previously fled major military operations in 1978 and the 1990s – Nur Alam was the first I had met to be made a refugee four times.

The nearly eight years spent working on *I Feel No Peace* was an experience filled with moments of learning. I started work on it very early on in my journalism career, at a time when coverage of the Rohingya was sparse and understanding of their plight was limited. I first visited the Rohingya refugee camps in Bangladesh in 2015, when thousands of Rohingya were being stranded by a transnational boat trafficking network that exploited their desperation. I met expressionless faces when I spoke to other journalists about writing a book on the topic. Frustration would stay with me while working on the book and remains with me to this day, as I see how neglect allows Rohingya suffering to continue and be expressed forever in new ways.

Through the course of researching and writing the book I discovered that this ignorance of decades of Rohingya persecution – which could be argued amounts to a long, slow-burning genocide – was not only present among general audiences but also those who should know more. When humanitarians flooded into Cox's Bazar area of Bangladesh to respond to the Rohingya expulsions, it was astonishing to find how many of them spoke of 'the Rohingya crisis' as a new phenomenon that had only just started. This view of what the Rohingya have experienced negated years of persecution that had not been dealt with by the international system, allowing conditions in Myanmar to fester over years and for the existence of camps in Bangladesh that had been there three decades. It made it seem like a temporary, unexpected problem rather than one that was entirely predictable. To be clear: the Rohingya have since the independence of Burma from British rule, and more aggressively since the 1970s, faced a systematic process of extermination. This has been enforced through military operations, the stripping of their citizenship, state-level violence and a system of total control over their lives that controls their freedom to pray, work, travel or access schooling and healthcare. They have been relentlessly demeaned in wider society, referred to by politicians, including the once-revered Aung San Suu Kyi, as 'Bengalis' to invoke an otherness. The more vitriolic freely use slurs referring to their darker skin. Beyond Myanmar's borders, their statelessness has opened them to abuse and exploitation, including human and sex trafficking.

When I met Nur Alam, he told me that the first country he fled to was Pakistan – something I found perplexing given that he said he had only fled for two weeks and Pakistan was a long distance from Myanmar. It was only when he told me he had arrived in Gundum – a Bangladeshi border town – that I understood he was talking about a period before Bangladesh's independence. This helped me put a rough date on his departure and I found some records in international newspapers of Rohingya being expelled from Burma, as it was then known, during the 1950s.

It was not coincidental that the Rohingya began facing problems soon after independence. They were victims of a post-colonial nation state model built to fit inside rigid borders that did not respect the historical shifting of people and boundaries in the region. Only a river formed much of the border between Bengal and Rakhine – which had historically been their own kingdoms – yet now the Rohingya were seen as intruders within their homeland because of a shared religion with those on the other side of the border and some similarities in religion and culture.

Nur Alam does not know his exact age so it was hard to pin down when exactly he fled Rakhine for the first time other than at some point in the 1950s. What was more easily established was that conditions for the Rohingya got much worse after he returned. He told me:

> I was around ten years old and my parents brought me to Pakistan. They brought us out from our houses and gathered us together and told us we had to leave the country. I arrived here holding my mother's hand. Then after about 14 days, the military here came and beat us and said go home.

> This has happened four times. Each time, the situation there has got worse. They don't let us pray in the mosque, they took everything from us, they closed the schools. There is no persecution they didn't do to us. There is no word to describe our suffering. That time we suffered little compared to what happened this time.

The real deterioration in the lives of the Rohingya happened after the 1962 coup that brought to power the dictator Ne Win and an unforgiving vision of nationalism that did not have space for the Rohingya or other ethnic groups on the country's frontiers. In 1978, this led to the expulsion of at least 200,000 Rohingya from Myanmar to Bangladesh as a result of Operation Dragon King, which saw Rakhine state flooded with military personnel ostensibly tasked with carrying out a census but seen as a way to root out the Rohingya from the wider population. While there had been smaller arrivals of Rohingya refugees in Bangladesh (and East Pakistan, in its previous form), this was the first time there were large-scale refugee camps being set up and a major international humanitarian operation.

If you speak to humanitarians who have worked in Cox's Bazar over the past seven years, you are quite likely to find many who know little to nothing about 1978 and how the Rohingya response was handled. That is despite it being incredibly important to understanding what has happened to the Rohingya in the decades afterwards and to this day.

The way Bangladesh handled that refugee crisis has been a blueprint ever since. It accepts refugees during the moment of most intense pressure but soon afterwards, not wanting to bear responsibility for them longer-term, it begins making the camps unliveable in order to coerce a return.

At a meeting with humanitarian officials in 1978, including UNHCR, Syed Ali Khasru, then Secretary of the Ministry of Relief and Rehabilitation, said: 'well, gentlemen, it is all very well to have fat, well-fed refugees...but I must be a politician, and we are not going to make the refugees so comfortable that they won't go back to Burma'.

The resulting policy were cuts to food rationing so harsh that around 12,000 people died within a year – likely more than were killed in Myanmar's actual military operation. Accompanied by a regime of control on the Rohingya and arrests of any activists, it was successful in pushing back almost the entire Rohingya population to Myanmar. But it also showed Bangladesh that it could push these lines without consequence. The lines it pushed about refugees being 'spoiled' have come up repeatedly in the decades since. Alan Lindquist, who arrived in 1979 as the new UNHCR head in Cox's Bazar, said in an internal review of the agency's response that: 'None of the UN agency heads raised any objection to using food as a political weapon.'

> Can there be any excuse for an international organisation like the United Nations High Commissioner for Refugees – whose brief is refugee welfare – to acquiesce in a policy which results in more than nine-thousand unnecessary deaths among a group of refugees? Certainly a UN agency is constrained by the policy of the country it is working in, but the UN's responsibility goes beyond that to any member government.

The Rohingya returned to Rakhine state after 1978 faced a situation that almost immediately got far worse. In 1982 they were stripped of their citizenship, laying the ground for a system that would entirely control their lives and leave them at the mercy of a state that seemed intent on pushing them out of Myanmar. The pressure ratcheted-up, with Rohingya land being seized and Rohingya men being routinely taken by the military for forced labour, to the point that by 1990, Rohingya again felt unsafe staying in Myanmar and an estimated 250,000 fled to Bangladesh.

'There was no safety for us, even in our own houses. They would come in and torture the women. So after all these difficulties we came to Bangladesh,' said Shob Mehraj, who left for Bangladesh in 1992, after her husband was taken for forced labour and repeated harassment from soldiers who told them to leave their village and confiscated land.

Camps were again established to host them and the conditions were, once again, awful. Many died to hunger and disease and Bangladesh was quick to sign a repatriation agreement with Myanmar and begin the process of returning the Rohingya, believing it could quickly emulate the 1978 process. But the same policies did not produce exactly the same results. While many of the 250,000 did return, a number of Rohingya were far more hesitant than before. The conditions for them in Myanmar were far more dangerous by now and even hardship in Bangladesh was not enough to convince them to leave. So, Bangladesh cracked down even further, arresting Rohingya leaders it felt were responsible for this resistance and stripping ration cards from families who refused to leave. On a few occasions authorities actually resorted to forcing people onto boats at gunpoint.

After Lindquist's 1979 review, a stronger UNHCR response might have been expected. In reality, they were even weaker and even cooperated with Bangladesh in carrying out repatriations – with a brief break after controversy over forced repatriations. While the agency said it obtained consent for all sent back, this did not account for the coercive policies enacted by Bangladesh and it was also accused of not properly informing people of what they were consenting to by providing forms in languages like Bengali and English – which they could not understand. They were also accused of using mass registrations instead of individual interviews, where all who did not refuse to return were assumed to be willing. A US researcher who witnessed a repatriation told me they saw people burst into tears when they discovered where the boat was heading.

Just like in 1978, there was an internal review of UNHCR's repose. But this time, the report was so damning that it was never published. The report recognised that in 1978 and the 1990s UNHCR had arguably 'departed the furthest from its protection mandate and principles in any of its operations worldwide' and 'at a minimum, UNHCR showed reckless disregard for its protection mandate'.

Probably the most shocking revelation in the report was the following remark made by a UN official regarding whether the Rohingya should be given a voice.

'The Rohingyas are primitive people. At the end of the day, they will go where they are told to go.'

The question is whether this view of the Rohingya as 'primitive' has gone away. Such terms are certainly no longer uttered out loud any longer but is the treatment the same? In fact, does this possibly apply to how refugees and displaced peoples worldwide are seen by aid agencies who sweep in during crises and dictate how responses should be carried out?

There have been some steps towards giving the Rohingya more voice since 2017 but much of this symbolic and all of it hard-fought for. Shows of consultation are made but decisions on everything that matters - repatriation, relations with Myanmar, food distribution - are made above their heads.

I have found it striking how the Rohingya, like other Muslim groups facing state repression, have often been viewed through a 'War on Terror' lens. This is something Myanmar's military has worked on, pushing the idea that its violence against the group was only a response to the armed group Arakan Rohingya Salvation Army - who launched a series of attacks on the military prior to the August 2017 military operations. This framing almost justifies a crackdown on them with the suggestion that the Rohingya support terrorism. It has had some effect. At the time of the massacres in 2017, I remember being asked whether they were truly innocent – maybe Aung San Suu Kyi's Myanmar was actually responding to a security threat. In India, there is constant fear mongering about the security threat posed by Rohingya infiltration, while Bangladesh occasionally floats the idea that the camps could become a breeding ground for radicalisation if the refugees are not returned. Humanitarians, who seem to rarely have much understanding of Islam or Islamism, seem to see any form of conservatism as equal to radicalism.

During the course of writing *I Feel No Peace* and as a journalist covering development at *The Guardian* I have a constant rotation of humanitarian workers working in crisis and disaster zones. They come in for a stint and then leave. Meanwhile, those affected and with the most knowledge of what is needed are left behind. I think this is why I was so frustrated by the lack of institutional memory within the UN and among humanitarian workers in general. There were many, fatal mistakes made during the previous repatriations.

But what also seemed to be ignored was that Bangladesh's repatriation policy had not entirely worked. Around 70,000 registered refugees never return to Myanmar and just as it was sending the others back, more were returning – and they never stopped coming. In 2015, when I first visited the Rohingya camps, there were reported to be between 150,000 and 300,000 Rohingya living in Bangladesh. Most of them were not registered as refugees, living in horrid, cramped conditions with barely any support.

Exploitation flourished in these conditions. Refugees who accumulated debt were ensnared by local drug traffickers to mule the popular methamphetamine Yaba past Bangladeshi police checkpoints - resulting in the Rohingya acquiring an unfair association with criminal activity - and women were vulnerable to being kidnapped by sex traffickers. More broadly, the disillusioned young people who grew up in these camps where Bangladesh banned work, travel, and education were enticed by human traffickers to seek opportunity abroad. They were convinced to board boats in the Bay of Bengal that would head to Malaysia but on the way stopped in the jungles of Thailand, where they were held captive until their families paid a ransom – even if they had already paid a fee to the traffickers. This trafficking ring was abruptly exposed in 2015, when Thai police uncovered mass graves.

This was when I first visited the camps in Bangladesh - where there were very few journalists working in international media. While most of the coverage of this crisis happened in Southeast Asia, where there were dramatic shots of boats stranded at sea or reaching land with hungry, dehydrated passengers, I was able to visit some of the families who had been left behind. Almost all of them had lost young men who had grown up in Bangladesh and left because they felt they had no future in the country.

A large part of my motivation for writing this book was to show that there were serious challenges that would emerge for the new generation of Rohingya refugees in Bangladesh. The international system had to learn from its past mistakes and create a more human environment for the refugees and it had to push for a solution to their persecution in Myanmar, or risk creating an even bigger space for exploitation than ever before. The camps that existed now were the biggest refugee settlements in the world.

Unfortunately, it feels like little has been learnt. Bangladeshi authorities over the past few years have become increasingly draconian in their policies. They severely limit Rohingya movement, they cracked down on informal Rohingya education centres while not offering a formal alternative for secondary education and they ban work. At times there have been harsh crackdowns on Rohingya shops within the camps and for a long period there was an internet blackout to stop the refugees using mobile phones. Tens of thousands of Rohingya have been relocated to Bhasan Char, a remote island in the Bay of Bengal considered vulnerable to extreme weather. Every other month there seems to be a crisis, whether in the form of floods, landslides or fires that can wipe out thousands of Rohingya shelters in minutes. All the while, financial support has shrunk year on year, resulting in food rations being slashed twice in 2023.

Meanwhile, the camps have become increasingly insecure, with armed gangs emerging in the security vacuum of these sprawling spaces. Some of them dress themselves up as Rohingya resistance groups but are all largely seen by the wider refugee population as criminal entities fighting for territory and control over the population. They kill Rohingya community leaders and kidnap refugees for ransom.

The insecurity and the hopelessness within the camps cannot convince anyone to return to Myanmar but it is pushing people back onto the boats again. UNHCR said it documented more Rohingya boat journeys in 2023 than at any point since 2015. I travelled in early 2024 to investigate this and found a worryingly similar situation to my first visit, with families who had lost young relatives, often not knowing whether they were dead or alive. The traffickers were again employing the method of convincing refugees to leave the camps for Malaysia or Indonesia but then holding them on boats or islands, sometimes even inside Myanmar, for ransoms of up to £3,000.

A middleman I spoke to, who helped to recruit refugees for these journeys, said it was a phenomenon that would only grow. 'It has corrupted throughout the camp, so if someone tries to stop it they can't do anything. Every day the traffickers are calling, asking for more people,' he said.

Even more worrying is that the situation for the Rohingya remaining in Myanmar is also once again deteriorating. Around 500,000 Rohingya are thought to have remained after 2017, compared to a million in Bangladesh, and had largely stayed out of the news. Even after the Arakan Army - which represents the Buddhist Rakhine ethnic group - began a war for control of the state with Myanmar's military, the Rohingya were largely out of the picture, though occasionally caught in the crossfire. But the situation has seriously worsened in 2024, with both sides turning on the Rohingya. The military began forcibly conscripting young men to effectively act as human shields while the AA, which now controls large parts of Rakhine state, have lashed out at the Rohingya. On one occasion, a UN official said the AA expelled Rohingya from several villages to the same location, where they were then targeted by a drone strike that killed hundreds.

There are now thousands of Rohingya trying to enter Bangladesh - some have managed to get through but are settling in the camps without any access to aid, while others are stranded on the border. There are eerily familiar images of young babies washing up on river banks after their boats have capsised.

When the new arrivals of Rohingya were settling in to the camps in 2017, many showed a surprising level of faith in the international system to deliver justice and ensure safety in Myanmar to allow their return. That faith has not been repaid.

Diplomats, aid workers, journalists, and researchers came to the camps to interview the refugees – some of them many times - but results were never returned. An International Criminal Court Investigation into forced expulsion has not yet amounted to anything while an International Court of Justice case into genocide has barely progressed since being launched in 2019.

There was always something that bugged me about the ICJ genocide case: it focused on 2017. Perhaps there was a legal reason for this but for me, the wiping away of the Rohingya people inside Myanmar did not happen only in those months. That explosive, unprecedented level of violence was awful and vastly accelerated their expulsion, but it followed decades of systematic violence. The Rohingya have been stripped of citizenship and belonging since 1978 in every way. They could not pray in their mosques, they could not congregate with each other nor go to the markets. They were banned from higher education and needed permits simply to seek medical care. Media and politicians, including the once-adored Aung San Suu Kyi, were involved in actively demonising them. Yet none of this seems to have ever really warranted concern within the international system in which they still seemed to have faith. In fact, it seems to have been ignored. While the Rohingya were facing increasingly widespread hate in Myanmar society and becoming the target of race riots in 2012, the US administration sought instead to preserve a fragile democratic transition that put Aung San Suu Kyi in power. She ended up still being deposed but only after defending the military's violence against the Rohingya in the ICJ.

As a journalist, I have spent most of my career covering the impacts of conflict and crisis and often in regions where coverage is limited. But the way the brutal treatment of the Rohingya has never been taken seriously for any sustained period has been striking. I took time with *I Feel No Peace*, choosing to produce a work of in-depth research over several years rather than turning around a quick, topical response to the violence of 2017, when it had been covered widely in international media. Only a couple of years later, many in the publishing industry felt the moment had passed and there was enough coverage of the Rohingya. Anyone who searches through the catalogues will realise that is not the case.

I hold no illusions about the efficacy of the 'international community', having seen it repeatedly fail to stop the repression and killing of civilians on a mass scale but my time spent with the Rohingya have revealed to me just how tragic the results of this failed system can be. The lack of teeth that has allowed Myanmar to establish a genocidal system does not merely result in people being killed, it strips them of their home and a future and leaves them vulnerable to the vultures of the world who seek to profit from trading in human bodies.

In a world of constantly competing crises, this system seems to have given up on solving problems. At best it offers not peace but a temporary pause to the cause of suffering, or aid that might help to survive. Whether by assisting the Rohingya's return to Myanmar or in allowing them to suffer in the camps of Bangladesh, the message from the world seems to be that it is not very concerned in offering them real safety. It offers them only a place to be sheltered, temporarily, from the very worst. It offers them only a brief quiet.

I will always remember a Facebook post written by one of my oldest contacts in the camps, who I named Nobi in the book to protect his identity. 'When a small minority group is [on the] eastern side of this river, they are called Bengali Kola by the Burmese people. When they are [on the] western side of this river they are called Burmaya. No peace, no dignity, no state, no happiness, no justice, no hope and no home for them still in any corners of this world.'

DISPLACED AGAIN

Celine Kasem

My family has encountered quite a few genocides. My bloodline is infused with migration, packing up, leaving everything behind, starting from zero, over and over, due to injustice, to dirty power, and genocide. When someone asks 'where are you from', first, before anything – and I promise this is not a romantic idealist answer, it's simply how I feel – I always say I am human, and then I get into the intricately woven history of my blood, nationality, culture, and citizenship. I am a Syrian, Circassian, Armenian, Canadian, who has had the privilege to live in over five countries. This has taught me a lot about who we are as humans, what makes us treat one another with empathy or superiority, what makes us good or bad, kind or evil – what makes us, us.

The oldest genocide that lives in my blood but not memory is the Circassian genocide. According to my ancestry test, I am 97 percent Caucasian and Anatolian, which attributes to both my Circassian and Armenian background. The Circassian genocide took place around 1817–1864, when the indigenous people of the Northwestern Caucuses region faced, at the hands of the Russian Tsarist Empire, mass killings, expulsions, ethnic cleansing, and forced displacement. In a colonialist, imperialist move, the Russian Empire sought to expand southward into the Caucasus to secure its southern frontier and gain access to the Black Sea. To quell the Circassians' fierce decades-long resistance against the Russian empire, brutal military campaigns by the Russian army, ethnically cleansed us from our land, killing hundreds of thousands of us. According to various records, over one million people were killed in the Circassian genocide. Another reason for this extreme expulsion, was simply because we were Muslim, which the Russian Empire considered a hindrance in establishing its Christian Orthodox hegemony.

Circassians follow the religion of Islam but we do not impose it. The principles that govern our lives is referred to as *khabze*. It is a code of values and traditions, ethics, and law that shapes our behaviour, our consciousness, and memory of ancestors and home. The true 'religion' of the Circassians was, and still is to some degree, Adygage. It translates as 'to be Adyge', that is Circassian. These peaceful and beautiful traditions are what make us who we are, and what makes us have a home in every city in the world that has a Circassians diaspora. When I was accepted at the master's program in Qatar, and came to the country not knowing anyone, my grandma put me in touch with her distant relatives. I had never met or heard of them in my life. They hosted me at their family's home when I first landed in Doha, treated me like their own daughter, welcoming me wholeheartedly into a new place where I knew no one: that is Circassian Khabze.

The Circassians were anything but a threat to the Russian Empire. Following their conquest of our land in 1864, Russia made a deal with the Ottoman Empire to deport Circassians from their native land to the region of the Ottoman Empire which today is modern day Jordan, Palestine, Syria, and Turkey. Some of my ancestors were placed on boats, and shipped in a horrific trip across the Black Sea. There are stories of the ships getting bombed, people drowning and dying in the ocean, widespread disease, starvation, and death during this long transit. This is why a common saying amongst the Circassians emerged: we would never eat fish from the Black Sea, because it contains the blood of our ancestors that were murdered by the brutal imperialist Russian forces. Other Circassians were driven to Sochi, where they died by the thousands as they waited for ships to take them to the Ottoman Empire. Eyewitnesses describe staggering images of corpses of women, children, elderly persons, torn to pieces and half-eaten by dogs. Many emaciated by hunger and disease were too weak to walk and collapsed exhaustion and become prey to wild dogs while still alive. This is the same Sochi that hosted the 2014 Winter Olympic Games, on top of mass graves of Circassians that the Russian Empire had massacred. Every year on 21 May, we commemorate the 'Circassian Day of Mourning' which is the day the Russians hold a celebratory parade of their conquest of the last bastion of Circassian resistance in 1864.

My ancestors, with their unique culture that is quite different from Arab or Turkish culture, had to start a new life wherever they ended up. They ended up in modern day Syria; and settled together mostly in the mountains of the Golan heights. The environment and its agricultural possibilities reminded them of back home. They built villages for themselves by themselves. Some also settled in the countryside of Homs, Hama, and Aleppo. All of my grandfathers' grandfathers from my mother's and father's side had settled in Golan, and I heard the most beautiful stories about the Golan from the both of them.

My grandfather Nour al Dien Doughouz, who grew up in Mansoura, a Circassian village in Golan heights, told me how when you walk through a field, barefoot, you end up stepping on all kinds of fruits and vegetables your heart can ever imagine. They relied on farming as main source of income, with other job opportunities being scarce, and they all helped one another in their villages. They considered themselves as family, one community where everyone supported each other. They lived in poverty as did most of Syria during those times.

My grandfather also told me that he was the first in his class so he had won an inflatable bear as a prize, and everyone in the village was amazed by the plastic toy, he would make all his friends stand in a line to take turns to play with the bear.

He was in his thirties during the Six Day War. When Israel attacked the Golan Heights, he had to flee in a matter of hours. He told me that they were called by their mayor and instructed to leave Golan as soon as possible and go to Damascus as Syria was about to go to war with Israel. My grandfather and his family left everything behind, everything except the clothes they were wearing, and fled their home village, Quinetra. The journey to Damascus, which they took on foot, lasted around fifteen hours during which time they had stopped multiple times, trying to figure out where they were going, what their next steps were. My grandfather sat down on the side of the road, put his face in his palm with his head down, wondering: what now, what will happen, how will I take care of my mother and father and siblings, we have nothing, where are we going, why did they do this to us? He remembers being shaken by his mother after he had been crying for a long time.

After being displaced from Quinetra, most of my family settled in Damascus, but some also went to Homs and Aleppo. This is when they had to leave the agricultural life behind and abruptly learn how to get involved in industrial life. The values of our khabza, built on respect of the elderly and ancestors, kindness, compassion, shyness, appreciation of our community and culture, came into play. We rarely married outside of our culture even after being forcibly displaced. We built our neighbourhoods and villages to keep the community together. I heard stories from my friends about how it was really rare for Syrian Circassians to have any non-Circassian friends, which to me nowadays seems odd. While I think it is important to stay close with your culture and community, not interacting with the rest of the population in one's place of residence is not very strategic either.

My grandfather from my father's side, Sarkis, comes from Armenian descent. Displaced from their town of Sivas during the Armenian genocide, Sarkis, along with his two sisters, Marta and Heghna, and mother, Mary, were deported along with the rest of their village community towards Syrian territories. During their journey, Sarkis witnessed the death of his mother, who had to be buried by the roadside. He continued his journey with his sisters towards Syria.

When they reached the city of Homs, in central Syria, Sarkis lost track of his sisters. A Bedouin took Sarkis into the desert to live and work with him as a shepherd, and the Bedouin gave him the new name of Mohammed Kasem. Life was harsh for the young Sarkis, so he attempted to escape, but failed the first time. Repeating attempts led to success; he fled until he reached the village of Bir Ajam in the Golan Heights. There, he made friendships with the youth of the village, who, upon learning his story, asked him to stay in the village and leave behind the harsh Bedouin life. He was afraid of the Bedouin's reaction, but they assured him that they wouldn't be able to do anything to him.

Indeed, he settled in the village, which resembled his hometown of Yarhisar in Sivas in terms of landscape, building style, or the lifestyle of people living in it and the surrounding villages. The young Sarkis – now Mohammed Kasem – worked various jobs, such as farming and transporting sand and other construction materials to cover his living expenses. With time, he managed to build a small house and marry a Circassian woman,

Fatima, with whom he had three children, two sons and a daughter – one of them being my grandfather, Shariff. Mohammed Kasem (Abu Shariff) then moved with his family to live in the city of Quneitra and continued working in the field of transporting building materials. His wife passed away in 1957 and Abu Shariff did not remarry and continued to live with his son in their house in the city of Quneitra. In 1967, due to the Israeli occupation of the Golan heights, Abu Shariff faced yet another painful displacement, forced to flee to Damascus, having to leave behind his house and properties in Quneitra. He continued his life with his son Shariff, who now began to establish his life in the suburbs of Damascus, working in the field of driving various types of vehicles, from taxis to tankers. In 1969, Shariff married a Circassian woman (my grandmother), and had four children, the eldest being my father Tambi Kasem.

Abu Shariff, my father's grandfather, continued to live in my grandfather Shariff's house until he passed away on 2 January 1987. In 2011, Shariff, my grandfather, was forced to flee again due to the brutal crackdown by the Assad regime on the Syrian revolution. This time he left Damascus behind and sought refuge in America, where one of his sons resided. He took a DNA test and was able to connect and meet with his first cousins, who had also been looking for their uncle who went missing in Syria. They had migrated to America long before and became a part of the Armenian community in Upstate New York. When Shariff went to meet them, he had the most precious time at the family gathering, discovering that they all even looked alike. They welcomed him with open arms and even asked him if he wanted to convert to Christianity (the Armenian Church), but he respectfully declined their offer. For the first time ever, my grandfather found out what his Armenian last name is namely Yanidian – his forgotten and hidden history.

In the meantime, in Damascus at a Circassian youth gathering, my mother and father met and fell in love. These gatherings, called *telematch*, were a regular feature of the Circassian lifestyle, where exciting, very competitive games were played in teams. They were very young but wanted to get married, which they did, and then moved to Saudi Arabia to look for work opportunities, as Syria did not have many to offer. I was born in 2000 in Riyadh, as the oldest grandchild of Shariff's, the oldest – and as such rather spoiled – child of my parent's friends group. A few years later my parents got the opportunity to move to the United States, where we stayed for four years. I went to preschool and kindergarten in New Jersey, where my sister, who is three years younger than me, was born. My father made it a rule that we were not allowed to speak English at home, lest we forget our mother tongue, Arabic. There was a huge Circassian community in New Jersey that we became a part of as well. Then in 2006, my parents decided that America was too different for them, and they were unable to find decent jobs. When I was in the first grade, we moved back to Saudi Arabia where I spent most of my childhood. I went to international schools there and had many friends of different Arab nationalities. As everywhere else we went, we had a huge Circassian community and would see each other every single Friday, which thus became my favourite day of the weekend. We would go to *isteraha*, which literally translates to break, it's a private park that we would rent for all of us to meet each other as a community. Growing up, I always had a keen interest in the world out there, always watching Al Jazeera in the living room television with my father.

As the 2011 uprising started in Syria, the news we were hearing from our families back home sounded ominous. I was eleven and did not understand the true horror of what was unfolding but in my family there was no shred of doubt what the moral, humane, and right side was. It was the side of the people. I have school photos of me in school on the 'international day' – 26 December 2011 – when everyone wears their cultural clothes and brings their country's cuisine to school. I am wearing a huge revolution flag with my mum's *galabieh*, the revolution flag drawn on my face. Slowly we had to get my mum's parents grandparents out of the Damascus suburbs, where they lived, which were targeted early on. My father helped organise private protests where people would get together and fundraise to send to our loved ones in Syria, who were getting hit, detained, and killed for asking for their basic human rights.

The Syrian revolution is one of the world's most iconic revolutions, one of those very few that started with roses. Roses and bottles of water handed to, what the people would then find out, are their killers. Roses met with bullets, with detention, torture, disappearance, and death. For the first time in a really long time, Syrians were able to somehow finally build up the courage to break the decades-long barrier of fear of our police military state, where 'even the walls hear', where people were not allowed to gather in more than a group of five in one place. From 2011, onwards the Assad regime's obsession with power made it do the most inhuman things to its own people. By 2015, when Syrian rebels came very close to finally overthrowing the regime in Damascus, Russia came to support the Syrian butcher, and started carpet bombings that killed thousands of the civilians. In the Syrian genocide, the Assad regime used every known method of killing: chemical attacks, barrel bombs, rockets, snipers, tanks, torture, sieges, starvation.

The Syrian genocide is technically difficult to prove, as what defines a genocide according to existing international law appears to need amending to reflect reality. Currently, genocide is determined when 'any of the following acts committed with intent to destroy, in whole or in part, a national, ethnical, racial or religious group, as such: (a) Killing members of the group; (b) Causing serious bodily or mental harm to members of the group; (c) Deliberately inflicting on the group conditions of life calculated to bring about its physical destruction in whole or in part; (d) Imposing measures intended to prevent births within the group; (e) Forcibly transferring children of the group to another group'. In Syria what happened was a mix of all of these intents, together, to all degrees, all war crimes, all crimes against humanity, towards all the Syrian people, from all backgrounds, sects, and groups. Indiscriminate war that knows no child, woman, or elderly. The Assad regime is one of the most brutal dictatorships to have ever walked this earth.

Even though I have never lived in Syria, which I have only visited during the summer months, Syria is my passion. It is the home of much of my family history and memory; it is the light in my life and defines who I am. I hope one day my family's history of fleeing from genocide will come to an end with their return to a peaceful Syria.

HEBA ABU NADA

Luke Wilkinson

Writing is like fasting, it cannot be done without intention.

Heba Abu Nada

Words cascade around Palestine: calls for restraint, ceasefire, Israel's right to defence, or the mutual exchange of accusations of genocide. Beyond this stream of declarations, it is the poetry and literature from the people of Gaza, that makes us feel, if but briefly, the constant regeneration of suffering among the Palestinians. The work of Heba Abu Nada, a Palestinian poet in Gaza, takes us to that open plain of ever-evolving human pain. Whether the leading powers in the world agree that Palestinians are the victims of genocide or not, this makes little difference to the lives of those in Gaza. As she states in her novel *Oxygen is not for the dead*, 'the wave grows in the middle of the sea and attacks the land …The bodies float up and the souls are astonished, while scientists are busy finding out whether what happened was an earthquake or a flood!'. The experience of mass death and destruction in Gaza is not one that can be processed through reason, but must be *lived*. As she states in a short piece she wrote for *Al Jazeera* in 2017, 'whether we like it or not, we have no choice but to wake up, breathe, and live this torment skin by skin, sigh by sigh.'

Heba Abu Nada was born in 1991 to a family that had come from Bayt Jirja, a village that was occupied by Israel in 1948. Growing up in Gaza, she quickly developed a perspective that crossed multiple disciplines. As was the case with many past thinkers that lived under colonial rule, the option to restrict oneself to a single field when living under hegemony was simply not an option. She studied biochemistry at the Islamic University of Gaza and gained a master's in clinical nutrition at al-Azhar University in Gaza. She also extended her efforts to aid the education of Palestinian children through teaching science at the Rusul educational centre in Gaza. Simultaneously, she began publishing several poems as part of a variety of poetry collections, such as *The Devouring Storm*, which made her a much-loved poet among Palestinians. In 2017, she wrote *Oxygen is not for the Dead*, which was awarded the Sharjah Award for Arab Creativity, a literature prize administered by the United Arab Emirates. From the beginning of the war on 7 October, she turned to Facebook to try to narrate the experience in Gaza through writing—to make her social platform one of the many 'mourning houses, memorial tents, obituary newspapers' where Palestinians 'move from page to page as if we are walking in a funeral yard, divided and open to each other'.

Through her poetry and short lines written after the 7 October, Heba Abu Nada writes in a way that conveys the experience of an entire people being effaced. We come to feel briefly what it means when the Palestinians express that they are experiencing genocide. Her words are soaked with the overwhelming presence of death in Gaza. In *Oxygen is not for the dead*, she describes death with the intimacy of someone who has seen it close at hand many times. 'I cried over my father's body until the blood became pink when it mixed with my tears', says Adam, the protagonist. Through her short pieces on Facebook during the early Israeli bombing, she conveys how the overwhelming barrage of death does not detract from the fact that each new death is unique. From afar, we lose this very quickly: deaths become statistics, as Josef Stalin knew too well. This produces a 'numbers game', in which a shameful, calculative part of us may even be pleased to hear that there are more deaths in hope that the Palestinians finally gain international recognition as the victims of a genocide. But, for Palestinians, when each name sounds familiar or even directly known, the vast spectre of death never overwhelms the individuality of each corpse. The sudden extinguishing of each flame by darkness is witnessed, one by one, until the darkness feels complete. Hear the emotion in a short post that she wrote on the 19 October 2023:

> My friend list is shrinking, turning into little coffins scattered here and there. I cannot catch my friends after the missiles, as they fly off, I cannot bring them back again, nor can I pay my condolences, nor can I cry, I don't know what to do. Every day it [the list] shrinks further, these are not just names, these are us only with different faces, different names. O God, what do we do, O God, in the face of this vast feast of death.

The day after she wrote these words, Heba and her family—her sister, brothers, parents, and aunts—prayed maghrib, the sunset prayer, together. She had come, along with her family, to her aunt's house in southern Gaza, which they had been instructed was the safe zone. They sat in silence after finishing the prayer, each in a different corner of the room—overwhelmed by processing the destruction around them. 'In the blink of an eye, a hot flame full of smoke broke into the house. I could not see anything and my feet were trapped. I could not move them, but still felt that they were not hurt. It took me a second to realise that we were targeted by a missile.' Having herself been pulled from the rubble, Somaia Abunada then tells of what happened to her sister.

> I looked at my mother, her face bloodied and half of her body still trapped under the rubble. I saw both my brothers. I checked to see if other family members were okay, but could not hear or see my sister. I knew that she was completely under the rubble. I started screaming: 'My sister is here, please save her!' I ran to the street, begging anyone out there to help save my older sister, Heba. It took rescuers 10 minutes to pull Heba out. I asked them if she was alive, but no one responded. An ambulance arrived to transport her to the European Hospital.

I stood there barefoot and watched as it drove away. My older brother, who is a nurse, held my hand and began to cry. I asked him if she was alive, but he did not answer. He noticed that I was barefoot and gave me his shoes. Another ambulance drove all of us to the hospital, where I received the news that Heba did not make it. I couldn't understand. She had only been a few steps away from me. How did she not survive? With thoughts racing in my mind, I asked myself: 'Why can't I have the power to split my lifetime in half to share with her so she could stay alive?'.

The next day Somaia waited with her family in the long line to the mortuary to see Heba. 'The morticians eventually called us to see her. She was covered in white. Her face was peaceful. "Can I hug her?" I asked my mum, who readily agreed. I held my sister tightly and asked her to forgive me. The mortician tried to hand me Heba's necklace, but I refused to take it. It was not real to me and I didn't want to hold it. I did not want to believe that I lost my only sister for good. Nothing made sense to me. We were supposed to grow old together. My future children were supposed to be best friends with her future children. We were supposed to have plenty of time and many more memories to create together.'

The novel that Heba Abu Nada wrote six years before she was murdered by an Israeli missile tries to enter the shoes of the oppressor. It tells the experience of a character called Adam, who works for the office of state intelligence in an unnamed country. The state operates as the archetype of a despotic political system under which people suffer; which serves to encapsulate both the situation of Palestinians under Israel, and the wider Arab pain of living under despotic leaders before and after the Arab Spring. Adam, a senior figure in the intelligence services, and son to the Minister of Intelligence, designated the 'oppressor' rather than 'oppressed', is tormented by increasing protests and revolutions, which quickly escalate to the assassination of his own father. Heba Abu Nada shows how the 'oppressor' himself suffers and is oppressed by his own actions. Adam is so suffocated by his thoughts and his self that he is 'choked' by his shadow or reflection in the mirror. The protagonist is consistently overwhelmed by memories re-emerging suddenly in his daily life in the offices of the intelligence services, making him unable to process the present. His father seems completely deadened in the heart, refusing to allow Adam to call him 'father' or engage in friendly conversation at their shared offices. Consider a paper note that the Minister of the Interior reads in the opening of the novel. 'Don't try to turn off this revolution, we can reach to you in your fortified villages, you are surrounded by our corpses, our eyes, our dreams, and our revolution.' The minister 'clenched the paper in his hand'. This response of clenching in the hand is mirrored in the heart, which tightens within the archetypal oppressor more and more until it has become completely hardened; a walled settlement itself, violently hostile to any person suffering. The picture that emerges, then, is that the 'oppressor', whether represented by a despotic ruler or the Israeli government, loses their own vitality in their position of domination.

Two types of deaths emerge that Heba Aba Nada brings to the surface. One is the death of the body, the ephemeral death, and the other is the death of the heart—a much harder form of death. Ibn Arabi, the thirteenth century mystic from Andalusia, tells us that when the body dies, each particle remains alive, buzzing with energy. The immaterial element in the body, the soul, may be alive or dead. If a person developed a hardened heart across their lifetime, the soul is in some sense deadened and heavy unlike the alive-ness of the soul—a state that it will continue to suffer in eternity—while the soul of the one who overcame their ego and lived for the love of the Ever-living, *al-hayy*, is free and alive. To 'die before you die', as the classic mystical Islamic expression goes, then, is the aim, for it frees the heart of the heaviness of the ego; should the soul recede into the self-enclosure of the ego, it becomes rigid like lead. Surrounded by constant new waves of physical death in Gaza across numerous wars that stretch across the years of a life, Heba Abu Nada calls on her fellow Palestinians to not be drawn into the despair, to not allow their hearts to die.

Yesterday, a star said
to the little light in my heart,
We are not just transients
passing.

Do not die. Beneath this glow
some wanderers go on
walking.

You were first created out of love,
 so carry nothing but love
 to those who are trembling.

One day, all gardens sprouted
from our names, from what remained
of hearts yearning.

And since it came of age, this ancient language
has taught us how to heal others
with our longing,

how to be a heavenly scent
to relax their tightening lungs: a welcome sigh,
 a gasp of oxygen.

Softly, we pass over wounds,
like purposeful gauze, a hint of relief,
an aspirin.

O little light in me, don't die,
even if all the galaxies of the world
close in.

O little light in me, say:
Enter my heart in peace.
All of you, come in!

The beauty of this poem, as translated from the Arabic by Huda
Fakhreddine, cannot be polished further by exposition. I may, rather, try
to hold up a mirror so we can see its beauty reflected back to us. The use
of oxygen here we could consider pointing back to the theme of her novel,
reminding us of the dual meaning of its title, *Oxygen is not for the Dead*.
Recall how the Minister of the Interior clenched the paper, and along with
it the dreams of the dead into his fist. Immediately after this sentence, the
phrase 'oxygen is not for the dead!' comes, ringing in the ears of the
reader. This prompts the minister into a sudden moment of terrifying self-
reflection. 'Oxygen is not for the dead! I looked at myself, stared at myself

for a long time, and I saw my reflection on myself.' The outer meaning of 'Oxygen is not for the dead' could be the minister realising the scale of death for which he is responsible. But, deeper than this, when considered alongside the poem, we realise that this a commentary upon the heart of the oppressor. When welcomed by the heart that is free, oxygen opens and relaxes 'tightening lungs'. While for the heart that is hardened—or, as is more frequent in Qur'anic terminology, 'covered' (*kafirūn*), the literal meaning of what is often translated as 'disbelievers'—the heart cannot feel the releasing breath of oxygen. After seeing his reflection on himself, the minister says, 'I breathed myself in, but I choked on me!'. Like the lungs of an ageing smoker struggling to receive oxygen, the covered heart cannot breathe in the expansive-ness of life, of *al-Hayy*. 'Do not die', Heba Abu Nada pleads to her fellow Palestinians, surrounded by death and destruction. In other words, do not let hearts become constricted. Allah asks Muhammad in the Quran, 'have we not opened your breast for you?' (94:4). The Prophet was shown the truth through the opening of his chest, through breathing in reality beyond the barriers of discursive thinking. By inhaling, the chest, and the heart within it, expands with space, opening to the vastness of the Expander, *al-Bāsit*. As Abu Nada says in her poem, 'gardens sprouted' from the 'yearning' of oxygen into the expanding chest. Gardens grow in the open heart, intertwining themselves with the gardens of *Jannah*.

The recurring presence of light in the poem reminds Palestinians and us too that no matter how complete the darkness may seem in Gaza, we can trust the beautiful stubbornness of light. Oxygen and light exist together—even in the darkest night, the lighting of a candle in a pocket of oxygen shows that the darkness was non-existent. Throughout the poem, we feel like the speaker is reminding her own heart to trust the inextinguishable light in her heart; and, in trusting it, shining that light to others. I am reminded of the words of W. H. Auden on the eve of World War II and the genocide that it would witness:

> Defenceless under the night
> Our world in stupor lies;
> Yet, dotted everywhere,
> Ironic points of light

Flash out wherever the Just
Exchange their messages.

The sense of solidarity in the exchanging of light under the night
between open, trusting hearts features in another poem, 'I grant you
refuge', which she wrote ten days before she passed, on the 10 October
2023. Her ability to still find creative energy during the darkest nights
shows the warming lightness of her own heart. As Psalm 112 of the Bible
reads, 'even in darkness light dawns for the upright, for those who are
gracious and compassionate and righteous'. Read her words and feel the
inexhaustible courage that comes with the exchanging of light.

I grant you refuge
in invocation and prayer.
I bless the neighbourhood and the minaret
   to guard them
from the rocket

from the moment
it is a general's command
until it becomes
a raid.

I grant you and the little ones refuge,
the little ones who
change the rocket's course
before it lands
with their smiles.

...

I grant you refuge
from hurt and death,
refuge in the glory of our siege,
here in the belly of the whale.

Our streets exalt God with every bomb.
They pray for the mosques and the houses.

And every time the bombing begins in the North,
our supplications rise in the South.

Reading the words of Heba Abu Nada, we are taken into the un-imaginable experience of suffering that the Palestinian people are experiencing in the intentional destruction of their lives, families, homes, land, and culture. We feel the total darkness of the night in which Palestinians must live; and can briefly imagine what genocide must feel like. But Abu Nada points us to the possibility of light, of oxygen, that cannot be extinguished—no matter how many tonnes of bombs Israeli warplanes drop onto this people, no matter how overwhelming the pain may feel, no matter how many days, weeks, and months this people endure with empty stomachs and dry throats. Beyond this strip of land that suffers, we must try to be lights ourselves.

REMEMBERING AND FORGETTING

Robin Yassin-Kassab

In the enthusiasm of arrival, I nearly forget what has brought me here.

Sarajevo is a city in a low valley between tree-clad mountain slopes. The architecture is a mix of Ottoman and Austro-Hungarian, and a series of elegant bridges arch over a central river. It's a city, therefore, lying somewhere between Prague and Isfahan, connecting those distant cultures. It has a café scene, based around the distinctive Bosnian coffee, which betrays a Middle Eastern approach to time. Its cuisine merges Turkish, Slavic, and central European influences.

It looks like a multicultural success story. A few steps from my hotel room there are several mosques, a Catholic church, an Orthodox church, and a synagogue. And a few steps from the nearest mosque is a café serving alcohol. Some of the Muslims leave the mosque after prayer and greet their friends who are sitting drinking beer. Between a quarter and a third of the women wear some kind or other of hijab. Sometimes the religiously-dressed women are accompanied by men in shorts and T-shirt. That's a sight that can be seen anywhere in the Muslim world. But there are also religious-looking men, long-bearded, in sober, spacious dress, accompanied by women in shorts and T-shirt. You could say that a 'secular' sort of Islam is practised here, if you were to use only one, positive signification of that troublesome word. Better, perhaps, to say that there's an easy interplay of the secular and religious. A variety of beliefs and levels of belief, of different ways of living, jostle against each other not just politely but brightly and warmly. So, it seems.

There are Turkish and Arab tourists, and Muslim visitors from Germany, England, and France, no doubt feeling safer, more respected, and more comfortable here than they would in most European destinations.

I am visiting in the eleventh month of the full-scale Zionist genocide of Palestinians. The banners in support of Palestine are ubiquitous – in shop windows, car windscreens, or draped from the bridges. Not just flags, but the remembered dates of specific massacres. But beyond that, when you bring up 'Syria', the Bosniaks don't immediately regurgitate conspiracy theories, nor squint in confusion, but demonstrate political understanding and Muslim and human solidarity. This provides another good reason for me to feel at home, or at least among friends. I remember the large protest demonstration in Sarajevo in 2016 when Aleppo was being destroyed by Assad, Russia, and the Iranian militias. Other capitals ignored the disaster, but Sarajevo knows fascism when it sees it. It understands genocide.

This line of thought brings me back to my purpose. If it hadn't, I'd have been reminded by the bullet holes and larger shell damage still visible on many of the walls. So now I recall an earlier mental image of the city, one formed by news reports in the early 1990s. It shunts my sunny euphoria to the side, imposing itself over my vision. This older version of Sarajevo is grey, snow-cursed, painted with pain-scarred faces, puddles of blood, and smouldering tower blocks. This is what has brought me here. My purpose is to write about the genocide of the Bosniaks.

And that makes everything look and feel different. Even the beautiful, green mountain sides, from which Serb big guns and snipers once terrorised the city below. When I walk out of town to the Kozija ćuprija bridge, then upwards on a path towards Mount Trebević, I find a different flag displayed. Nobody stops me to ask for my passport, but I am now, very suddenly, in the territory of a different administration – the Republika Srpska. The officials of this entity don't recognise that a genocide of Bosniaks took place, or if they do, they believe it was necessary. They believe the Serbs, the genocidaires, were the real victims of the war, and are today the victims of the peace. Which makes the peace merely temporary. Nothing here has been resolved, only frozen. Inconvenient facts have been forgotten, while genocidal narratives have been carefully remembered. Sarajevo is surrounded, locally and globally, by immensely powerful interests that don't believe in the happy jostling together of different ways of life. The city is besieged by forces of history currently paralysed from motion but ready to fall, like axes or hammers, as soon as the spell of peace passes.

How then did this multicultural Muslim society in the Balkans come to be, and why is it so dangerously surrounded?

A mountainous land rising from the Adriatic Sea up into and beyond the Dinaric Alps, Bosnia and Herzegovina (or BiH for short – Herzegovina is the drier, warmer southern third) was known as Illyria before the slow Roman conquest. Slavic tribes settled in the sixth and seventh centuries, amongst them a tribe called Croat and another called Serb. But the area between today's Croatian and Serbian states has had its own distinct political identity at least since the medieval Banate of Bosnia and the Bosnian kingdom that followed. Ottoman forces first arrived in 1414. It took them the next 150 years to absorb the entire country into the empire. Then the Bosniaks gradually converted to Islam. By the early seventeenth century, Muslims formed a majority of the population.

Why did so many of the Bosniaks convert? Why them, as opposed to other communities under Ottoman rule in the Balkan peninsula, such as Serbs, Croats or Greeks? The answer surely has something to do with Bosnia's position in the borderlands between western (Catholic) and eastern (Orthodox) Christianity. Most Bosniaks rejected both. In the early medieval period, they had their own Bosnian Church, and were charged with heresy by the larger churches as a result. The two related theories presented by historians to explain the Islamic conversion are both connected to medieval Bosnia's alienation from official Christendom. The first theory is that membership in the Bosnian Church – a less hierarchical version of Christianity – facilitated the passage to anti-hierarchical Sunni Islam. The second is that most medieval Bosniaks still lived in mountain hamlets and thus had no strong connection to any organised form of religion before the arrival of Islam. By this reading, the Bosnian Church was an elite affair, known to only a tiny minority.

It is certainly the case that complex urban society in Bosnia developed for the first time under Ottoman control. Centers like Sarajevo, Mostar, and Travnik were endowed with mosques, madrasas, baths, and markets, and their populations rapidly grew. Bosnia was no longer an independent state, but it retained its identity as an Ottoman administrative unit, an *eyalet*.

There was opposition to the empire in Bosnia as there was elsewhere. Muslims as well as Christians staged uprisings and tax rebellions. The most significant was the Great Bosnian Uprising of 1831–32, led by Husein Gradaščević, a figure later shaped by the Bosniak imagination into a folk hero and national symbol. This history had to be forgotten by Serb and

Croat nationalists so that the myth of the Bosniaks as traitor Slavs and Ottoman agents could be constructed.

Later in the nineteenth century, as nationalism spread from western Europe, ethnic differences in BiH became more clearly defined and more politically salient. The distinctions between the peoples were religious first, but were cemented by competing state ideas. Orthodox Christianity was identified with Serb nationalism, which defined itself in opposition to the Ottomans and 'Turks'. Catholicism was identified with the Austro-Hungarian empire, and the more 'western' Croat identity. 'The Bosniaks,' on the other hand, as Ahmet Alibašić, professor of Islamic Studies, told me in his Sarajevo Old City office, 'didn't build up their national identity at that time because, as Sunni Muslims, they were members of the empire's majority community. It was the other religious groups that formed "millets". But today we live in a world of national groups, not of religions.'

In the nationalist convulsions which ended Ottoman rule throughout the Balkans, Muslims were usually marked as those who didn't fit. Almost all the native Muslims of Serbia were exterminated or expelled, and their mosques destroyed, in the decades after the First Serbian Uprising of 1813. Then in the aftermath of the Ottoman defeat in the 1877–78 Russo-Turkish War, up to 300,000 more Muslims were exterminated in Serbia and Bulgaria, and another million expelled. A cycle of targeting and killing Muslims had set in. Other groups would soon be added to the target list.

In 1878, the Austro-Hungarian empire inherited BiH from the Ottomans, adding a new architectural layer to the cities. The nobles accepted the new rulers, while both the Muslim and Serb peasants resisted. But the western empire didn't last long. Famously, Archduke Franz Ferdinand was assassinated by Bosnian Serb student Gavrilo Princip while leaving Sarajevo's City Hall. That was the spark that lit an already very flammable interstate rivalry, catalysing the First World War. 'The twentieth century began in Sarajevo,' wrote Susan Sontag in 1993 as the city burned. 'The twenty-first century has begun in Sarajevo too.'

The World War ended with BiH's incorporation into the Kingdom of Yugoslavia – land of the southern Slavs – dominated by its Serb king. Land reforms of this period made the Bosniak community poorer. According to political scientist Jasmin Mujanović, 'both upper and lower class Bosniaks were targeted for socioeconomic marginalisation by a policy that was clearly ethno-national rather than economic in its intention and character.'

The Yugoslav kingdom lasted until the outbreak of World War Two. Then a new round of genocide rolled over a new generation of victims. The Jewish community – descendants of Sephardim expelled from al-Andalus by Christian supremacists – was largely wiped out by the Croat Ustashe as well as Serb Chetniks, both Nazi-aligned. The Ustashe also committed genocidal violence against Serbs, and the Chetniks slaughtered Croats. In some cases, Bosniak Muslims participated in these crimes. In more cases, Bosniaks were slaughtered, especially by Chetniks. In particular, there was a 'cleansing' of Muslims from eastern Bosnia.

At a certain point in the course of the fighting, most of the Chetniks gave up their alliance with Germany and joined Marshal Tito's anti-Nazi partisans. So as not to disrupt the new multiethnic resistance, their previous atrocities were carefully forgotten.

Following victory over the Germans, Tito set up the only Communist state in Europe independent of Russian control. Economically, it did a lot better than the rest of the Communist bloc. Ahmet Alibašić remembers wide-eyed visitors from neighbouring states amazed by the quantity and quality of goods in Bosnian shops. The urban working class, he tells me, enjoyed free housing and a reasonably good standard of living. Class differences were slight.

As for ethno-sectarian diversity, the state ideology was 'brotherhood and unity'. This required an officially-directed forgetting of religious and cultural specificity. Ahmet explains: 'For 45 years we obliterated difference. We all went to the same schools. We all did the same military service. There was no separation between the communities. There was intermarriage. And it didn't work. In the 1990s, the narratives that had been submerged re-emerged. There is a lesson here for those who oppose multiculturalism. Here we tried assimilation, and the erasure of difference, and it didn't work at all.'

Nevertheless, signs of 'Yugonostalgia' abound. In a park in Travnik, a statue of Tito still stands, and the leader's face decorates T-shirts and fridge magnets sold in the Sarajevo tourist markets. I mention this to the activist and researcher Azra Imamović, who gives me a few more examples of the phenomenon, then comments: 'sometimes we idealise the Communist period because we knew nothing else, and because when it ended the war began, and then everything we knew crumbled.'

'But in those days, Islam was not valued, structurally. It was described as backward and reactionary, associated with the backward Ottomans. My grandfather was an imam. Of course, he wasn't paid. My grandmother was veiled until Communists forced her to take it off, in the name of emancipation. And the Bosniak identity was not recognised.'

Waqf endowments were seized by the state, madrasas were closed, mosques destroyed. In 1969, however, Muslims were recognised as one of the constituent Yugoslav 'nations'. This represented a kind of progress; at least there was now formal acceptance that the Muslim community existed. But it was a questionable progress. If the state portrayed Islam as backward and reactionary, then the Muslims implicitly carried the same labels. Hasan Nuhanović, a survivor of the Srebrenica slaughter, tells me, 'it is unfair and illogical to refer to an ethnic group by religion.' But there was a logic to it. Describing the people as Muslim meant they weren't described as Bosniak, which meant the connection between the people and their land could be forgotten. For Jasmin Mujanović that connection is essential. 'BiH is the Bosniak community's only homeland; they perceive themselves as its indigenous people, and it is the source of their identity as a community.'

A Bosniak isn't inevitably a Muslim, though most are. The minority of Serbs and Croats who believe in BiH might also identify as Bosniak. A couple of centuries ago they were more than a minority, before the ethno-nationalisms swelled.

When Tito died and Communism collapsed, such exclusionary nationalisms took their place. The strongest and most extreme version was Greater Serb nationalism, and this was fattened on propaganda – though propaganda may be too narrow a term for the cultural work underpinning the murderous ideology. The crimes against Serbs during World War Two were carefully remembered, while the memory of Serb crimes against others was suppressed. But the remembering went much further back, far enough to cast a sense of eternity over the conflict. In particular, the 1389 Battle of Kosovo, an indecisive clash between the Ottomans and a Christian coalition led by a Serb prince, was remembered with so much care that a myth was constructed from the paltry historical facts. A tale of sacrifice and treason had been made of it at least since the development of Serb

nationalism in the nineteenth century. *The Mountain Wreath*, an epic poem
of that period which portrays Slavic Muslims as Christ-killers and calls for
their extermination, was a standard school text in Yugoslavia.

In this endlessly repeated poem, and in the speeches of Serbian president
Slobodan Milošević, among others, Serbs cast themselves as eternal
victims. Victimhood is often assumed to grant its holders a moral
immunity, and thus recasts 'retaliatory' or even 'pre-emptive' violence as
self-defence. This – the powerful imagining themselves to be weak – is one
of the key elements of fascism. Every case of genocidal violence is
preceded by a narrative of victimhood.

Alongside tropes of victimhood and 'blood and soil', Serb propaganda
relied on the Islamophobic scare stories that have become more widespread
since, conjuring Bosniak Muslims who wished to build a purist Islamic
state stretching from the Great Wall of China to the Adriatic. In reality, the
Bosniaks were the only ones in ex-Yugoslavia appealing to pluralism. While
Serb and Croat nationalists sought to build states that would defend and
exalt their respective ethnicities, the Bosnian referendum question was as
follows: 'Do you vote for a sovereign and independent Bosnia and
Herzegovina, a state of equal citizens and peoples of Bosnia and
Herzegovina – Muslims, Serbs, Croats, and of other peoples living in it?'

Demographics as well as principle favoured a pluralist system, for the
country had no clear majority community. The Muslim proportion of the
population had fallen since the Ottoman heyday – a result of Ottoman
forced conscription as well as of Christian oppression. By 1992, when the
referendum was held (on 29 February and 1 March, to be precise), 43
percent of the population was Bosniak, 33 percent Serb, 17 percent Croat,
and 7 percent other. The 'other' category comprised those of mixed heritage
who self-defined as 'Yugoslavs', as well as Jews, Roma, and Albanians.

Many Bosnian Serbs boycotted the referendum, following the directives
of their nationalist leaders, but of the 63.7 percent of the population that
did vote, 99.7 percent supported the independence of Bosnia and
Herzegovina (BiH) as a 'state of equal citizens'. 'This means,' says Satko
Mujagić, a lawyer and a survivor of the Omarska concentration camp, 'that
the new, independent Bosnian state was conceived as multicultural. But it
wasn't a new idea, because that's the way it always was. Bosnian society
was the first multicultural society in Europe.'

'The first after al-Andalus,' I add in my mind, drawing some connections. Andalus: another European and Islamic society which had practised *convivencia* – a multicultural flourishing, even if it wasn't always truly convivial – and which had been ended by Crusader genocidaires.

Did people see the trouble coming? Why didn't they prepare for it better?

I remember a conversation on this subject many years ago in London with a woman called Natasha, who had recently married my friend Mick. Natasha was the product of a marriage between a Muslim mother and a Croat father – which made her 'other' or 'Yugoslav' according to the census. She was only sixteen when the war erupted, and she left almost immediately, first to Belgrade, then to London. She told me she'd had no idea before the war who of her neighbours were Muslim, Catholic, or Orthodox. She remembered the men of the neighbourhood drinking vodka together on the Catholic and Orthodox Christmases, as well as at the Eids. All the men drank vodka – that was their defining identity as far as she was concerned. Then one night her father was driving the family home from a restaurant when the car was stopped by angry militiamen. But these men pushing the nose of a gun through the car window were the kids who until that day had played football at the bottom of the building, who had usually been friendly. Now someone had handed out guns and armbands, and all of a sudden, they were defined as Serbs. The next day Natasha went with her parents, her sister, and tens of thousands of others to demonstrate for peace in central Sarajevo. Serb snipers shot and killed people in the crowd, and the unexpected war was underway.

Hasan Nuhanović had a very different experience. He was older than Natasha and, more to the point, came not from the capital but from rural eastern Bosnia. However much 'brotherhood and unity' discourse he'd heard growing up, the reality was that Serbs and Muslims lived in different villages, or at least in different quarters of town. 'We knew who was who,' he says. 'We knew by geography, and by people's names.'

Azra Imamović knew too, but still, she says, it was hard to imagine the differences between communities resulting in actual violence. 'Yes,' she says, 'we could see it coming. There'd already been a war between Serbia and Croatia. But even then, there was a lot of denial that it could happen here. And that denial continued even when snipers were taking positions on the roofs. It continued, in fact, even after people had been killed.'

Long before the snipers, there were more than enough warning signs. Serb nationalists themselves warned of the damage they would soon do. 'Don't believe you won't lead Bosnia and Herzegovina to hell, and possibly the Muslim people to extinction,' raged Bosnian Serb leader Radovan Karadžić to the BiH parliament in October 1991, 'because the Muslim people cannot defend themselves if war breaks out here.'

But many didn't take the threats seriously. Because people were always threatening things which never happened. Because it was mere political rhetoric, even if there'd been a war in Croatia. Because it was only a joke.

Haris Hindić was living in Norway when the war started. He was working as an interpreter for the Norwegian immigration service, which meant he heard many stories from those who had fled. One was told by a Bosniak who had been a policeman in a rural area. This Bosniak officer had been on night shift with two colleagues, one Serb and one Croat. It was a quiet night, so the three men were relaxing together in the station, talking and laughing, drinking coffee. And then the Serb abruptly changed his expression, pulled out his gun, and ordered the others to disarm. At first the Bosniak and the Croat continued laughing, assuming their friend was performing a practical joke. But there was nothing funny about it. Their colleague threatened to kill them if they didn't hand over their weapons. So they did, and just a few minutes later they heard buses and trucks on the road, and then smelled the smoke as houses began to burn. The buses were intended to transport surviving non-Serbs out of town.

As Bosnian Serbs disarmed Bosniaks and Croats, arms were distributed to Bosnian Serb paramilitaries. The war began, therefore, with the Serbs bearing the most weapons and the Muslims the least. When the UN imposed an arms embargo on the former Yugoslavia, the (always ill-named) 'international community' locked the Bosniak disadvantage in place. Serbia inherited the former Yugoslav army and its stocks. Croatia by now had achieved independent statehood, and possessed a long coastline, which made it easier to smuggle or deal for weapons. But the Muslims had to manufacture weapons from whatever they could find, or buy them from their enemies.

Well-armed and well-prepared, combined Serb forces seized over 60 percent of the country in the first six weeks. But they couldn't seize the capital.

Activists of the Serb Democratic Party barricaded the approaches to Sarajevo in early April 1992. The minority of Serbs and Croats who remained loyal to the idea of a multicultural BiH remained in the city, organising themselves into the Serb Citizens Council and the Croat Citizens Council respectively. But most left. And so began the siege, which lasted for 44 months, or 1,425 days. Families huddled in basements, in the dark, and starved. They burned their books to keep warm. Upstairs, in the streets, there were massacres. An average of 329 shells a day hit the city, ripping apart schools, hospitals, markets, and residential blocks. 11,541 people were killed, including 1,601 children. At least 50,000 were injured.

That was the period that provided my early idea of Sarajevo. I had pictures in my mind because there was media coverage. But I had no pictures from rural eastern Bosnia – not until Srebrenica in 1995 – because there was no TV coverage of the events there.

After a few days in Sarajevo, I hire a driver to take me to Srebrenica. Just outside the capital, the flags change from the Bosnian lilies to the red, white and blue stripes, and the mosques become much fewer. The Cyrillic alphabet accompanies or replaces the Latin on the street signs. Once again, I've entered the Republika Srpska.

The driver, Afan, points out a village in which one resident – a woman whose husband was murdered by Serbs – recently won a long-running court case. Apparently, the locals had built an Orthodox church in her garden. Right on her land, right up against her window. Not so much a place of worship in this case as a symbol of ethno-sectarian triumph, and a further urging – following the first, which was the murder of her husband – for her to vacate the property.

But this was a mere echo of the war in the early nineties, if 'war' is what it was. That may not be the most appropriate word, given that the main targets of the violence – as in Palestine today, as in most genocides – didn't have a strong, unitary, functioning state to defend them. The violence was very one-sided, and its point was genocide.

Bosnian Serb militias under Serbian state control, reinforced by the old Yugoslav army, burnt whole families in their homes. Sometimes they crucified men before burning them. They shot parents in front of their children, and children in front of their parents.

We descend from the hills, past a sign advertising a not-yet-built ski resort, and then down to the plain where Vlasenica lies. This town once had a Muslim majority, but no longer.

I read in Edina Bećirević's book that in this municipality boys as young as twelve were mobilised, 'armed not only with machine guns but also with fear,' because they'd been told the Muslims wished to kill them.

Ordered to hand over their weapons, the Bosniaks of Vlasenica complied. They believed compliance would calm their neighbours' passions. Instead, in the town and the surrounding villages, the neighbours summarily executed men, women, and children. The murderers were known to the victims. Some survivors managed to flee into the forests, and some joined the Bosniak resistance. Others were gathered in concentration camps, such as the Sušica camp, which consisted of a warehouse and a hangar, which held 8,000 people between May and October 1992. The majority of women and girls in the camp were raped.

An estimated 50,000 people were raped during the genocide, most of them Bosniak women and girls. Some camps were entirely dedicated to the purpose. This means a harvest of many tens of thousands of thoroughly traumatised lives, and of lives born into trauma. There is testimony by Alen Muhić displayed in Mostar's Museum of Genocide titled 'My biological father raped my biological mother'. Edina Bećirević quotes the man who raped Bakira Hasečić, who told her as he was raping her (in Višegrad, in 1992) that the rape was not personal but systematic, so that Bosniak women would be 'inseminated by the Serb seed.'

Rape is an element common to almost all genocides, with the curious exception of the Nazi Holocaust, when taboos on intercourse with racial inferiors, as well perhaps as the abstracted, 'scientific' justifications for the slaughter, worked against such messiness. But other than in the Nazi case, organised rape is as ubiquitously connected to genocide as patriarchy is to most human cultures. This arises from the conception of women as property. Spoiling the enemy's property is a war aim. To make his property ours.

In Sarajevo's Galerija 11/07/95, there is a photograph of a woman pushed across a frontline east of Travnik. Bosniak fighters are kneeling to her level, asking gentle questions, and she is sitting on the grass, her dress torn, hair matted, face horror-shocked. According to the text accompanying the photograph, she is mute. Those traveling with her reported she'd been held in a Serb-run detention camp.

The car rolls onward. If it weren't for memory, eastern Bosnia would be bucolic. Steep-roofed wooden-plank houses stand between stands of corn, piles of firewood, and beehive haystacks. There are actual beehives too, and home-made honey on sale at the roadsides. Cattle stroll the road, bells around their necks. Afan says there are wolves and bears in the hills. We see an eagle.

Afan offers me a cigarette. 'I gave up three years ago,' I say. 'That was a big mistake,' he says, very seriously. 'If you can control yourself, you can smoke only one pack a day, and that is good.'

We're driving alongside a river now. It's sinuous, emerald clear, foaming over rapids, and banked by elegant green. I remark on its beauty. 'These rivers are full of bodies,' says Afan, in the same serious tone he uses for discussing cigarettes.

Edina Bećirević's book is called *Genocide on the Drina River*. That's the next river to the east, and the natural frontier with Serbia. Serbs who wished to erase the frontier aimed to eliminate all Bosniaks from the towns and villages on the river banks. So, in mid-April 1992 a Bosniak woman watched through her window in Višegrad as Serbs shot people at the bridge over the Drina unceasingly for thirty-six hours. The corpses that fell into the water clogged up the culverts of the dam serving the hydroelectric plant downstream.

So there are bodies in the river beds. The grains of river silt consist of corpse dust. The fish of these rivers have bred on corpses over many generations. 'The bodies are not just from the 90s,' Afan frowns. 'But from every war, from all of them.'

The same quiet, slightly sour seriousness settles on all his words throughout the day. He was a boy when the last genocide was perpetrated. He comes from the Krajina region in the north, also part of the Republika Srpska today, and cleansed of most of its Bosniak natives. He lives in Sarajevo, near his father, who has not been the same since the 90s. 'He is angry,' Afan says. 'He isn't able to be happy.'

For a while I stop asking questions. The day is balmy. A warm September. There are one or two mosques between the churches, the fields, the patches of forest, but these mosques are newly built.

'It is not just one genocide,' Afan says. 'It is one after another. The Serbs don't give up their aim.'

From the Bećirević book I learn the story of Hasan Tufekčić: In 1943, Chetniks killed his wife and ten children on the Višegrad bridge. He married again, and had five more children. In 1992, Chetniks killed three of these children, who were named after their brothers killed fifty years earlier.

But now the car pulls in at the Potočari memorial, just a mile or two out of Srebrenica. The memorial is opposite the old battery factory, where Dutch UNPROFOR troops were once barracked, where – when Serbs captured Srebrenica – Bosniak families once rushed for help, and where the Dutch UN troops handed the Bosniaks to the Serbs, who murdered 8,000 of them.

I've seen pictures of this memorial, the engraved names and serried headstones officially inaugurated by President Bill Clinton, all very somberly institutional, suggesting the formal recognition of the crimes committed, a degree of restitution, and closure. What I hadn't realised before I came – what, in fact, makes very little sense to me now – is that this memorial is under the control of a regime of official forgetfulness. It's in the territory held by the genocidaires.

When I mention Potočari to my Bosnian friend and correspondent Adnan Delalić, he responds with indignation. 'The sheer absurdity of it,' he writes. 'Imagine if the Nazi state were allowed to continue existing, with Auschwitz in its territory. And everyone "remembers" it and declares "never again", but barely anyone mentions the fact that the political project that committed the genocide still controls the territory. Which means the conflict is not really resolved. In some ways, the genocide continues. This is what official/international Srebrenica discourse feels like. Detached from the material reality and the facts of how it came to be. Sentimental, if not kitsch.'

The memorial in this context is almost an insult. At the same time, it's necessary, and meaningful. But I don't quite know what to do with the meaning. How does one commemorate a genocide? How does one recognise, or do something positive with, the objectification of a group of humans, and their consequent slaughter? How to make meaning of the fact that their lives were considered by their murderers to have no meaning at all? How to acknowledge, and comprehend, and make amends for, the enormity of the pain and fear felt by the 8,000 murdered here, the 100,000 killed throughout BiH, and all their surviving relatives and friends?

I take a photograph of one section of the stone installation. Dozens of names from the same family: Ibrahimović. I send the photograph to my son, whose name is Ibrahim. Two old ladies, meanwhile, have picked their way to a certain spot among the gravestones and are reading the *fatiha*. During the genocide they would have been in early middle age. Mothers, sisters, daughters. I read the *fatiha* too. What else can one do? I read the *fatiha* several times at different locations in the cemetery. Conscious as I read that I am overlooked by the partisans of Republika Srpska. Conscious too of the bereaved Syrians eking out an existence in this same moment in the tent cities of Idlib. Conscious of the carpet bombing of Gaza, and of the abandoned Rohingya drowning at sea, and the Tigrayans and Ukrainians, the Uyghurs and Yazidis, everyone who has had a turn, the same evil turning again and again and again. Not sure what use there is in reading the *fatiha*, but anyway reading it.

I walk across to the battery factory, which is now a museum. The factory itself – its cavernous inhuman halls – is a testament to man's tendency to alienate himself, to act against his own interests. It's a shadowy place, cold even on a hot day. The exhibits seem small in its holding. There are the piled shoes of dead people. There is racist, sexist graffiti left by the Dutch, mocking the people they were about to send out to die. There are maps and plaques recounting the details of what happened.

Srebrenica had been under siege for months before the Serbs moved in. The locals were starving alongside tens of thousands of refugees from the 'cleansed' villages of the Drina valley. When the town fell, thousands of men and boys tried to march to free territory. They were strafed by artillery, picked off by snipers, and they starved even thinner. Many died; many others eventually arrived in safety, having seen their relatives die.

Of those who sought and were denied shelter with UNPROFOR, most women and young children were deported – though many of those too were killed. But the Serbs demanded access to the men and older boys, claiming they wished to filtrate them, to check if they had committed crimes. And the Dutch UN soldiers handed these men and boys over, though the Serbs until that point had respected the battery factory boundaries. Hasan Nuhanović, who I met in Sarajevo, was an interpreter for the soldiers who handed the rest of his family to the Serbs, who then murdered them – his father, mother, younger brother – 'before my eyes'. Dutch officers continued to send Bosniaks to their deaths despite the pleas of people like Hasan, and even after reliable information came back that men were being murdered.

Years later, Hasan took the Dutch state to court in the Netherlands, and won. In 2013, the Dutch Supreme Court found the state liable for the killing of three Bosniak men, including Hasan's father and brother. Liable only for those three, not for the rest. So Hasan's was a partial victory – like the official recognition of the Srebrenica slaughter as a genocide, but not the slaughter of Bosniaks in general; and like the trial and conviction of Serb military leaders at the Hague, but not the punishment of the foot soldiers. Partial, symbolic, but a victory nevertheless. Another of my Bosniak interlocutors referred to Hasan Nuhanović as 'an institution'.

Another human institution, at least in Srebrenica, is Ahmed Hrustanović, the imam of a rebuilt mosque. I met him in a Srebrenica café over coffee and crepes.

His father and uncles were murdered when the Dutch troops handed them to the Serbs. Ahmed's last sight of them was from the back of the truck which carried him and his mother into internal exile. He grew up in this exile, and studied Islam, and then came home to the scene of the crime.

'I've spent 11 years back here,' he tells me. 'And these have been the best years of my life. This land, these streets, this is where my memories with my father are. It's like a treasure.'

But is it easy living here? 'No,' he says, 'It's not easy at all. Our neighbours are those who committed crimes against us. We suffer constant discrimination. All the official jobs go to Serbs. In schools, the children are taught what they call the "Serb" language, and Serb versions of history and geography.'

'So why did you come back?' I push him further.

'Living here again,' he says, 'is treatment for my trauma. That's the main reason I came. To fight with my trauma.'

There were 13,000 Muslims native to the area before the genocide. Now there are 2,000, people like Ahmed who decided to return. 'But the conditions are uncomfortable. And the young go to the west in search of jobs. There are many empty houses. But despite that, there is a community again. Before, everything was destroyed, the mosques and the houses. Now there are five mosques in Srebrenica.'

Not a single mosque in eastern Bosnia was left undamaged by the Serbs. 'This is a clear difference,' says Ahmed. 'The churches in Sarajevo survived. In Srebrenica, the Serbs destroyed all the mosques, every sign of Islam, even our graves, in a couple of days. They bulldozed everything and then buried the rubble. They made mass graves for the mosques.'

But first they made mass graves for the people. And when investigators arrived in the years following, they dug up and reburied the evidence. They moved the remains from site to site, trying to cover their tracks. This means that Ahmed has buried his father's bones several times. 'In 2012 we buried 40 percent of his bones. They were identified by DNA testing. In 2021 we buried another 40 percent. So 20 percent are still missing.'

Beside me Afan frowns into his coffee cup. I remember something else he told me in the car: 'There is a type of butterfly that is attracted to calcium. This was a clue for those searching for mass graves. The butterflies like the calcium in the bones.'

We return to Sarajevo, and the next day I take a bus to Travnik, an alpine town in central Bosnia which served as the Ottoman Empire's first Bosnian capital. Once called 'the European Istanbul' and still packed with historical buildings, it feels to me like a psychic relief. I notice the relief before reading why: this part of central Bosnia never slipped Bosniak control. There was some fighting with Croat militias, and the town hosted refugees from elsewhere, but there was no siege here, no genocide. The Sulemanija Mosque – wooden, lushly painted, with floral decoration reminiscent of the Umayad Mosque in Damascus – is one of the most beautiful I've seen anywhere. The wonders of the architecture suggest how much has been lost elsewhere. The place, in any case, feels much less interrupted than the war-damaged locations I visit. The people, like the buildings, feel somehow more intact. I'd like to return with my hiking boots, for the mountains, and with time to enjoy more grilled trout at the spring-side restaurants.

Then I take a bus to Mostar, which is in the southern, Herzegovina part of the country. The route passes through remarkable scenery, jagged blue peaks, and Jablanica Lake, which justifies another potential visit…

Mostar is built in a valley between hills, like Sarajevo, but the hills here are drier and the valley is still steeper than Sarajevo's, so even more at the mercy of those who control the heights. In the early days of the war, Serb forces came from the east, 'cleansing' the villages of Muslims, then setting up their big guns on the summits to blast the buildings below. 'You could call it urbacide,' Haris Hindić says, using a term invented specially for the Bosnian war. Homes and civilian infrastructure were incinerated, roads were cratered, food sources cut off. And Haris's mother was killed in the shelling.

I meet him and his friend Jasmin Maksumić for evening coffee in a Mostar hotel — because coffee seems to regulate every meeting here, at every time of day.

They run through the history for me. The Serbs were attacking Croats as well as Muslims, and at first the two targeted communities made natural allies. They fought shoulder to shoulder against the aggressors. 'But the politics of the Croatian state were different,' says Haris. 'Blaz Kraljević was an honest Croat, a local. He wanted to deepen the cooperation between us. But the Croat leaders killed him.' This was because Croatian president Franjo Tuđman had made a deal with Serbian president Slobodan Milošević to divide BiH between Croatia and Serbia, leaving nothing for the Bosniaks. In Mostar, therefore, the Bosniaks were soon hemmed in between the Serbs on the eastern heights and the Croats to the west. Once again, neighbours turned on neighbours. Croat forces took the Muslims they captured to the stadium in Mostar, and from there distributed them to their own network of concentration camps. 'It is difficult to understand,' says Haris sadly. 'We were allies first. Before that, we were neighbours. But anyway, they couldn't finish us off here. Their plan didn't work. There was resistance.'

The resistance was fierce, and in some cases epic. The Croats held almost all the west of the city, where their community was in the majority. They soon destroyed all the bridges across the River Neretva, including the old Ottoman bridge, the high-arched Stari Most. As well as a tactical loss, this was a blow to Bosniak morale. The bridges had given Mostar its name — the men who guarded the bridges in medieval times were called *mostari*, or bridge keepers — and the Stari Most served as a Bosnian national symbol. But despite its destruction, a Bosniak presence remained on the west bank. Two small neighbourhoods, Donje Mahala and Cernica, were held throughout the eleven-month battle by only 'eight or nine men' and the surviving Muslim families who shared their meager food supplies. These eight or nine 'kept shifting positions, one place to the next, so the Croats thought there were hundreds of defenders.'

The Croats, though better armed and benefiting materially and politically from the support of an independent state, were not ultimately helped by their reliance on Zagreb. Young troops belonging to the Croatian state's army were sent to fight in a city they'd never seen before, in a land which only belonged to them according to a recently-forged ideology. So, the advantage remained with local Bosniak defenders.

Jasmin Maksumić was one of them. He tells me about the battle of 15 July 1993, when non-Bosnian Croats arrived from the south, planning to cut the road between Mostar and Blagaj. The Bosniaks were able to surround the Croat advance force, and to kill the commander. When they found the commander's Motorola phone, they shouted 'retreat! retreat!' into the receiver, which caused confusion in the Croat ranks. 'Our soldiers killed many of them. Their panic that day saved Mostar.'

The east bank of the city was almost entirely destroyed. The west bank, in general, was not. Pictures in Mostar's Genocide Museum prove that the impressive, stone-walled, tourist-crammed Old Town is not actually old but has been recently reconstructed. Today the tourist throngs are the only physical obstacle to moving from one side of town to the other, but Mostar is still socially divided. A huge cross has been mounted atop the hill on the west bank on exactly the spot where Croat artillery once sat. I ask Haris what he thinks of it. 'It's not just that one,' he says. 'They put up crosses on any land they claim. They are marking their territory, just as dogs do.'

After years of international inaction, a few days of NATO bombing brought the slaughter to a halt. At the same moment, the US intervened to prevent Bosniak forces retaking the northern city of Banja Luka. In the same spirit, the agreement made at Dayton, Ohio allowed the initiators of the war, the worst criminals, to mark almost half of BiH as their territory. 49 percent of the country fell under the administration of the Republika Srpska. In the words of my correspondent Adnan Delalić, 'the genocide was institutionalised.'

Nothing was resolved. The conflict was frozen. But ice is better than murder. 'The fact that we haven't had a war for twenty-nine years is a good thing,' says Hasan Nuhanović. He directs a similar glass-half-full rhetoric at the attempts towards accountability: 'There are thousands of war criminals living in our neighbourhood, but their entire political leadership was tried at the Hague.'

He's referring to the International Criminal Tribunal for the Former Yugoslavia (ICTY), which sent dozens of men to prison. It was the first time that top officials had been held accountable for the crime of genocide. This gave legal and some emotional validation to the survivors, and seemed to go some way towards ensuring their future safety. 'Had there been no ICTY,' Azra Imamović asks rhetorically, 'can you imagine this place today?'

An estimated 19,500 men participated in the massacre at Srebrenica – soldiers, police, drivers, and various other facilitators. Throughout BiH, very few Serbs actively protected their Bosniak neighbours. This is not because they are Serbs, but because they are human. Very few Germans actively protected their Jewish neighbours. Dissenters in matters of blood are always very few. Almost the entire Serb population was complicit in the genocide, even if only by averting their eyes at key moments. These people were not put on trial. Neither – at the other end of the scale – was the most powerful perpetrator of all. The February 2007 verdict of the International Court of Justice (ICJ) in the case of the BiH state against the Serbian state held Serbia accountable for failing to prevent genocide, but not for perpetrating it. BiH had asked the court to consider the minutes of the Serbian Supreme Defense Council, which would have showed the state's intentions and its behind-the-scenes acts, but the court refused to do so. This let the Serbian state off the hook, and eased the way for denialist narratives.

Milorad Dodik, the current Bosnian Serb leader, calls the genocide 'the greatest myth of the twentieth century'.

I ask Ahmad Hrustanović if he ever discusses the past with his Serb neighbors. The answer is no. 'They don't want to speak, certainly not to apologise. They are proud of what they did.' Ahmet Alibašić agrees. 'The problem isn't so much denialism,' he says, 'as triumphalism.' And Hasan Nuhanović confirms it. 'Beyond certain outspoken activists – who are usually Serbs from Serbia, not Bosnian Serbs – they all deny the genocide, including representatives sitting in the Sarajevo parliament. The Banja Luka [Republika Srpska] parliament has actually passed legislation to deny it.'

When I ask Azra Imamović if this level of denial means that the genocide could happen again, she responds, immediately and energetically. 'Yes! Certainly, it could happen again, and many people feel it. Some keep their suitcases packed. The outbreak of war in Ukraine made us afraid. Gaza too. We are waiting.'

If it does happen again, who will the Bosniaks be able to rely on? My interlocutors cultivated no illusions.

'Without America,' says Hasan Nuhanović, 'the Europeans would have tolerated the genocide even longer.' This seems to be a fact as much as an opinion. Comments made by Bill Clinton support it, as reported by his confidant Taylor Branch. Clinton told Branch that, 'privately, key allies objected that an independent Bosnia would be "unnatural" as the only Muslim nation in Europe. He said they favoured the [arms] embargo precisely because it locked in Bosnia's disadvantage … President Mitterand of France had been especially blunt in saying that Bosnia did not belong, and British officials also spoke of a painful but realistic restoration of Christian Europe.'

But America is no more reliable a guarantor of Muslim safety than Europe, as the current bloodbath in Palestine and Lebanon proves. The provision of arms, funds, and propaganda for the slaughter shows how little Muslim blood matters when weighed against Israel's 'painful but realistic' maximalist aims. As the west distances itself from its previous interest in law and human rights, western Muslims even beyond BiH find no reason at all to feel secure. In the UK, those demonstrating against the genocide of Palestinians – surely the segment of society that currently cares most about law and rights – are called 'hate marchers' by those in power. In this climate, riots broke out in northern English towns a few weeks before I left for Bosnia. Provoked by big-name disinformants on social media, the mobs attacked a mosque, a hotel housing refugees, and random brown and black people in the streets. In the following weeks (reversing the ICTY pattern), the often-lumpenproletarian foot-soldiers were rapidly tried and sentenced, but the upper-class rabble-rousers were left free to disinform another day.

Rabble-rousers, propagandists, the powerful nursing a sense of victimhood. When such types dominate the media, in a time of uncertainty, whether in a fractured post-Communist state or in an internet-drenched late-capitalist state, then deadly trouble follows. Then the demons of the past return with a vengeance.

There is a problem with the ownership of the media, most certainly, and particularly in societies whose media have replaced or smothered their cultures. There is a culture war, in the truest sense.

So what can we do? I mean, those of us who don't own media platforms. We can read the *fatiha*. And against forced forgetfulness, we can place our own efforts to remember.

This is what the Bosniaks do. They try to remember, and to remind everybody else. Museums in the cities remember the sieges, the war crimes, the genocide. Wall plaques at massacre sites throughout Sarajevo remember the names of the victims, and flowers remember their hearts. In Sarajevo pavements, at intervals, the impact holes from the heaviest shells are filled with the memory of blood-red paint.

Genocide is always an attack on culture, because a people's existence is carried in their culture as much as it is in their bodies. Hence the destruction of all the mosques, shrines, madrasas, and graves. And hence, in reply, the Sarajevo film festival, begun in the siege and still continuing today. Hence the burning of the National Library's 1.5 million volumes, and hence the performance of Mozart's Requiem in the ruins. For every act of erasure, a corresponding act of inscribing. This is most steadily apparent in the lived business of everyday culture. All my interlocutors, secular and religious, stressed how the genocide had solidified Bosniak and Muslim identity.

I walk again through Sarajevo's Galerija 11/07/95 (the title remembers the date of the Srebrenica massacre) – and stop at Tom Stoddart's famous photograph of Meliha Varesanović. It remembers a moment in 1993 as this Bosniak woman was moving through the besieged capital. She's wearing high heels, and a flowery dress showing off her shape, and pearls, and on each wrist a bracelet, her chin high, her dark eyes energetically engaged with the eyes of the viewer. To her left is a soldier's body and gun, and the cigarette burning in his fingers. Sandbags are piled high behind her.

The picture channels her defiance. And the beauty of the body – the spirit of the body – while all around men are obliterating bodies, reducing them to chunks of raw matter.

ARTS AND LETTERS

RESERVING SERIES

Ruth Cuthand

I was born in 1954 in Prince Albert, Saskatchewan of Plains Cree and Scottish ancestry. I grew up in Cardston, Alberta, near the Blood Reserve, where at the age of eight I met artist Gerald Tailfeathers and decided that I, too, wanted to be an artist. As a child, my first art materials included the orange paper that was discarded in the processing of the Polaroid chest x-rays that we were subjected to annually as Indigenous people in routine tuberculosis screenings; they collected the peculiar-smelling eighteen-inch squares of paper and gave them to my Anglican minister father for use in Sunday school. Early fascination with disease, First Nations living conditions, and settler/Native relationships informed by childhood experiences have become key elements in my creative practice, which has encompassed printmaking, painting, drawing, photography, and beadwork.

The 1876 Indian Act was passed into law as a means to protect, civilise, and assimilate the Indian population. Today it remains a barrier to improvement in First Nations standards of living and a paternalistic system of governance devoid of transparency. My personal experiences with this system are reflected in work that throughout my career has included subjects such as 'white liberal' attitudes towards Indigenous women, the Canadian response to the 1990 Oka crisis, Mormon-Native relations in Cardston, Alberta (my childhood home), the diseases that ravished First Nations upon European contact, and the deplorable living conditions in Indigenous communities that exemplify the social issues that have affected Canadian First Nations people.

In my early work, I adopted a consistently anti-aesthetic stance, refusing to be stereotyped by forcefully rejecting the authority of both Western high art and traditional Indigenous art and design. In true anarchic style, however, I borrow freely from both when it suits my purposes. This approach has allowed me to challenge mainstream perspectives on colonialism and the relationships between 'settlers' and Natives, addressing the frictions between cultures, the failures of representation, and the political uses of anger in Canada, employing stylistic crudeness to counter the stereotype of Canada as the great polite nation. In my work, I challenge the status quo by exposing the inequities that have plagued for centuries Canada's relationship with its First Peoples, while proudly claiming a complex and self-determined Indigenous identity.

Adopting the traditional craft of beading in my recent work was a way to continue to centre the Indigenous woman in my art while addressing other issues of concern. Maintaining the anti-aesthetic principles on which my practice was founded, I have traded crudeness of style for materials and techniques that have long been denied status as serious art. This shift has allowed for a more sophisticated end-product that capitalises on my fascination with the attractive and repellent subject; the simultaneously beautiful and abhorrent. This dichotomous relationship between appearance and content, or between style and subject creates a cognitive schism; it is that gap that creates a space for contemplation about the work and what it means. Though humour softens the blow of a critical message, I have found that making work which confronts the most difficult truths about Canadian society and the impacts of colonisation on Indigenous people are made remarkably palatable when delivered in a strikingly seductive package.

'Smallpox, from the Reserving Series', 2011. Glass beads, thread, backing, 25 1/4" x 19 1/4". Collection: National Gallery of Canada, Ottawa, ON.

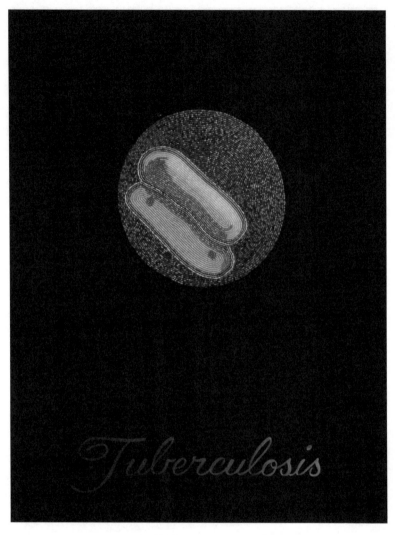

'Tuberculosis, from the Reserving Series', 2011. Glass beads, thread, backing,
25 1/4" x 19 1/4". Private Collection.

'Polio, from the Reserving Series', 2011. Glass beads, thread, backing,
25 1/4" x 19 1/4". Private Collection.

'Spanish Flu, from the Reserving Series', 2011. Glass beads, thread, backing,
25 1/4" x 19 1/4". Collection: National Gallery of Canada, Ottawa, ON.

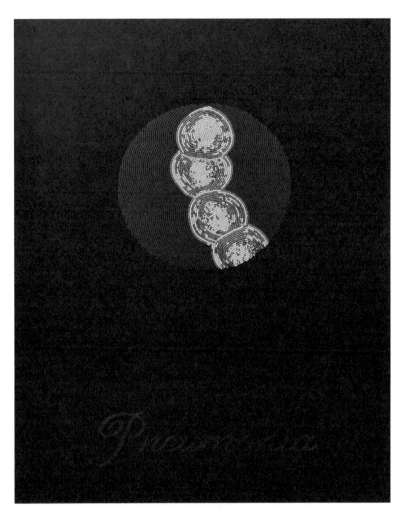

'Pneumonia, from the Reserving Series', 2013, Glass beads, thread, backing,
25 1/4" x 19 1/4". Collection: National Gallery of Canada, Ottawa, ON.

'Smallpox, from the Reserving Series', 2018. Glass beads, thread, backing,
25 1/4" x 19 1/4". Collection: Claridge Inc., Montreal.

'Extirpate this Execrable Race no. 3.', 2018. Glass beads, Canadian Forces blankets, ribbon, dimensions variable. Collection: Claridge Inc., Montreal.

HOW TO BURY THE DEAD

Andleeb Shadani

Marriage, Marriage, Marriage—these three words echoed in our house like a muezzin's call to prayer. Aunt Sadiya didn't want to get married. She wanted to study. But Grandma said she had been studying all her life. Grandma said if she didn't get married on time, she would become old, her beautiful slender hands would become wrinkled, her Rapunzel-like hair would go grey like Grandma's. 'No one wants to marry an old woman. Not even old men.' Grandma would blabber day and night, like old men and women reciting the verses of the Koran. It was seven months later we got to know that Aunt Sadiya was secretly married.

Aunt Sadiya was doing her MA at Christian College. She would go to the college in the day, and come back around two pm. She would then lock herself inside her room. She only came out for dinner. She read a lot – the Urdu digest *Shama*, Ibney Safi's detective fiction, and sometimes the English novels of Virginia Woolf and Katherine Mansfield, with the help of a dictionary. When I had completed my homework, I would sneak into her room. I would knock on the door thrice, and then say 'It's me, It's me' twice. That was our code to help her know it was me and not her mother. Aunt Sadiya would open the door. She would then sit against the mirror table and apply kohl to her eyes. When she wasn't reading, she would sit against the mirror table, put talcum powder on her rosy cheeks, and apply kohl to her eyes. On days when she was sad, she talked to her reflection in the mirror, and told her in detail, the long list of her miseries

She was beautiful, like those women on the cover of *Urdu Digest*. 'Aunt Sadiya, why I ain't beautiful like you?' I would say. She would look back with the bottle of kohl still in her hand. She made me sit on her chair and applied kohl to my little button-like eyes. 'Who told you you aren't beautiful?' 'Those boys at Colvin.' 'They are blind. Boys of your age are blind. When you become of my age, you will be the most beautiful woman in Lucknow.'

I knew she was lying. She lied most of the time. Like the way she told Grandma that day, that she wanted to do a PhD. She said she was writing a book about Grandpa's works. My Grandpa was a historian. But he was more famous for his imaginary fictitious work about the life of Nawab Kaleem Kaiser, a fictitious King he created. The book was in fourteen volumes. Every volume dealt with a facet of his life. One volume was called *The King's Horses*, the second, *The King's Enemies*, the third *The King's Wives*. The fourth, a book of poems called *The King's Recipes*, had all kinds of lost Awadhi recipes written in the form of poems. One later volume was called *The King's Dreams*, another he had called *The King's Killers*. The work was almost on the verge of getting lost. It was highly controversial as many around Lucknow felt that Grandpa had written a parody of the Kings. Not many understood that the King he was talking about was his own fictional character. The book was written first in Persian, then Grandpa spent the rest of his life translating it into Urdu and trying to publish it. It was published and some reviews appeared in Abdul Halim Sharar's *Dil Guzda*, and *Avadh Akhbar*. He was famous for two years, but then the publishers stopped publishing new editions, and soon his memory faded from the public life, so much so that after a point, his life also became fictitious, like the King he created.

Aunt Sadiya said she would translate all of Grandpa's works into English and achieve for him an international fame. She said she would translate all the fourteen volumes, and had even spoken to a publisher in Delhi, who was interested in the work. But I knew Aunt Sadiya was lying. And the reason was to buy more time so that the family didn't get her married off. She didn't want to get married, because she was already married, secretly to that mathematics teacher at the Christian College. His name was Joseph. At the college, they all knew about them. The news soon broke out. Grandma pulled her hair. She went mad. Abba slapped Aunt Sadiya. She sobbed like a young bride cries when she is about to leave her paternal home. 'He is a nice man. And he loves me. So what if he is a Christian? He isn't asking me to change my religion.' 'He would ask at the right time. He would make you a nun someday. He would make you leave Islam. He would make you wear a cross. And someday get crucified in an abandoned desert.' 'No he won't,' Aunt Sadiya cried, moving her face from the pillow wet with her tears. 'What would I tell my friends? They would mock me' Abba shouted. 'You are only concerned about your image. You are all concerned about your feelings, and your worries. I don't matter to anyone.'

The house echoed with their fights day and night. Aunt Sadiya cried all the time, with her face in the pillow. When she was done, she would sit against the mirror table and watch her face carefully. 'Joseph will get angry at me. He says my eyes get puffed up when I cry a lot.'

That week Abba said that Abdel Malek, the shopkeeper was ready to marry Aunt Sadiya. She said she would rather die. Grandma talked to her the whole night, telling her about the difficult life of a nun. Around dawn, she cried aloud. Aunt Sadiya was lying dead on her bed, her hair disheveled, and her eyes wide open, like that housemaid's when she saw a ghost seated on the solitary tree of the mango orchard. I stood at the door and watched Abba and Grandma try to bring her back to life. But they couldn't. I noticed that her eyes were still adorned with kohl. The beautiful eyes of my beautiful aunt. That was the first funeral of my life. When Amma died I was newly born. I watched very closely how my female relatives washed Aunt Sadiya's corpse and then buried her at the Karbala.

The dead body of a Muslim man or woman, about six hours after life is extinct, is placed in a coffin and conveyed to the place of burial, with a parade suited to the rank he or she held in life. The body is washed preferably at home, or at the corpse washing place in the graveyard, where water is available for washing and preparing the dead body for interment. The female relatives and neighborhood aunties usually wash the corpse, thoroughly bathe it; when dry, they rub pounded camphor on the hands, feet, knees, and forehead, these parts having, in the method of prostrating at prayer, daily touched the ground; the body is then wrapped neatly in a white line, covered with particular chapters from the Koran. After this, the body is taken up with great gentleness and laid in the grave on its side, with the face towards Mecca. The officiating Moulvi steps solemnly into the grave, and with a loud voice repeats the creed; after which he says, 'These were your good and holy leaders, O daughter of Eve!' Here he repeats the womans's name, then continues. 'Now when the two angels come unto you, who are the messengers from your great and mighty God, they will ask you, "Who is your Lord? Who is your Prophet? What is your faith? Which is your book? Where is your Kiblaah? Who is your Leader?"

'Then you should answer:—

'"God, greatest in glory, is my only Lord; Mohammed, my Prophet; Islam, my faith, the Koran, my book, the Kabah, my Kiblaah;

'"Imam Ali, son of Abu Talib, Hasan and Hosein, Ali Zainul Abidin, Muhammad al Baakir, Jaffer Saadik, Moosa Kadhim, Ali Reza, Muhammad al Jawaad, Ali ul Hoodah, Hasan al Askari, Mahdi, the standing proof that we are waiting for. These are all my leaders, and they are my intercessors, with them is my love, with their enemies is my hatred, in the world of earth and in the world to come eternal.'"

Then the cleric says:—

'Know you for a truth, O woman (repeating her name), that the God we worship is One only, Great and Glorious, Most High and Mighty God, who is above all lords, the only true God.

'Know also, that Mohammad is the best of the Lord's messengers.

'That Ali and his successors (before enumerated, but always here repeated) were the best of all leaders.

'That whatever came with Mohammad is true (meaning the whole work of his mission);—Death is true; the Interrogation by Munkar and Nakeer (the two angels) is true; the Resurrection is true; Destruction is true; the Bridge of Sirraat is true; the Scales are true; Looking into the Book is true; Heaven and Earth are true; Hell is true; the Day of Judgment is true. Of these things there is no doubt – all are true; and, further, that God, the great and glorious God, will raise all the dead bodies from their graves.'

Then the cleric reads the following prayer or benediction—

'May the Lord God, abundant in mercy, keep you with the true speech; may He lead you to the perfect path; may He grant you knowledge of Him, and His prophets. May the mercy of God be fixed upon you forever. Ameen.' This concluded, the cleric quits the grave, and slowly moves forty measured paces in a line with it; then turning round, he comes again to the grave, with the same solemnity in his steps, and standing on the edge, he prays —

'O great and glorious God, we beseech You with humility make the earth comfortable to this your servant's side, and raise her soul to You, and with You may she find mercy and forgiveness.'

'Ameen, Ameen,' is responded by all the mourners.

I watched everything standing near the graveyard's dilapidated brick wall. When my family and the other mourners started coming out, I ran very fast like a horse, outside the stable, when he gets to know that his master the horse cart driver has died. When I entered the courtyard at home, my heart raced like that of a horse still galloping on that empty road towards Rumi Gate. I heard a slow wailing sound coming from Grandma's room. Like the wailing sound you hear, coming out from a house where all the residents are dead. Aunt Sadiya's room was locked. Who could lock the room from inside, when now she was inside a grave? I knocked on the door twice, and then said, 'It's me, It's me.' She moved from the bed and opened the door. Then she sat against the mirror table and applied kohl on her eyes, like the eyes of a dead woman. I kept on staring at her. She moved back and asked, 'Why are you looking at me like that?' 'I thought you were dead.' I went closer to her, I tried to touch her hands, but the moment I touched her, she became a ball of smoke, like the smoke from camphor, rising beside a corpse.

That was the first death I saw closely. I was a child, and it was hard for me to understand the implications of death. What happens after death? How do the dead live alone in that grave? Would they ever come back? Grandma said there is a world inside the graves. A world made of mirrors. The world of the dead. I saw dreams, hallucinations. I saw Aunt Sadiya inside her grave, seated in front of a huge mirror table, combing her hair, applying kohl to her dead eyes. Sometimes the comb would fall from her hand, and then she would call my name, 'Sheeba, Sheeba, can you pick my comb?' I would wake up in a pool of sweat. I would look at the mirror table, at the lipstick and kohl bottles, Aunt Sadiya's portrait, in which she is standing beside Abba, trying her best to control her laugh, Abba while shaving having cut his mustache in half. I see the chair on which she used to sit and apply kohl to her eyes, the chair empty, silent, like chairs in those houses where no one lives.

I went to school, and then after twelfth to Karamat College for my BA. I never fell in love, nor confessed my love to any of those boys, not even to that boy whom I also loved. The boy with broken front teeth, and sky-blue tinted spectacles, always waiting outside the school, with a branch of rose, and piece of paper in his sweaty palm. I once saw him coming out of Lalbagh Methodist Church. I knew his religion. Though when I asked him, he said he wasn't a Christian, he said he took a neighborhood aunt to Church every Sunday, whose sons and daughters had died. He pointed towards that aunt seated on one of the wooden benches of the Church, but I knew he was lying, or maybe he wasn't. I was scared. I didn't want to become a nun, neither get crucified in an abandoned desert. I looked at the piece of paper, in his hand, which he always carried, like those old clerics carried the rosary bead. I knew what he had written in that smudged love letter. 'I don't love you' I said, my eyes besieged like that of a dead woman I knew the consequence of falling in love, and then marrying outside religion. I didn't want to die. I was too scared to die. I had seen the faces of the dead, I knew about their dreams.

Before Grandma's death the house had started echoing again, with the sounds of marriage. Grandma talked to Abba, day and night, as if I didn't get married on time the world would come to an end. They called the barber Rashid's wife who fixed the neighborhood marriages. She came with photographs of men – old Nawabs, blind saints, fat butchers, mathematics teachers, and landlords (who already had two wives). Grandma showed me their photographs. They all looked the same. Like it was the same man who got photographed, by putting prosthetics and fake mustaches over his face. Maybe that boy who always had a letter for me in his sweaty palm.

I asked Grandma to get me married to any of them. But before she could fix my marriage, she died. And the house became silent again. My father wasn't concerned about my marriage. He had retired from the archive's department. He was old. I knew he didn't want me to get married. He wanted me to work and find a job so that he didn't have to sleep on an empty stomach. He was working on his father's incomplete encyclopedia – about the King's Horses, Wives, Recipes, Enemies, Dreams, and Deaths. Maybe he was the one who killed Aunt Sadiya, so she didn't work on that book. My father wanted to work on that book. He wanted to play that game that his father had played all his life. It was all a game, to pass through old age and then die. Like the games that a little girl plays, hopscotch, and hide and seek, while waiting for her father, who would come back from work and take her to movies. The father never comes, and the games never stop. I can still hear the sound of a little girl playing hopscotch on the roof of my house. Like I can still see my deceased aunt applying kohl to her dead eyes inside that old grave, over which now, large grasses, a tree of berries and one of plums have grown.

Abba never died. Every day when I came back from college, I found him seated on his desk, writing something on those little pages. He would tell me about a King's death, which he found in a book of Farid Attar's poems, about a lost recipe he found in *Shama*, and a letter to King Wajid's wife he discovered inside a dictionary. I would eat, cold bland food. I would go to my room and put my bag on the mirror table. I would stare at my face. I was old like my Grandma. No one would marry me. 'Even the old men won't marry old women.' Her voice echoed in the lonely house. I tried to sleep. I tried not to think of my past or future. There is no past, there is no future. There is no present also. I see dreams, hallucinations, I see wailing women, washing my corpse, Aunt Sadiya applying kohl to the dead eyes, and then they dress me in a beautiful maroon gown, laced with golden borders. My father, and that boy with tinted glass who loved me, and always had a letter for me in his sweaty palms, they take me to the graveyard. I see the red-bearded cleric, stepping solemnly into the grave, and with a loud voice repeating the creed; after which he says, 'These were your good and holy leaders, O daughter of Eve! Now when the two angels come unto you, who are the messengers from your great and mighty God, they will ask you, "Who is your Lord? Who is your Prophet? What is your faith? Which is your book? Where is your Kiblaah? Who is your Leader?"

Then I answer:——

'God, greatest in glory, is my only Lord; Mohammed, my Prophet; Islam, my faith, the Koran, my book, the Kabah, my Kiblaah;

'Imam Ali, son of Abu-Talib, Hasan and Hosein, Ali Zainul Abidin, Muhammad al Baakir, Jaffer Saadik, Moosa Kadhim, Ali Reza, Muhammad al Jawaad, Ali ul Hoodah, Hasan al-Askari, Mahdi, the standing proof that we are waiting for. These are all my leaders, and they are my intercessors, with them is my love, with their enemies is my hatred, in the world of earth and in the world to come eternal.'

Then the cleric says:——

'Know you for a truth, O woman (repeating my name), that the God we worship is One only, Great and Glorious, Most High and Mighty God, who is above all lords, the only true God.

'Know you also, That Mohammad is the best of the Lord's messengers.

'That Ali and his successors (before enumerated, but always here repeated) were the best of all leaders.

'That whatever came with Mohammad is true (meaning the whole work of his mission);—Death is true; the Interrogation by Munkar and Nakeer (the two angels) is true; the Resurrection is true; Destruction is true; the Bridge of Sirraat is true; the Scales are true; Looking into the Book is true; Heaven and Earth are true; Hell is true; the Day of Judgment is true. Of these things there is no doubt—all are true; and, further, that God, the great and glorious God, will raise all the dead bodies from their graves.'

Then the cleric reads the following prayer or benediction—

'May the Lord God, abundant in mercy, keep you with the true speech; may He lead you to the perfect path; may He grant you knowledge of Him, and His prophets. 'May the mercy of God be fixed upon you forever. Ameen.'

This concluded, the cleric leaves my grave, and slowly moves forty measured paces in a line with it; then, turning round, he comes again to the grave, with the same solemnity in his steps, and standing on the edge, he prays,

'O great and glorious God, we beseech You with humility make the earth comfortable to this your servant's side, and raise her soul to You, and with You may he find mercy and forgiveness.'

'Ameen, Ameen,' was responded by all present, but I only heard the voice of my father, and that boy who said he loved me.

My funeral ended, like all funerals. The mourners left the graveyard. I thought the first night in the grave would be scary, but it wasn't. The moment everyone left, I felt a hand over my shroud, someone uncovered my face, my beautiful aunt – 'Aunt Sadiya,' I cried with joy. 'You thought your Aunt would have become a Grandma, and died even in the world of dead.' I kept on staring at her beautiful face. She sat against that huge mirror table, the size of Bada Imambada, she stared applying kohl to her eyes, then combed her long hair. I was still staring at her, she looked back, 'I am ready, now let's go to the roof and play hopscotch.'

THE HOST

Tam Hussein

What do you reckon that is?' Abu Imad said, tapping the scope. He regarded me thoughtfully, rubbing his bushy beard. He wanted me to make the two-meter journey to take a look.

'I'm all right here to be honest,' I said, peering at Abu Imad's powerful frame. In my experience, God creates two types of men who stay on for the long haul. Either the rugby player variety or the wiry knife-wielding sort, used to taking down bigger opponents. Abu Imad belonged to the former. 'Come,' he insisted, 'come.'

I didn't really feel like giving him my opinion. I didn't want to entertain the mad shit bouncing around his head. What's it going to be? Either some mountain goat or a hardy plant that has somehow emerged out of this cruel valley where we'd been stuck for years. We hadn't progressed against the enemy, not because we were weak but because the commanders were arguing sometimes over strategy, sometimes over tactics, most of the time over honour and on rare occasions about God. In spite of them, we held this crag. We were mountain lions in courage and mountain goats in stubbornness. What new excitement could this brother show me?

'Come,' he pleaded, 'check it.'

Nope. It would just lead to him putting his finger on the trigger and the whole desolate valley would be ringing out. So I said it again, 'I'm all right here to be honest with you.'

I wasn't lying. The night was cold. The blanket I was wrapped in was just about taking the edge off its bite. The little miserable heat from the kerosene stove was about to go out, my hands were wrapped round a cup of tea and I had four hours till someone would relieve me. 'I'm fine here, praise be to God.'

'No, seriously, what are those things? Come here, bredrin.'

'I'm not feelin' it,' I insisted, getting annoyed.

'I swear to God, man is going to throw the blanket off this rock and you'll freeze till dawn.'

I still sat there. But then I saw that look found only in hunting animals when they pick up on something and block everything out apart from the object. Abu Imad's whole being was intent on whatever it was in the red dot reticule in his optic device. I could see him toying with the safety, I could see that finger dancing around the trigger.

'Wait!' I said, knowing that the thirst for blood is a terrible, terrible desire. Sometimes you cannot resist it. 'Don't you even think about it!'

Abu Imad looked as if he had woken up. He grinned at me childishly. Now that grin would have been endearing ten years ago. It was probably once charming to women, but on the wrong side of thirty it had the opposite effect.

Abu Imad had looked this way just the other day. Abu Walid, a knife wielding pirate of a fighter, had given us an earful as a result. It was embarrassing to hear his gravelly voice. We weren't new to this thing. Even he felt embarrassed to scold us like a headmaster. He was right though. I just didn't get it; I wanted to give Abu Imad a good kicking. I kept reminding myself of his virtues, the man had risked his life for us plenty, saved me from some nasty scrapes but still, what was going through his mind?

I remember Abu Walid pitifully regarding the lifeless body that had just started to smell. Abu Imad was a poor marksman and had shot him through the stomach. The American must have experienced excruciating pain. Abu Imad didn't even tell us till it was too late. The soldier had expired by the time we went down to the desolate spot. The corpse lay there amongst the shards of rock that punctured the landscape like wolves' teeth biting into flesh. It was a lonely place to die. Abu Walid gazed at the piercing blue eyes that reflected the clear sky, beautiful in its tranquility. Things seemed simpler up there.

The soldier was well-formed and handsome, as unshaved men go. His torso was muscular. His right arm was bent at the elbow and on his forearm sat a tattoo of a naked woman. She sat suggestively under the words PHILLY written just above his clenched fist. Our emir gently bent down and covered her up, unrolling the dead man's sleeve. It was strange how lightly the American was dressed. There had been no thought behind his garb, like it was rushed. He carried only a side arm, a knife and a day sack. The other arm had a curious bite on it which smelled like shit and rotten meat. Abu Walid turned his face away as soon as he got a whiff of it. Must have been some rabid dog or something. It couldn't have been a black bear or a snow leopard. He would have been mauled. Apart from that single wound, the man was in fine health. A bit of a stubble, smooth sunburned forehead, a true American soldier from the movies.

'Why did you do it?' Abu Walid frowned. After all these years, whenever he got upset, he reverted back to his old profession, a stern school master.

The effect on the questioned was one of embarrassment. Abu Imad looked down to the ground.

'He was alone,' Abu Walid continued. 'He could have been a deserter. We could have ransomed him; we could have found out things. Why didn't you radio?'

'We can still ransom his body,' said Abu Imad in Arabic.

That got Abu Walid vexed.

'Calm down,' said Abu Imad. 'He's just an American, it's not such a big thing, the more dead the better. If he was our prisoner, he'd eat up our resources.' He looked to the others for a bit of support, especially Abu Muslim who had the most experience fighting Americans. But even Abu Muslim looked upset. He had this elemental scowl full of loss, blood, sweat, love, hate, yearning and faith, and he was wearing it now.

'We don't revel in taking people's lives,' said Abu Walid angrily. 'Why exactly are you here? If you just want to kill people, go and do that somewhere else.'

'No,' said Abu Imad, blushing. 'It's not like that.'

'Or if you are here for booty,' continued Abu Walid, 'get it somewhere else.'

Abu Imad stayed silent and lowered his head. Abu Walid did a body search on the American. He didn't care for all the equipment. Abu Imad would take care of that for sure. The soldier had a good set of boots for starters. Abu Walid found his dog tag and gently took it off. He always did that. During those moments the wiry man in the tank crew overalls and Afghanka jacket turned into a lotus flower emerging out of a dark, muddy pond. Abu Walid was a father and I knew he would let Marcus's father know that his son had died a soldier's death. Abu Walid would use his channels to pass it on to the Americans. In fairness, the Americans did the same. Then he started to look for something else. He patted him down. Eventually he found it. It was a letter in English. He handed it to me and I translated it.

The Americans had been ambushed and overwhelmed by an enemy the likes of which they had never seen before. They needed reinforcements – fast.

After the message, Abu Walid was even more upset with Abu Imad. He closed the soldier's eyes. He looked ashamed in front of the dead man. He ordered Abu Imad to bury him and mark the site with a stone.

'I'm sure,' said Abu Walid, 'we will pay for this.'

We left Abu Imad to sulk. I made sure he did his tasks properly and gave him an earful.

I didn't want a repeat of that incident. I threw off the blanket and made my way to the Dragunov to look into the scope. I saw his point. About eleven kilometres away, trudging slowly towards the pass under cover of darkness, was a menacing swarm. Abu Imad was itching to have a go but whoever the fighters were, they wouldn't be in range for a while unless they suddenly increased their pace. I came off and went for the binoculars. Abu Imad looked at me, concerned. I knew why: turning on the night vision would give away our location. But curiosity got the better of us. Besides, the swarm didn't move like any enemy that I had seen before. So I chanced it and took a good peek.

'Well?' said Abu Imad after a few moments.

'I don't know to be honest,' I replied.

'That's a first,' Abu Imad said, surprised at my response. 'I think we should call Abu Walid.'

I didn't usually agree with him, but on this occasion I did. He got on the silky and spoke in that rough Arabic accent that was steeped in Iraq, requesting that Abu Walid respond. He didn't need to repeat himself, for Abu Walid replied promptly.

The emir leapt up to the vantage point like an agile mountain leopard. The air was cold and the night was slowly turning blue. You could see the rugged contours of the mountains and the road that everyone had to pass through, friend or foe. Of late, apart from the odd goat herder who'd give us a kid out of his innate generosity to guests, no van or lorry had passed.

Abu Walid was clear-eyed. I don't think he had rested like the others. He wore a black woolly hat over his curly hair. His beard was as fragrant as ever. He always made sure it was, even during the toughest of times.

'May I?' he asked.

Abu Imad deferentially moved over. He had forgotten about the incident a few days past. Our commander peered through the scope, surveying everything. What was he to make of faces whose eyes shone in the darkness like cat's eyes?

'They don't blink,' he said, amazed, and kept on staring. 'How many?'

'Hard to tell,' I said, 'maybe three hundred.'

'In formation?'

'No, they are moving slowly.'

'Are they civilians?' he asked.

'They don't look like civilians to me.'

'May I borrow your binoculars, brother?' he asked.

I handed them over. He stood staring for a long time.

'What are those things? There's four of them on a dead carcass that has been there for weeks,' he said.

'Are they human?' Abu Walid said.

'What do you mean?' I asked.

'There is something of the beast in them.'

'I don't know what they are,' I said.

'There's only one way to find out,' said Abu Imad, about to go for the Dragunov.

'Wait,' I said, 'you're out of range. You might startle them and we don't know how they'll behave.' I looked to Abu Walid who was still staring through the binoculars, studying them.

'Get the American,' he said.

Abu Imad jumped down and eagerly brought out the American sniper rifle that was kept lovingly where I sat.

It took a while to set up. Our target was one at the back. Abu Imad hit him right in the skull. Should have died immediately. Should have stopped him in his tracks, but the thing kept stumbling on for a while till it slumped over for lack of direction. Abu Imad looked on incredulously. The others in the pack looked at the slumped-over victim slightly startled, but just carried on with what they were doing.

'They must be zombies or something,' he said.

'You been watching too many Hollywood movies,' I said.

'It's either that or they're Jinns,' said Abu Imad. He started to recite the surahs from the Quran that protect from the satanic forces of this world.

By the time they were within eight hundred metres, Abu Imad started firing two rounds a minute, but then he's never been that accurate, that was always his problem. Never had any patience. That was how we got ourselves in this mess in the first place. A long time ago, when Iraq was happening, he pulled up on his mountain bike and told me we had to do something.

'What?' I asked, unsure of what he meant.

'Man needs to hold it up for the man dem, bredrin,' he replied. 'Come!' Abu Imad looked bored in those red shorts, hairy calves and baseball cap.

'Man don't even pray though,' I had said.

'Don't worry, both are an obligation,' he said. 'Come.'

I did start to pray. I also learned how to live with fear on account of doing a whole lot of fighting, a whole lot of killing for God knows what reason. God forgive us for our mistakes. In the end, we found our way here.

So patience was never one of Abu Imad's virtues. He preferred to fire off rounds. And now, he was just doing it because he hadn't done anything but wait. He was always like that, he'd marry then divorce, marry then divorce. I used to warn fathers against him. But he was handsome, and in hard times a handsome strong man with a gun, hair down to his shoulders and a broad smile can win any girl's heart. So he'd disappear for a few weeks and return divorced. He was still like that now, even more so as he got older. Pricks don't change their nature with age.

I took over and we increased our accuracy to about seventy percent. The creatures seemed to have been caught in an ambush and didn't know where they were drawing fire. They were like a bunch of women in a market when a car bomb strikes. They fell so easily that at one point I felt maybe they were civilians. Their high-pitched screams sounded like soldiers trapped inside a BMP struck by an RPG and unable to get out. Maybe that's how it all began with the American soldier. Maybe the soldiers just opened up on them and now all that these creatures wanted was revenge. I couldn't develop my chain of thought; all eight of us were giving those things a good licking. I could even see Abu Imad and Cenk smiling as they fired. It's hard to police the monster in the soul once it's out. Sometimes it just feels too good.

'Enough,' said Abu Walid, peering through his binoculars. When Abu Imad continued firing Abu Walid shouted, 'That's enough! Conserve your ammunition. God knows how many more there are.'

He was right. It had been two weeks since we heard from the commanders and God only knew when we'd get more ammo.

We prayed the dawn prayer behind Abu Walid, ate rich tea biscuits dunked in sweet tea, watching the pinkish summits gleaming in the rising sun. To Abu Imad they were serrated wolves' teeth, to me they were tent pegs that held the earth still, and to Abu Walid they were the thrones of Angels. Then, we went to inspect our handiwork.

Abu Walid left Cenk and Jan Mohammed to cover us from our crag, just in case. Me and Abu Imad took the rear, Khaldun and Abu Waqqas took the flanks, whilst Abu Walid followed Abu Muslim, a huge Chechen brother who took point. Abu Muslim's confidence gave us certitude, even though he looked wild with his unkempt blonde reddish hair and beard over loose fatigues. Everything about him looked ragged, apart from his belt which framed it all perfectly. Only his weapons were expensive and, like his forefathers, he had a knife even though he didn't need one. The Mountains must have been the man's mother.

When we got to the bodies, we held our hands to our noses. The bodies were already decomposing. Some of the creatures wore Shalwar Kamizes, others ripped trousers and shirts, some were even in combat khakis. They looked like men and women that had emerged from a cemetery. I looked at one head that had separated itself from its body. It lay there lifeless until we walked past and it revived. For a moment its one eye stared wide awake at us and its mouth started to snap. We all flinched except Abu Imad.

'Man this thing is meant to be dead!' Abu Imad said and kicked the head like he was taking a free kick in Stamford Bridge. 'GOOOOAAAAL – and it's Zidane,' Abu Imad mock celebrated.

Abu Walid glared at him. I poked roughly between Abu Imad's shoulders. And he soon returned to reality. We walked past several strewn limbs that still wriggled like the tails of geckos.

'This must be the army of Gog and Magog,' said Abu Imad, convinced, almost exultant. 'Like the Prophet said, they have finally crossed the barrier and there is nothing to stop them – except us.'

'God knows best,' replied Abu Walid. He hadn't forgotten that the Prophet said: no one can stop the tribe of Gog and Magog that will be unleashed at the End of Time. All that will remain will be heroic deeds solely for His pleasure. As we say in Beirut, there are many ways to die but death is one and the same.

We might have been dead men, but we still felt alive. That whole day, like a grizzled pirate crew, we prepared for them. For two weeks we had been waiting to be relieved. We had sent Abu Yahya to the commander but he hadn't returned. There had been much uncertainty and endless speculation. There had been radio silence apart from a brief interruption when we thought we heard shooting on the frequency. At first, Abu Walid had tried to get in contact every hour. But now he communicated with Command only when it was absolutely necessary, in case the enemy was listening.

We each did a four-hour shift keeping watch, while the others slept uneasily in the cave. Abu Walid did an inventory and quietly discussed the issue with Abu Muslim. After 'Asr he sat there, reciting Quran and twisting his beads, stroking his grey beard, deep in thought. After the Maghreb prayer, as the sun set on our crag, which for so many years had served as my home from home, he gathered the men around the fire. After praising and magnifying God and His Messenger he addressed us. 'Brothers, I wanted to ask you all what you thought about these creatures. God knows what they are, who sent them and why. Maybe the Americans have devised a new weapon, maybe they are sent by God or maybe this is the End of Time. It is only right that whatever decision I take must be with you in mind.'

We didn't say anything, and he searched our faces to divine our inner thoughts.

'It is not cowardice if we retreat,' he said. 'You men are experienced enough to know when a tactical retreat is called for. My question is, should we retreat or remain? I don't know if we should hold this pass.'

He looked at us again. 'Advise me.'

'I don't think we should retreat,' said Abu Imad, as if he had been accused of cowardice. 'I think we should take down as many of these infidels as we can. I have never run from a fight and I don't intend to do it this time. I'm not frightened of these devils. We have fought devils, haven't we? What's the difference between them and the Americans?' He looked at the men sitting round the fire. Their eyes were frightened but his bravado gave them succour.

'Shush man!' I said.

'No, let him speak,' said Abu Walid, 'let him speak.'

'If they are American-made,' continued Abu Imad, 'then we will be wasting their assets.'

There was nothing I or Abu Muslim could say to dissuade the younger brothers, they went with the thinking of Abu Imad and so the meeting went his way.

'Right!' Abu Imad said, 'then it's decided.' He got up and checked that his Stechkin pistol was secure in the holster across his chest. He adjusted the curved Yemeni dagger of his tribe around his waist. 'I'll take first watch.'

I walked up to Abu Walid and told him there was still time to reverse the decision. I could get the men to change their minds.

'I've put my armour on,' Abu Walid said, as if determined to follow through. 'Don't worry, brother.' He slung his Kalash with his modified night scope round his shoulders and nodded to the other brothers to follow as it was time to take the first watch of the night.

'Get some sleep,' he told us. 'It's going to be a long night.'

He went out of the entrance and started going up the roughly hewn stairway that led to the vantage point. We had carved it out over the years. Might as well get comfortable.

Jan Mohammed spotted the second wave around the same time as the night before. This time, though, we were all ready for them. The first wave had trudged forward, this one behaved differently. Two or three crept forward cautiously and seemed to almost sniff at their dead comrades, the way dogs do, as if they were trying to understand what had happened. Then they gave out loud piercing screams at different intervals, like some sort of primitive Morse code. Another followed, sniffed again at his fallen comrade, and then these trudging creatures started to move at a speed you wouldn't expect them to move at. They spread out, they hopped and tumbled and started not for the pass but towards us.

At first Abu Walid discouraged us from using the PKC mounted guns – he wanted to conserve ammunition as much as he could. He encouraged us to use the Makhanazmas and Dragunovs, but the creatures were moving too fast, they were incredibly agile. In the end, to the great delight of Abu Imad, he let the PKC rip and the regular fire of the machine gun mowed the things down however much they hopped, twisted and screamed. A few made it to the bottom of our cave and started to climb up the walls, but we dispatched them with little effort.

'Didn't we show them?' said Abu Imad, elated. 'Didn't we show the Americans?'

'Yes,' said Abu Walid perceptively, 'but they are learning.'

We spent the whole next day preparing for the night to come. It was tiring but we were in good spirits. We had scored a great victory against the empire that had orphaned our sons, invaded our lands, raped our women and stolen our resources. Here we were teaching these invaders how it's done.

But the next night they didn't come at us as we expected. Cenk saw two sniff at some of their comrades and then return to where they'd come from. We did not see them all night. There were no high-pitched Morse code-like screams. Silence. But they were there alright. Their foul odour permeated the air. We felt they were so close that they were listening in on our conversation.

We only realised they had changed tactics when Abu Waqqas and Khaldun didn't return by mid-afternoon. They had been sent out to scout and stock up on water in the morning. The two were experienced, they had fought on many fronts all over the Muslim world. Men like that didn't just disappear. We knew they had been taken. We found their muddy boots in our cave. Now only two brothers could rest whilst the rest of us kept a lookout.

'We should go after them,' Abu Imad said. 'They may still be alive.'

'I think,' said Abu Muslim, 'there is little chance of that.'

'How do you know?' Abu Imad said.

'I don't think these creatures take prisoners,' replied Abu Muslim. 'They are martyrs, God willing.'

'What sort of infidels,' asked Abu Imad, 'are we dealing with here?'

'I don't think they are infidels,' I said.

'If they are not infidels', asked Abu Imad, 'what are they?'

'God knows,' I replied, 'some sort of scourge that feeds on the souls of men.'

'Is there anything that the Prophet, peace be upon him, said about these creatures?'

'Not that I have heard,' said Abu Muslim, 'unless they be Gog and Magog or Jinns.'

That night, we heard a sort of jittery, high-pitched laughter as if there were hyenas surrounding our cave and pill box. The smell of rotting meat enveloped us. Following the loss of our two brothers the creature appeared enriched, seemed wiser, more knowing as if they'd figured out how to come at us. We felt it. Sometimes we saw their bright cat eyes in the night and then there were none. We thought we heard them behind us. We became increasingly undisciplined with our fire and more careless with our ammunition. None of us could sleep. We drank Red Bulls and Cenk kept us going by making us strong Turkish coffee whilst we kept watch. I could see that the usual calm that God bestowed on us whenever we fought the enemy wasn't quite there. Few of us could crack those jokes. I looked at Abu Imad and his eyes were wide open. He was pale.

'What!' he said when he caught my worried stare. 'What! I'm tired, what do you expect, bredrin?'

But he wasn't tired. He was uncertain. I reckon that Fear itself had got one over him and he was fighting it off.

In the morning, when all those polytheists were worshipping the ascent of the sun, the host, for this is what we had begun to call them, sent us two messengers. They wore fatigues that were familiar. Their faces, though gaunt and pulled back with tufts from their beards missing, looked familiar.

One had lost an arm. Yet, as they trudged towards us, they seemed to be laughing.

'It's the boys, it's Khaldun!' Abu Imad said joyfully over the radio. He was close to Khaldun because Khaldun never ribbed him for anything. 'Praise be to God,' he kept saying, 'praise be to God. They have returned to us!'

Abu Imad was about to rush out and help them but Jan Mohammed held him back. As soon as the creatures saw Abu Imad, they bounded on all fours and leapt towards him as if they were greyhounds at the races. We opened fire but they kept coming. No human could have survived the amount of lead we were putting their way. We stopped them but nothing of them remained. All was quiet.

'Get some rest,' said Abu Walid grimly. 'We need to dig some trenches around our perimeter.'

We were too tired to think we had just wasted two of our closest companions. Two pious comrades. Only Abu Walid kept watch, till I got up and relieved him a few hours later.

Just before noon when Abu Walid, me and Abu Muslim were sitting down chatting amongst ourselves, Abu Imad who had been watching us intently asked, 'Aren't they supposed to have been martyred?'

'What do you mean?' I said.

'I mean Abu Waqqas and Khaldun, aren't they supposed to be martyred? They are meant to be smiling, this isn't meant to happen to them. We buried many brothers with their clothes on because they were martyrs. This doesn't feel like martyrdom to me.'

'They are martyrs, God willing,' said Abu Walid.

'If they were martyrs why were they like that?'

'Snap out of it,' said Abu Muslim, 'those Americans, they experiment and create monsters. It's probably a disease. They used to inject their own soldiers with syphilis. Don't worry. They are martyrs, God willing.'

'What do you reckon they are?' said Abu Imad, turning to me nervously. 'Come on, bro, no use being silent now! You always have something to say.'

'Maybe,' I said, 'it's a punishment from God – like locusts or jellyfish.'

'Jellyfish?' Abu Imad said, surprised. 'Why do you always complicate things?'

'It's just an epidemic, no conspiracy nothing. Epidemic, that's all there is to it. It's just a disease like AIDS, the plague and all others before them. They turn into jellyfish and consume everything until there is nothing left.'

'That's just the human race,' said Abu Walid, ruminating.

'Well, well,' said Abu Imad, 'man gets an 'A' GCSE science and man becomes an oceanologits as well.'

'Oceanologist,' I corrected. I didn't know anything more than what I picked up in Beirut and on TV when I was a kid. Whenever things got hot on the Green and I was getting into too many scrapes, mother, God have mercy on her, would send me to Beirut. I could let off steam during the summer months, behave myself or my uncles gave me a good licking. In all honesty, God forgive me, the girls in Beirut were just off the scale in comparison to the ones on Green. The girls on Green had teenage pregnancy written all over their faces and my mother knew it. They'd bring shame to the family. At least, with a Beiruti girl you could approach their parents if things progressed. Sometimes, when Beirut got a bit hot and oppressive, you could grab a bus to Jubail and visit Uncle Sami. Uncle Sami was great. He had a small restaurant right by the harbour and served freshly caught fish. Sometimes Uncle Sami would take out his boat and catch the fish himself, that's how fresh they were; a bit of lemon juice, chips, mayonnaise – and nothing else. But when the jellyfish came that was it. Sometimes there'd be thousands of them just floating there. They consumed everything. They clogged everything up, you could even get stung by them on the beach when they were dead. Uncle swore the catch was less.

'There's no anchovies, there's nothing!' He would complain. 'They're damn locusts, a punishment from God!'

Aunty would still him. But when the catch was bad for weeks and people stopped visiting, even she would say. 'Maybe your uncle's right.' And she'd start praying again.

'No, no,' said Abu Muslim, rejecting my explanation. 'Trust me, it's the Americans and the Jews. I've been fighting them for years, this is their handiwork alright.'

'I just don't see them doing this,' I said.

'Why not!' said Abu Muslim, offended. 'These people have no morals, they blow up whole cities. Why wouldn't they do such a thing? The means justifies the end. It's them, believe me – it's them.'

'I don't know,' I replied, 'I just think these creatures are out of control, completely. Americans like control, they can't control this thing. That's why I don't think it's them.'

'It's them alright, it is them,' repeated Abu Muslim. To some people fighting Americans had become a religious creed, an act of worship equal to praying.

'It must be,' added Abu Imad. 'God wouldn't do such a thing against us.'

'Why not?' I asked. 'We've done a whole lot of killing in His name and it probably wasn't right. We believed that the means justified the end. We found a fatwa that allowed torture if needs be. We reintroduced things which we shouldn't have.'

'What is it they want?' Abu Imad began to wallow in it, sounded panicked, scared even. 'Has it all been for nothing?'

'Shut up, all of you!' Abu Walid ordered.

He snapped us out of it. He set us to work, to dig trenches and booby trap them with trip wires, replenish the ammunition we had collected over the years. We opened the boxes, placed our PKC heavy machines guns ready for the night. A reminder that he didn't want anyone to be slacking. He didn't allow us to think about it too much. By the time we finished, I don't care who you were, you needed to be some amazing Spec Op to enter our perimeter. We didn't even have time for praying Maghreb before we could smell that rotten odour surrounding us.

The host weren't shy about their intentions. They leapt towards the booby traps caring little for their own self-preservation. The Mon 50s just burst and you heard their laughter as they fell on the ground, immobilized. A high-pitched sound screamed out and then the others followed, trampling over their comrades. There were hundreds of them coming for us and we mowed them down like we were soldiers in the Great War killing Germans. We ate the ammunition like children go through packs of haribos. The six of us fought all night and just about managed to repel them, though we had some close shaves. Our efforts should have been preserved in song or poetry, but no one saw our valiant deeds.

The next day we left Cenk to guard the entrance whilst we snored. In the evening we grew concerned about the level of ammo. We were discussing this issue when Abu Muslim got bit. One of those things jumped out of nowhere and bit him on his left hand. He calmly blasted his pistol and the damned creature fell to the ground wriggling and laughing. We couldn't stop the bleeding though, due to the relentless attack that followed. So he had to treat himself.

It was only in the morning that we could give Abu Muslim proper attention. He seemed fine and in good spirits, but his hand had a gangrenous smell to it: rotting flesh and shit.

'How does it look?' said Abu Muslim, sounding uncharacteristically cheerful.

'Looks like it's spreading,' I said, turning his hand against the light trying not to sound too worried.

'Can we stop it?' he asked.

'Hope so.'

'Is he turning?' Abu Imad said, looking disturbed. 'He is, isn't he? He is?'

'Calm down,' I said, putting my hand on my Beretta. 'Calm down. What do you mean, "turning"?'

'He's turning into one of them!' shouted Abu Imad. 'We need to kill him before he turns!'

Abu Muslim looked frightened. First time I'd seen that.

Abu Walid got up from the kerosene heater and gave Abu Imad the biggest backhander I had ever seen him give. It wasn't one based on anger, it was the sort you saw in the old black and white movies, where the actor gives the hysterical heroine a slap so she'll snap out of it.

'No one's doing any killing here,' he said, looking at Abu Muslim, reassuring his old comrade. 'He's our brother, he's my brother. We don't know what this thing is. Good and bad, all of it, is from Him. So no one's going to do any killing on my watch. Now we are going to get some rest and then we will decide what we are going to do later.' He went up to the vantage point and left Abu Imad there to watch the cave's entrance.

We woke up two hours later and Abu Imad had gone. Abu Walid didn't seem too angry about it.

'Had he waited he could have left with you,' he said sadly. 'Now he has to bear the sin of desertion.'

'I'm sorry,' I said.

'Don't be,' he replied, 'we're better off without him.'

A good platoon commander always knows when it's time to retreat. So he ordered us to get going. We looked at Abu Muslim and realised that he was in no state to move.

'Look,' I said, 'we will stay together to the end.'

'No,' said Abu Walid. 'I will stay with Abu Muslim and see this disease out.'

'You take the rest and make your way.'

'Where?'

'You'll find your way, go and collect our wives and kids and give them my love.'

'Has it all been a waste?'

'No,' he said, hugging me, 'you don't have much time before darkness comes. Go. I'll see you there.'

'Where do I go?'

'I will find you.'

We packed hastily. Cenk, Jan Mohammed, and I hugged Abu Muslim as if for the last time. We carried him to the vantage point and cuffed him, leaving Abu Walid well stocked with ammunition waiting for the night battle knowing that it would probably be his last. Perhaps he let us go because he wanted our deeds to be preserved in song. We made our way praying to God that we were all on the right path.

POEMS FOR GAZA

Carol Rumens

Danger. Store Upright. Avoid Contact with Skin

Another child, another face. Forget
that look it gives back to the dot of light
in someone's phone. It's not easily read
(the eyes sun-narrowed, ritual smile turned shy,
reclusive, even). Still, it's clear enough
the kid sees something kind, something like love.
Click it away. Don't wonder. You might spot
the hand, resting easy on his right
shoulder – some soft touch he barely felt
but felt was on his side, though urging him
to trust his small pride to the dot of light.
Forget that trust. It's not as sweet and bright
as the trust of little girls. He didn't ask
to be included in that bloodied casket
of screaming smiles he made. Forget, forget
how nearly child he was, how near, and far,
he stands, and always stood, their murderer.
Let him be name alone, sharp, difficult name.
Keep him wrapped up in it. Don't open him.

Dolls

The children aren't coming back for
their babies; they took off
on wings of dirt and blast. Those pink Mattel babies,
the grownups said, had cost them an arm and a leg.

Most were factory seconds,
and every child had a story
whenever hair-glue melted, or an eye stuck open.

The children were playing as usual
on the floor in the flat above
or below or next door to
the flat the drones were eyeing.
The flats were crushed into one
by the world's most moral army.
How would you recognise
the dolls, their old mad look
in the mad-look pit, *without form, and void?*

If anything's coming back for the dolls it won't be
kind. It won't have arms
to catch a baby, or a smile to remember
the lipsticked lips, the little holes
between the lips, the hilarious wetting-play
with tiny bottles; how the babies never
slept for long, how someone always shook them
over and over to hear them crying "Mama,
I'm thirsty…"

Smoke

Out of its grave-in-the-air a drifted column
circled, touched a similar vague form
of caught breath and particles of soot.
They were smoke-brothers, they'd already met
under spilled streets before this half-embrace
they struggled in and out of, tired and weapon-less.

Suddenly tall, one spat a shower of curses:
"OK, you see a murderer's face in mine

but why d' you see him in the children's faces?
Are they my children – all the thousands dead?"

"Yes, yours. You should have kept them hidden.
I targeted an arms-cache, not the poor
flammable skins that were your roof and door."

Fires roared where smoke had sighed. The air was emptied.

POEMS FOR GAZA

Michal Rubin

Once they started invading us.
Taking our houses and trees, drawing lines,
pushing us into tiny places.
It wasn't a bargain or deal or even a real war.
To this day they pretend it was.

Naomi Shihab Nye

So many stones
burying your story.
I pick one,

it collapses into powdered specks
of words or letters or punctuations.

The specks darting in the air
like my words,
like my letters,

like my attempts to find the right turn
in the thick river of howls.

I am baptized in your pain
or in the truth of your telling,
bathe in the air carrying
the dust of your demolished home,
bathe in the oud notes,

its broken strings—my handcuffs.
Wet shame drips at my feet
as I stand in the still of time.

So many stones
burying your story.

Still

You lie on the ground,
a misshapen form you did not choose.

A fly buzzes by, chasing your neighbour's
scent, your silence cuts the sound

of background booms and sirens.
I am far, you are just a photo

on a screen,
a painting of our capabilities.

I am far,
far from the sounds I imagine

but your stillness quakes inside me,
your silence—a scream

into which words are swallowed—

you lie on the ground,
forbidden to live.

New Republic

1.

> *I grant you refuge*
> *from hurt and suffering.*
> —Hiba Abu Nada

We lived in the second century
of world wars inside seas

I drowned with you
and we sank to the bottom

of the sea of salt
where drowning is not possible

2.

> *You were first created out of love,*
> *so carry nothing but love.*
> —Hiba Abu Nada

We carried nothing
but each other, in the deep sand

we built another castle
share its floors and words

braided melancholy tunes
into unseen ceilings

3.

> *O! How alone we are!*
> —Hiba Abu Nada

You and I painted the shadows
we brought along

gave them colours
hung them on the walls of water

to be washed off
in the third century.

The translations of Hiba Abu Nada's work quoted here are by Huda Fakhreddine. Naomi Shihab Nye, the family of Hiba Abu Nada, and Huda Fakhreddine have granted permission for the publication of the epigraphs in [untitled] and 'New Republic'. The name Hiba means 'Gift from God' and can also be transliterated as Heba.

POEMS FOR GAZA

Adrianne Kalfopoulou

The Evening Began with Cardamon
for Reem Razem

And ended in the kitchen
Looking at a map on the wall
There was also sage, cinnamon tea
Conversation about the quality of the bark

How to steep it in boiling water
How long to leave it

And that map had all the names of villages
Scattered over its length and width
Like embroidered stitches
Wavering and linked and minuscule
Letters like the patterns
Particular to the regions famous
For their stitching, oranges, and cloths
Some are still the same, she said

Hebron and Jaffa, or Yafa… she paused
They weren't changed, and then she smiled

And explained the Canaanite symbols
On the cloths, that *Yafa means beautiful* in Arabic

This was how she introduced each tea
Each food had its own scent and story

Each place too once belonged to its name

See, Unsee

The soldier with his bras
And panties
Wrapped around a rifle
Hand on a gun
Face leaning toward a friend
Lighting his cigarette
Is this sex? They can be
Very close, we're told
Death and sex, and here
The dark story
Of tortured flesh
The ways humans
Take pleasure
In acts I can't unsee –
A blond man in uniform
Fondles an absent woman's underwear
Maybe she's dead
But the panties are pink
The bras too, perhaps
Size C, perhaps
She kept them
Scented, or just
Washed, these
Intimate pieces
Of clothing
Dangling from a
Soldier's wrist, casually
Against his rifle
A day's cull
His kill

Ashlaa'

A notebook accumulates, helps write the scattering intention. Find
language to gather what was once a home, a body, a body dispersed, still
a family homed in the ruin, the limbs, mangled columns, the no-longer
walls, the gashed ceilings, this mother who cannot find her child, this
mother who tries to urge her son towards her, his legs gone, this son
who wants to know if his legs will grow back. *Ashlaa'* in Arabic is
without equivalent in English, these images on our screens are without
equivalent. These screams. *Ashlaa'* – you can see what was once, you can
see this was a home, there are utensils on what was a kitchen floor. Bisan
walks through a part of Khan Yunis, shows us names on walls, the
numbers tell us how many once lived within them, 19 in this one, the
number 5, circled, is the number of bodies found, this home now the
family grave, there's the family name, it belonged to them, it homes
them again. *If you tear a Palestinian into pieces, each piece will resist and fight
and would go on fighting...* a post tells us *our will is God's will.* Inside the
redacting, inside this strike/through a child barely smiles, a plastic jug in
her hand almost as large as she is, it's just been filled. The water from a
hose on a container truck, the water splashes as it fills the jugs, the
child's bare feet stand wet in mud. Shy with large, terrified eyes, Bisan
asks if she's happy to have her water, she nods, she has a lovely name I
only remember the sound of. An hour later the screen is in flames, a
scene of burning tents, a man offers a headless child to the night sky, his
screaming grief rocks him to his knees, the child still in his hands. Flames
are everywhere and Allah's name. We hardly see the shapes, we see the
smoke of bombs, hear Allah's repeated name. I am writing this the night
of May 26, 2024, 1:23pm local time in the UAE, now May 27. The ICJ
has ordered Israel to stop the assault on Rafah, the ICJ votes to issue
arrest warrants for Hamas leaders, Netanyahu and his several ministers,
this emboldens more Israeli strikes, more massacres. Israel accuses the
ICJ of being anti-Israel. Israel is anti-Israel if Israel truly wishes to be a
part of a world that believes in peace, a peace not policed, a peace not
pieced by checkpoints, ruined orchards, destroyed schools, corpses:
Ashlaa'. Language has no container for the uncontainable – how to
contain a grief that keeps spreading. *Ashlaa'* breaks platitudes. An

American professor spat in the face of a student wearing a hijab, an American police officer pushed a professor at Emory College to the ground when she stood up for a protesting student. The burnt bodies are unnuanced, not a platitude if an absolute. Mosab posts *if you can't look at it, this is* … a mutilated child. Language leads, language falls apart, how to follow this savaged space, a place, once homes and trees and growing mint, now the calling out of names inside the flames, bodies woken burning, where there are flames and Allah's name, there is a U.S. diplomat whose name makes no sense to name asking media outlets to 'Tone down the images.' No mention of stopping bombs. Two boys scoop up rubble. *Ashlaa'* is Day #234 of the genocide, also Day #235, #236… The living room is still a room the boys will live in that now looks out to unobstructed sea. The buildings are leveled. Like a leveled sentence, the buildings no longer order space, once a neighborhood, a leveled sentence like a leveled building has lost the structure to shelter what it once sheltered. The boys are putting together what is left. Cement chunks. The space that once sheltered is now dangerous. Letters and words, letters that make up words no one understands within a blown structure, as flesh and blood scatters, *Ashlaa'* … so too this line I keep trying to put together, a sentence that might re-collect parts I don't want to name. To write what I see, and others are living. Day #241, "The Harvest of 24 hrs" Bisan writes, a man runs with his dog as buildings around him explode, what happened to this man, and his dog, Bisan wants to know. Children are rounded up and stripped naked by the IDF, a young boy, maybe 10, is holding his younger sister who looks like she might be 5 or 6. Another reel shows a woman being pulled by two young men, she just lost a leg, you can see she's only got one as they drag her belly down, screaming. Her blood leaves a path. She'd gone out to find food for her kids, it's the Jabalia camp, a safe place people were told. The displaced keep trying to find a space to keep themselves in place, these sentences too need to somehow stop. Day #309. Al Tabaéen school, 4:30 am, the *Fajr* prayer. They were all men, 100 worshippers piecemeal from the missile. Bisan keeps repeating, *they were praying. Ashlaa'* means the scattered parts, they are gathered, each 70 kg bag once a body. There is so much blood, its many paths from start to finish, when will that finish, *Ashlaa'* has no equivalent in English.

REVIEWS

THE GAZA PRISON

Hassan Mahamdallie

The majority of Jean-Pierre Filiu's monumental account *Gaza: A History* covers the period from 1948 onwards, the year of The Catastrophe (Al-*Nakba*), until the present day. However, at the start of his historical narrative he chronicles what he describes as 'Gaza before the strip'. 'Travellers who have visited Gaza over the centuries have often remarked on the fecundity of its vegetation and the diversity of its agriculture, both of which are the products of its underground waters and the gentle nature of its prevailing climate'. The first-century Greek philosopher and historian Plutarch is said to have described Gaza City as *aromatophora* – the dispenser of perfumes, due to its central position on the trade route from Yemen, the main producer then (and now) of high-quality Frankincense

Jean-Pierre Filiu, *Gaza: A History*, Hurst, London, 2024
Ilan Pappe, *The Biggest Prison on Earth: A History of Gaza and the Occupied Territories*, Oneworld, London, 2024
Fida Jiryis, *Stranger in My Own Land*, Hurst, London, 2024
Rashid Khalidi, *The Hundred Years' War on Palestine: A History of Settler Colonial Conquest and* Resistance, Profile Books, London, 2020.
Norman G. Finkelstein, *Gaza: An Inquest Into Its Martyrdom*, University of California Press, Berkeley, 2018.

In 1932, a French tourist guidebook described the 'bustling bazaars' of Gaza, and its accessibility, situated as it was at the halfway point on the Palestine Railways coastal line linking Haifa in the north to the Suez Canal southwards. And today? In January 2014, Palestinian photographer and writer Mohammed al-Hajjar described how 'throughout the Gaza Strip, it only smells of death, debris and decay'. He reveals how dogs root amongst the rubble, devouring semi-decomposed human flesh, and 'chasing after a stray dog to retrieve a tiny baby's leg from its mouth.'

The plan for the partition of Palestine, with the creation of a Jewish state and an Arab state, was presented in 1931–1932 by Victor Jacobson, World Zionist Organization delegate to the League of Nations. To expand the Jewish state in preparation for future immigration and economic growth, Jacobson proposed the transfer of more than 100,000 Arabs off their land, and the handing over of the nascent Arab state to the Hashemite rulers of Transjordan. The rise to power of Hitler and the Nazis swelled the number of Jewish immigrants entering the British mandate of Palestine, increasing it from 9,533 in 1932, to 30,327 in 1933, then 42,359 in 1934 and 61,854 in 1935.

In *Stranger in my Own Land*, Fida Jiryis writes that the majority of Palestinians were ill equipped to grasp the wider implications of this and earlier waves of immigration, and the preparations that the Zionist movement were making, both through international lobbying and organisation on the ground, to dispossess and drive out the indigenous population and form an exclusive Jewish state.

Jiryis, who is the daughter of prominent civil rights lawyer, activist, and member of the PLO leadership, points out that the Palestinians had been 'under four centuries of backward Ottoman rule and were beleaguered by ignorance and poverty'. It is a cruel twist of historical fate that the Palestinian people's own yearning to follow the rest of the Arab states in modern nation-state building on the European model was suppressed, cut short and finally crushed, first by British occupation followed by the aggressively expanding Zionist European colonial-settler project that, like all colonialists, regarded Palestine as *terra nullius*, 'a land without a people for a people without a land'.

In his incisive and compelling book *The Hundred Years' War on Palestine:*, Rashid Khalidi argues that the war waged against the Palestinians to force them to relinquish their homeland can best been seen as both a colonial and a national conflict. Khalidi writes that 'World War One and its aftermath accelerated the change in Palestinian national sentiment from a love of country and loyalties to family and locale to a thoroughly modern form of nationalism'. Khalidi points out the ascendancy of the United States and its antipathy to the old empires and the Bolshevik Revolution of

1917, initially guided by Lenin's maxim of the right of self-determination of small nations, 'the apparent endorsement of the national aspirations of peoples the world over by ostensibly anticolonial powers had an enormous impact'. This was manifested by a renewal of anti-colonial struggles in Asia, Africa, and across the wider Arab world, but by the turn of the century, it was often expressed within a nationalist framework. No sooner had the suffocating yoke of the Ottomans been lifted, the Palestinians came under British military occupation, and with the 1917 Balfour Declaration, as Khalidi terms it 'found that their home had been promised to others as a "national home"', even though Jews at that time represented just 6 percent of the country's population'.

It is striking how much language, and the turning of meanings on their head, played an important part in the establishment of the Greater Israeli settler-colonial state, and continues to do so today. Gaslighting is not a recent phenomenon. In 1901, when Palestine was still under Ottoman rule, the Zionist Organization set up the Jewish National Fund (JNF) to 'acquire' land in Palestine with the aim later described as wiping out 'all trace of these people to make room for Zionist settlers'. The JNF referred to this process as 'liberating', 'emancipating', and 'redeeming' land, as if, as Jiryis points out, they were freeing land somehow held 'captive' by Palestinians who had lived on and worked the land for numerous centuries.

Even if at the outset only a minority of the population fully understood the ultimate goals of the British plans for partition and Zionist expansion, resistance was not long in coming. In line with the earlier period of anti-colonial struggles across the Arab world and north Africa, the Palestinian struggle was, in its initial phase, led by Islamic religious leaders, with the difference that those engaged in it were fighting on two fronts. Filiu describes how Ezzadin al-Qassam, who had previously led resistance against the Italians and the French colonists, 'was determined to mount a revolutionary jihad against the British and the Zionists...The discovery that arms were being delivered to the Jewish Haganah militia gave fresh impetus to the secret preparations that were being undertaken in Arab circles. Ezzedin al-Qassam was the first to go into action, leading a guerilla force of a dozen men before being killed in an ambush set by British troops in November 1935'. This in turn fed into the 1936–1939 Arab revolt across Palestine, triggering a general strike combined with civil protests and guerrilla actions against the occupiers and strategic infrastructure such as the railways and telegraph lines. Increasingly the uprising took on both a nationalist and revolutionary character. The response of the British was brutal. The legitimate Palestinian national aspirations were to be crushed with the upmost ferocity in disregard for any international conventions and basic human rights.

As Khalili writes, the ensuing British action,

> left 10 percent of the Arab male population killed, wounded, imprisoned or exiled…Well over a hundred…sentences of execution were handed down after summary military trials by military tribunals, with many more Palestinians executed on the spot by British troops. Infuriated by rebels ambushing their convoys and blowing up their trains, the British resorted to tying Palestinian prisoners to the front of armoured cars and locomotives to prevent rebel attack, a tactic they had pioneered in a futile effort to crush resistance of the Irish during their war of independence from 1919 to 1921. Demolitions of their homes of imprisoned or executed rebels, or of presumed rebels or their relatives was routine, another tactic borrowed from the British playbook developed in Ireland.

Little wonder that the Irish people and government have proved to be such stalwart supporters of the Palestinians. They share a collective memory of trauma and injustice at the hands of the British.

The Zionists and later Israeli state proved to be eager disciples of the British counter-insurgency tactics, 'refined' after World War Two in attempts to crush anti-colonial movements, perhaps most notoriously against Malayan freedom-fighters and the Mau Mau uprising in Kenya. In June 2024, the BBC reported that Israeli soldiers in the West Bank had thrown or tied Palestinian onto the bonnets of their army jeeps and drove them at high speed along village roads. One victim, twenty-five-year-old Samir Dabaya, was shot in the back and then left for hours until IDF soldiers finding he was still alive beat him with their guns before picking him up and throwing him onto the bonnet of their jeep. 'They took off my [trousers]. I wanted to hold onto the car, but [one soldier] hit my face and told me not to. Then he started driving,' he said. 'I was waiting for death.'

Norman G Finkelstein, in his powerful forensic account *Gaza: An Inquest Into Its Martyrdom*, shows how these war crimes came to be codified in various military stratagem, including the 'Dahiya doctrine', named after the southern suburb of Beirut, flattened by Israeli bombing during the 2006 war on Lebanon in punishment for their perceived support for Hezbollah. The Head of the IDF's Northern Command stated that 'we will wield disproportionate power against every village from which shots are fired on Israel'. The Head of the Israeli National Security Council pledged that 'the next war...will lead to the elimination of the Lebanese military, the destruction of the national infrastructure, and intense suffering among the population...The suffering of hundreds of thousands of people are consequences that can influence Hezbollah's behaviour more than anything else'. Finklestein points out that the use of disproportionate force and targeting civilian infrastructure constitute war crimes under international law.

During and in the aftermath of the 2006 war, the Israeli political and military establishment strained at the leash to visit the Dahiya doctrine upon the people of Gaza. The descent into hell, as Jean-Pierre Filui describes it, was not long in coming. On 27 December 2008 the Israelis launched a barbaric air and land assault on the Gazan population – Operation Cast Lead. It lasted three weeks, at the end of which one estimate calculated 1,417 Palestinians had been killed (in comparison nine Israeli soldiers were killed, four of which were casualties of 'friendly fire'). Over 46,000 homes were destroyed in Gaza, making more than 100,000 people homeless.

Top Israeli government and military officials openly glorified in their disproportionate ability to wreak death and destruction. Finkelstein singles out for 'sheer brazenness and brutality' the words of the then Deputy Prime Minister Eli Yishai. It should be, he declared, 'possible to destroy Gaza, so they will understand not to mess with us...It is a great opportunity to demolish thousands of houses of all the terrorists...(they) should be razed to the ground, so thousands of houses, tunnels and industries will be demolished'. Finkelstein concludes that the civilian death and destruction of 2008–2009, followed by further deadly assaults in 2012, 2014, and now 2023–2024, were not the result of 'the fog of war', 'collateral damage', 'unintended consequences', and other euphemisms: 'what happened in Gaza was *intended* to happen, by everyone from the soldiers who executed the orders to the officers who issued them to the politicians who approved them'.

Furthermore, Finkelstein argues that the 'land and air war on Gaza was not a war at all – it was in fact "a non-war"'. During Cast Lead the Israeli army rarely engaged Hamas forces. An Israeli strategic analyst concluded 'in reality, not a single battle was fought in twenty-two days of fighting'. IDF soldiers sent into Gaza reported that 'there was nothing there', 'no one ran into the enemy', 'there was supposed to be a tiny resistance force upon entry, but there just wasn't'. So if Hamas couldn't be found, who were the enemies the Israelis were confronting on the ground? The truth can be discerned from the musings of a Hebrew University philosopher on the challenges facing an Israeli soldier: he had to 'decide whether the individual standing before him in jeans and sneakers is a combatant or not'. Of those killed during Operation Cast Lead 350 were children.

Later on in his book, Finkelstein quotes *Haaretz* journalist Zvi Ba'rel's description of the 2014 assault on Gaza (The Israelis dubbed it Operation Protective Edge, in the pretence that it had some element of self-defence). Ba'rel saw that the IDF had in truth 'turned the entire Gaza population into an "infrastructure" to be destroyed'. By this measure, a house, a power-plant, a factory, a mosque, a school, a bridge, a young child, a teenager, a grandmother, are indistinguishable; to blow up one or the other is all the same. Finkelstein poses this question in relation to Operation Cast Lead (although it applies to those operations that went before and those that came after): 'What was Israel really trying to accomplish?' Finkelstein, as he does throughout his book, allows the aggressor to describe their own intent. He quotes Israeli commentator Guy Bechor, who in an 2010 article entitled 'Israel is Back', wrote, 'if Israel goes crazy and destroys everything in its way when it is being attacked, one should be careful. No need to mess with crazy people'.

Finkelstein ends his account by drawing a historical parallel between Gazans and the ethnic cleansing of the Cherokee Nation, which in the nineteenth century 'was expelled from one tribal homeland after another, forcibly marched across territory along what became known as the 'trail of tears' and finally stripped of its tribal holdings by the US government. He cites a historian of the period who wrote that 'there is no record so black as the record of its [the US government's] perfidy to this nation'. The author hoped that although the Cherokees had been ethnically cleansed, the truth of what had been done to them should remain, in the hope that future generations might read and learn what was done to them. 'Truth is on the side of Gaza' Finkelstein concludes. 'If this book rises to a crescendo of anger and indignation, it's because the endless lies about Gaza by those who know better causes one's innards to writhe'.

Illan Pappe suggests that the decades of Israeli occupation of the West Bank and Gaza Strip should be understood as a prison. In *The Biggest Prison on Earth*, he argues that there are two models of prison that Israel has used.

> One is the open prison model – which is 'granted' by Israel to the Palestinians in the occupied territories as a reward for 'good behaviour'. The 'open prison' includes limited autonomy for the Palestinians for the administration of domestic policies...In return the Palestinians had to give up any struggle for liberation or national independence. The best they could hope for in the future was a Bantustan, with no right of return for refugees, with a significant presence of recent Israeli Jewish settlers and with no capital in Jerusalem.

The second is the maximum-security prison model. It is used whenever the Palestinians rose up against the open prison system, as they inevitably would. For who can live under such a suffocating and hopeless existence? This includes 'collective punishments such as arrests without trial, killings, serious injuries, house demolitions, expulsions and a free hand to vigilantes among the Israeli Jewish settlers to assault and harass Palestinians'. But whereas maximum security prisons in the US are often built in the midst of poor populations, scooping up local inhabitants and throwing them into jail, in Gaza, the prison has been built around the entire population, incarcerating men, women, and children, young and old.

The prison paradigm also explains the intensifying bloody spiral of Israeli 'operations' carried out in 2008, 2012, 2014, and 2023–2024. Pappe, writing in the context of the 2014 military assault, likened the failed ground incursion into Gaza by Israeli troops as

> a bit like a police force entering a maximum-security prison in which the prisoners are besieged and running their own lives: you control them mainly from the outside parameters and you put yourself in danger if you try to invade it, to confront the desperation and resilience of those you are trying to starve and slowly squeeze the life out of. The Israelis knew all too well that such confrontation had to be avoided and therefore they...opted to use massive

firepower, which in the words of the army, contained the situation in the strip rather than leading to the destruction of Hamas.

Pappe documents how successive Israeli leaders, faced with continual refusal by the Palestinians and their political leadership to conspire in their own erasure, devised the Gaza open prison system as a way of both minimising the 'problem' whilst simultaneously pursuing strategies to take more land away from the Palestinians, for example the seizure of Arab East Jerusalem and subsequent Israeli expansion eastwards, almost bisecting the West Bank.

To the outside world the Israelis marketed the open prison model as a 'peace plan'. Pappe uses the example of foreign minister Moshe Dayan (veteran of the Zionist militia the Haganah, whose hero was British pro-Zionist war criminal Orde Wingate). In the 1979 Israeli-Egyptian peace talks, conducted over the heads of the Palestinians and their political representatives, Dayan proposed an 'autonomy plan' that was in reality its opposite, in that it 'assumed that the territory's sovereignty, control and resources were to remain forever in the hands of Israel'. The Egyptian president Anwar Sadat duly signed the peace treaty with Israeli prime minister Menachem Begin, with both of them sharing the Nobel Peace Prize as a reward. The Israelis withdrew military rule in the occupied territories and replaced it with an 'autonomous' civil administration. In an attempt to supress Palestinian Liberation Organization (PLO) influence, the Israelis, using the services of a former Jordanian minister of Agriculture, Mustafa Dunin, created Village Leagues, that were in Pappe's account hated by most of those they pretended to represent. In 1994, as a result of the Oslo Peace Accords, the Israelis allowed exiled PLO leader Yasser Arafat, who they had been attempting to assassinate for decades, back into Gaza. This was part of the agreement between Israel and the PLO that for a five year period a Palestinian Interim Self Government Authority would be established 'in order to guarantee public order and internal security' with 'a strong police force, while Israel will continue to carry the responsibility for defending against external threats'. This new iteration of the prison model would effectively be by the agreement of both the warders and the inmates.

It was perhaps inevitable that the Palestinian Authority and its police and security services, controlled by the Palestinian Liberation Organization (PLO), would eventually, as the Israelis turned the screw, be forced to turn inwards on their political opponents, principally Hamas. This group was founded in 1987 under the leadership of Sheikh Ahmed Yassin, although organisation's roots lie in the Egyptian Muslim Brotherhood of the earlier period. Sheikh Yassin was assassinated by the Israelis in 2004, however, in its formative days his organisation proved useful for the Israelis. As Pappe writes, 'Hamas...both complicated life for the Israelis and helped them in branding the Palestinian struggle as part of a global anti-Western Islamic force involved in a clash of civilisations.' In truth the emergence of Hamas was principally a domestic phenomenon. 'Yasin and his fellows were able to create a new movement mainly because there was a desperate search for a new national outfit that could deliver salvation where the old ones had failed so abysmally. The secular organisations were considered helpless in finding a way of liberating their homeland'.

As Fida Jiryis, whose father Sabri Jiryis was very close to Yasser Arafat, recalls, 'the Palestinian sovereignty provided for by the [Oslo] accords was a mere façade...Worse, the new Palestinian police force became a tool for security coordination with Israel, trailing and handing over those who engaged in resistance. No one could have imagined such a scenario. Objectors to the new setup found themselves excluded from the jobs and perks of the Authority or imprisoned'. The Palestinians saw that the Oslo Accords could bring neither peace nor freedom. Jiryis writes that 'tensions simmered between the Fateh-dominated Palestinian Authority and Hamas, Israel pressured Arafat to rein in "terrorism", as it termed any act of resistance, and he, though reluctant, often complied'.

Under pressure from the Israeli government to stop armed militant raids inside Israel, the Palestinian police rounded up hundreds of Hamas and Islamic Jihad members. Interrogations, torture, and extrajudicial killings followed. On 18 November 1994, Palestinian police fired on protestors after Friday prayers, killing fourteen people and wounding hundreds. Arafat, faced with this rising threat, doubled down, implementing a policy of 'Preventative Security'. The pressure of these events then set in motion criticism of Arafat within both the PLO and the Fateh movement that he had founded, weakening his internal power base, and making him less and less use to the Israelis in his role in containing Palestinian aspirations. The open prison model thus became a less and less attractive strategy for the Israeli state, which instinctively then turned to extreme violent repression as it had done many times before.

Despite all efforts of the Israeli state to snuff out Palestinian resistance 'the ghettoised community continued to express its zest for life' as Pappe terms it. The First Intifada (1987–1993) protests, civil disobedience characterised by stone-throwing children, had been met with lethal force, as was the SecondIntifada (2000–2005). With the defeat and withdrawal of the IDF in southern Lebanon in 2006, 'the army intensified its punitive policy even more against one and a half million people living in the most densely populated 40 square kilometres on the planet'. Pappe argues that the kind of weapons deployed by Israel in Gaza: '1000-kilo bombs, tanks, missiles, from the air and shelling from the sea against civilian areas – were not intended to deter, wound or warn. They were intended to kill'. This murderous intent met the United Nations Article 2 definition of genocide:

> Genocide means any of the following acts committed with intent to destroy, in whole or in part, a national, ethnical, racial or religious group, as such: Killing members of the group; Causing serious bodily or mental harm to members of the group; Deliberately inflicting on the group conditions of life calculated to bring about its physical destruction in whole or in part.

Gaza, blockaded, besieged, and helpless before Israeli weaponry, was transformed into a maximum-security mega-prison, with the key thrown into the sea. Pappe argues that the period from 2007 onwards, has seen both the consolidation of an open prison on the West Bank continually degraded by creeping settler incursions, and the 'measured genocidal policy' of the closed prison system that the Gaza Strip has become.

REASONING WITH CATASTROPHE

Zain Sardar

On 18 July 2024, five 'Just Stop Oil' activists were handed record sentences for conspiring to orchestrate a daring climate action. Their plan: to block the M25, the London Orbital Motorway, to draw attention to the righteousness of their cause. Climate change – the defining and existential challenge of our times – and the extraction of fossil fuels that continues to accelerate it, in the judgement of the activists, provided the overwhelming moral imperative to act. This was to be 'the biggest disruption in British modern history'. The logic behind this implying that the scale of the action ought to correspond to the enormity of the challenge.

The activists were given lengthy custodial sentences of four to five years each. The severity of the punishment for a peaceful protest is unparalleled in recent British legal history and was decried, perhaps unsurprisingly, by the UN's special rapporteur on environment defenders. The environmental NGO Greenpeace also weighed in, condemning the chilling effect of the judge's verdict and the succour it would give to 'the polluting elite'.

The presiding judge, in affirming his decision, told the defendants upon the conclusion of the two-week trial that, 'you have taken it upon yourselves to decide that your fellow citizens must suffer disruption and harm…simply so that you may parade your views…You have appointed yourselves as the sole arbiters of what should be done about climate change, bound neither by the principles of democracy nor the rule of law'. In response to this judgment, one of the convicted, in a plea to mitigate the length of her sentence, described her actions as an obligation in the face of the real and present threat of runaway greenhouse gas emissions. She explained that 'earth's life-support systems are breaking down due to human activities, whether we believe it or not…I maintain it was a necessity and I stand by my actions as the most effective option available to me'.

Travis Reider, *Catastrophe Ethics: How to be Good in a World Gone Bad*, Duckworth, London, 2024

This case, the crux of which is reflected in the judge's assessment and the defendant's mitigation plea, offers up several salient questions. Foremost amongst these is how we could possibly start to work through the moral reasons for our actions in a world engulfed by multiple, intersecting catastrophes; the paradigmatic case being man-made climate change. Another question arises from the Just Stop Oil activist's firm belief, expressed above, that there was a 'necessity' to act using all available means to address an imminent emergency. One can therefore ask whether there is a duty placed upon all of us as individuals to act in a similar manner? A secondary and related question then presents itself: how do we triage our moral projects in a context of 'First World' complicity in harmful and resource depleting socio-economic structures?

There is also a qualifying concern here, invoked by the judge's rebuke that despite the currency of their cause, the activists had effectively become self-anointed crusaders 'parading' their convictions and sliding into a 'fanaticism' inimical to the public interest. This seems to suggest that they had somehow missed the crucial collective dimension of the ethics required to respond to planetary-scale challenges. In other words, the activist's project had failed to grasp, and accommodate, the pluralism of moral projects amongst the public and the varying degrees of commitment to them (the 'principles of democracy' in the judge's statement on the sentencing).

The pertinent issues raised in the case of the five Just Stop Oil activists are tackled head on by climate change ethicist Travis Reider in *Catastrophe Ethics: How to be Good in a World Gone Bad*. Reider attempts to construct a framework or, perhaps, provide guidance for making collective and individual ethical decisions in a world where the magnitude of the problems confronting humanity can easily unsettle well-meaning people. This endeavour carries greater resonance when traditional moral theories fail to equip us with the supple, ethical decision-making agility required to respond to the catastrophes assailing us.

Sitting at the centre of the author's thesis is a paradox that he calls, somewhat cryptically, 'the Puzzle' — after the fashion of some beguiling spiritual guru leading a meditation session for highly stressed financial executives. The Puzzle refers to the disjuncture that opens up between the very limited, small-scale impact of individual ethical agents and the almost insurmountably large, structural, and planetary-wide problems that rudely confronts humanity. Reider's argument throughout the book — which is blended with some striking and relatable autoethnographic passages as well as a few crude Americanisms, for which we shall forgive him — is that the solution to this mismatch is the revival of a participatory, collective ethics. It is an ethics that must hold steady in a world where many intellectuals, the Marxist philosopher Slavoj Zizek amongst them, have observed that 'it is easier to imagine the end of the world than the end of capitalism'.

The opening chapter gives an indication of what is at stake with the Puzzle. The author is at pains to marshal much of the evidence that points to the reality of climate change in the current geological age many climate change scientists refer to as the Anthropocene, that is, an era defined by humanity's insidious mischief in upsetting the earth's living systems. The science, or climate realism, suggests that CO_2 emissions are contributing to increases in average temperatures above 2 degrees Celsius within the next thirty years. This is ruinous for humanity and the planet by virtue of causing rising sea levels and raising the likelihood of more extreme weather events (not to mention any amplifying feedback loops and the unexpected ramifications that arise from them). There is also the attendant impact this will have on the Global South in generating displaced people, wars over resources, and so forth. This scenario, projected by UN modelling, is reminiscent of a hellscape from Dante's *Inferno*, with much of the gratuitous suffering and none of the poetry.

What, however, makes climate change the ideal demonstration of the dynamics and intricacies of the 'Puzzle'? The answer partially hinges on the derisory nature of a single individual's contribution to CO_2 emissions, as evidenced by Reider. The consequent harms that can be attributed to an individual's carbon footprint are low (even in the Global North), particularly when one bears in mind 70 percent of CO_2 emissions are emitted by the one hundred biggest global companies. One should also factor in that a person's average emissions are a miniscule proportion of our collective carbon budget (the level of emissions permissible to humanity within the constraints of keeping global warming below manageable levels). If individual moral agents do not contribute to the problem at hand in any significant way, we can legitimately query where a subject's moral responsibility comes into play in the collective endeavour to curb climate change.

Much of the moral subtlety that Reider is trying to introduce into these debates invariably seeks to sidestep the polarising nature of discourses around moral duty and structural powerlessness. Hence, his argument, in for example citing the vanishingly small CO_2 emissions of individual people, tries to release the individual from an overweening moral duty that is no respecter of moral pluralism, agency, and personhood.

This argument is also a subset of his critique of both deontological ethics and utilitarianism. It reflects on his willingness to explore a new terrain of practical moral reasoning that captures the insights of these major traditional theoretical redoubts of ethics (the other being virtue ethics) without being reduced to them. Reider is determined not to get sucked into the 'grand theory syndrome' that impels modernist, formulaic responses to a deeply 'textured' moral reality. Finding the right tools for efficacious moral reasoning is more fundamental to living a good life than 'high moral theory' and the distorted lens through which it occasionally peers at the world.

One of the advantages of this turn towards the microworld of moral reasoning could perhaps be to devise a method to deconstruct or dissolve the modern political binary that so dominates public narratives. That is, the dichotomy between the so-called 'virtue signalling' woke brigade on one side, and the reactionary, populist purveyors of cultures wars on the other (MAGA Republicanism a mind-boggling variant of this). Indeed, most of the 'demos' would fail to identify with either side of this (artificially constructed?) divide but would arguably remain committed to an authentic engagement with the challenges of our time in ways that feels and seems empowering.

It is also worth very briefly mentioning Reider's analysis of utilitarianism in relation to the influence still exerted by the 'master discipline' of macroeconomics on world affairs. The 'moral mathematics', in Reider's phraseology, of utility seems to be perfectly aligned with an economics that envisages GDP growth as the holy grail of development in the Global South. I shall return to this point below.

One of Reider's main targets in *Catastrophe Ethics* is Utilitarianism. As a school of thought it is variant of consequentialism, or the moral theory that dictates the most important consideration in making ethical decisions is the outcome of actions. One of the most celebrated utilitarian thinker and proponents of this theory - as well as serial deployer of thought experiments that seeks to justify altruistic actions - is Australian moral philosopher, Peter Singer. Reider admires and cites Singer, author of the influential book *Animal Liberation*, as an inspiration in his own work. But Singer's high-fidelity ethics imposes a weighty moral burden on individuals to make choices that increase the overall welfare and wellbeing of humanity – for example, giving all excess resources to charity as this maximises the overall wellbeing of people.

The underlying issue, as with consequentialism in general, is that the utilitarian moral calculus treats individuals with little dignity (a critique made with great acuity by the late English philosopher Bernard Williams), undermining our autonomy in ordering and sorting moral projects – one of the key driving forces of ethical agency. It is a fascinating point of comparison that the same critique can be levelled at development economics. Both the moral theory and the abstract forces of classical economics (some of which has its grounding in the ethical theories of Adam Smith) impose from a distance (in the same way that gravity is described by classical physicists as a force acting at a distance) and fetishise metric-based decision making (game theory being the most recent manifestations of this).

Deontological ethics, which emphasises the relationship between duty and the morality of human actions, fairs little better. Inadvertent recourse to deontological rubrics from climate change activists such as the Just Stop Oil protestor may fall into the 'narrative trap' of legitimising these high moral theories. We see this with the darling of climate activism, Greta Thunberg, who frequently frames the fight against climate change in moral language, using the parlance of duty, betrayal, and the importance of building on moral foundations. This certainly tells us something - and aligns with many – of our moral intuitions.

Nonetheless, this approach to theoretical ethics privileges duty regardless of outcome. Hence, duties such as keeping promises that conform to some universal rule ought to be adhered to despite circumstances in which the immediate outcome leads to harm. Duty-bound imperatives, while undoubtedly compelling, suffer the fate of downplaying the active role of moral rationality in ethical subjects, once again minimising the autonomy of moral actors. Moreover, duty-based obligations appear heavy handed and lack the suppleness of a more nuanced exercise of moral reasoning.

The foundation of a participatory, collective ethics, in Reider's view, is then affirming the heterogeneity and integrity of moral personhood. Both consequentialism and deontological ethics fall foul of this prerequisite. We ought to, Reider suggests, refuse to be drawn up the narrow, steep, and weed laden paths of these ethical theories. Instead, we should continue onwards to reach the accessible upland in front of us, and peer out over the cliff edge into an immensely rich moral universe, brimming with contending reasons to act ethically.

Moral reasons provide motivations to act one way or another, and we encounter many of them daily. They are worthy of deliberation but do not amount to ethical obligations. This is, it would seem to me, a sensible way to conceive ethics, at a point in world history where moral purity is negated from the outset by our complicity in a highly interconnected global system, lubricated through rapid information flows and complex supply chains.

Leading an ethical life today would appear a most daunting prospect. The atomism of Western societies privileges an ethics caught between the attempt to completely withdraw from systems of harm and a browbeaten zombie state of listless indifference. In an involuted world that regularly leads one to feelings of cognitive overload, the complexity and superabundance of contending moral causes can, much of the time, congeal into disorientation and paralysis. One only has to mention but a few of the current protracted crises to accentuate the point: the civil war in Sudan, the continuing Israel-Palestine conflict, the escalating violence over resources in Democratic Republic of Congo. Disorientation is undoubtedly a true postmodern condition. And it is heightened by the way in which neoliberal forms of capitalism appropriates its own critique – the iconic Che Guevara image appearing on a mass-produced t-shirt, the Banksy graffiti taken and sold to a private art collector!

To expand on this point, capitalism is said to actively perform and parade the discontentment it produces. This is a phenomenon that induces what the late cultural theorist Mark Fisher referred to as 'interpassivity'. The notion can be rendered explicable through reference to cultural forms such as Hollywood blockbusters. For instance, the Disney film *Wall-E* – which depicts a ravaged, polluted and waste filled future vision of Earth – in Fisher's opinion self-gratifyingly derides the excesses of capitalism while rendering the intended audience of this message passive. Put otherwise, capitalism can offer up the simulacrum of change and critique in a manner that strips the consumers of it of all incentive to translate it into reality.

Interpassivity of moral participants at a time of catastrophes – and these, beyond climate change, Reider identifies as structural racism, pandemics, and so on – is, needless to say, highly concerning. In the absence of a foundation built upon the dead ends of moral duties and utilitarian formulas, Reider's practical approach depends on alternative tools and heuristics ('mid-level principles' taken from methods deployed by bioethics: maxims and general rules that one adopts to live by) that operates across a broad spectrum of moral reasons, and not simply just at the edges.

Hence, a new moral perception and sensitivity is needed to replace the calculus of moral abstractions. Moral reasons to act on some issue must respect a plurality of moral projects by requiring an assessment of competing reasons that may militate against them - which can be mundane but meaningful, for example having to spend time with family, having limited financial resources. These reasons can span different spheres of action, such as at the individual behavioural level (trying to limit one's harm), the social, and the structural (advocacy, protest, policy change). The evidential strength of these reasons to act in one way or another can also vary in relation to the force of competing reasons not to.

Through all of this, we must not lose sight of the reality that we are still called upon to justify the decisions that we make in our lives. The respect owed to the pluralism of moral projects does not in any way protect us from legitimate scrutiny of our actions and ostracization by others in the moral community. This is despite Reider's ethical heuristics being shaped around protecting our ability to commit to personal moral projects, even when at times they may clash with the need to respond to catastrophic challenges.

An intriguing example he raises is the case of procreation. Procreation is an enormous contributor to climate change, and hence one of the biggest life decisions that one will make in a world actively and acutely being reconfigured by climate change. Many ethicists have made the argument that adoption would be the most ethical way of assuming parenthood, one that neatly rescues another life from the jaws of disadvantage while minimising one's own carbon footprint. Nonetheless, Reider defends the substantive moral project of creating new life as an intimate and highly meaningful one, worthy of the veil of dignity. It is a project in which moral autonomy is sacrosanct.

Reider does not, however, intend to let anyone off the hook. He does not capitulate to a form of relativism that would only serve to further the 'utopian project of capitalism', in the words of the American art theorist Jonathan Crary. The point is that as no one can completely withdraw from the system (Crary states that not even sleep can act, as it once did, as sublime respite from the monstrous restlessness of a twenty-four-hour neoliberal capitalism), we are given plenty of moral reasons to act, including participating collectively to instigate structural reform.

Acting as a moral participant is integral to a meaningful life: disentangling the ethical messiness of one's own life is a substantive project that will actively engage the full powers of our moral reasoning. The question is whether Reider's confidence in moral rationality can be justified. Certainly, catastrophes such as climate change and systemic racism furnish us with exceedingly potent reasons for action, both individual and collective. These demand due consideration, and through sustained processes of deliberation, the idea is that we ought to enrich our own lives profoundly. The myriad moral reasons that trigger moments of introspection furnish us with their 'own abundant reality'.

We must therefore find ways to make our own meaningful contributions to solving the collective challenges facing humanity in the context of reasonable degrees of pluralism. But within the autonomy that we exercise, lurks a chastening reminder of the stakes involved as we edge ever closer to catastrophe.

QUR'ANIC RENDERINGS

Shamim Miah

The first Muslim representative to the US Congress was elected in 2007. During the ceremonial oath to office, Democrat Keith Ellison, who converted to Islam at the age of nineteen, used Thomas Jefferson's personal copy of George Sale's 1734 translation of the Qur'an, *Alcoran of Mohammad*. The translation, which resides at Rare Books and Special Collection Division of the Library of Congress, is one of over 6,000 titles transferred from Jefferson's private collection to the Congress Library. As an avid reader and true bibliophile, Jefferson had purchased Sale's *Alcoran* in 1765 from the Virginia Gazette, the local newspaper in Williamsburg and the only book shop in the colony. There is some scholarly debate over whether Sale's translation held at the Library of Congress is the personal copy of Jefferson, or was his personal copy destroyed in his house-fire along with his valuable collection of books and papers.

George Sale was an eighteenth-century Anglican lawyer. His translation was commissioned by the Society for Promoting Christian Knowledge, and published in two-volumes. The first volume consists mainly of 'preliminary discourse' which provides an outline of the history of the formative years of Islam. Whilst the latter part of volume one and two include the translation of the 'Koran' with detailed footnotes and commentary. Sale in his introductory remark's captures the essence of the translation: 'I have thought myself obliged, indeed…to keep somewhat scrumptiously close to the text; by which the language may, in some places, seem to express the Arabic a little too literally to be the elegant English'. This is clear from the following rendition of the Surah al-Fatihah:

> Praise be to God, the Lord of all creatures; the most merciful, the king of the day of judgment. Thee do we worship, and of thee do we beg assistance. Direct us in the right way, in the way of those to whom thou hast been gracious; not those against whom thou art incensed, nor those who go astray.

Combing through the Sale's translation and footnotes it is evidently clear that Sale had a working knowledge of the both the orientalist and the Muslim Qur'anic exegesis. Whilst Sale had a good command of the Arabic language, he relied mainly on the Latin translation of the Qur'an published in 1698 by Father Lewis Maracci. The principle laid out by the Latin translation of the Qur'an as early as twelfth century by Robert of Ketton provided a format for future Qur'an translations. Despite the influence of Latin in the European translation movement, many historians have questioned the theological and political motivations behind translating the Qur'an into High Latin – the language of high cosmopolitan culture for advanced Catholic theology. The objective behind Sale's translation was to convert Muslim's to Protestant Christianity whilst 'reminding' the devoted Christian reader that 'Alcoran' was the works of 'Muhammad' and that Islam was a 'false religion'. Despite the flaws within Sale's translation, it had a profound impact throughout Europe as it was reprinted four times during the eighteenth century and was further translated into various European languages including Dutch, French, German, and Russian. Bruce Lawrence in *The English Koran: A Biography* describes the Sale translation 'as the longest lasting, most popular and influential English translation'. He further argues that for the most English readers of the eighteenth and the nineteenth century, it was 'the Qur'an of record'.

Sales's translation wasn't the only translation of the Qur'an. In fact, as early as 1649, Alexander Ross, a chaplain to King Charles I, translated the Qur'an into English. Ross having no access to the Arabic language used the French translation by Andre du Ryer published in 1647. Since Sale's 'Alcoran of Mohammad' there has been several translations of the Qur'an into the English language. Another noteworthy work is that of Rev. R.J. Rodwell's translation published in 1861. The challenging feature of this translation is that it re-arranges the verses based upon chronological order of revelation. Rodwell's translation titled *The Koran: Translated from the Arabic, the Suras arranged in chronological order with notes* was widely used and circulated especially given that it was reissued as part of the Everyman's Library series beginning in 1909. Both Sale's and Rodwell's translation was based upon the orientalist assumption that the Qur'an was not divinely inspired, rather it was the 'work of Muhammad'.

It would be another eighty years before Abdullah Yusuf Ali, an Indian British barrister, would publish, in 1937, his *The Holy Qur'an: Text Translation and Commentary*. This was followed by Muhamad Marmaduke Pickthall, a novelist and a Muslim convert, who translated *The Meaning of the Holy Qur'an* in 1939. Both translations would have an important status within the English-speaking Muslim diaspora. However, the Yusuf Ali translation would be marred by controversy, especially following the 'orthodox' edits, changes and erasing of most of Yusuf Ali's footnotes at the request of the Saudi patrons of Yusuf Ali's American publishers – Amana. The overt political influences on the Qur'an translation would further impact the crucial and novel translation of the Qur'an by the celebrated scholar-adventurer Muhammad Asad, a Jewish convert to Islam. The distinguishing features of Asad's *The Message of the Qur'an* (1980) lies in the unique idiomatic and rationalist translation of the Qur'an by using al-Zamakhshari's twelfth-century linguistic approach to the Qur'anic exegeses.

M.A.R Habib and Bruce B. Lawrence, *The Qur'an: A Verse Translation*, W.W. Norton & Company, New York and London, 2024.

Recently, there has been a resurgence in the field of Qur'an translation in the English language. *The Study Qur'an: A New Translation and Commentary* (2017), published by Harper-Collins, has attracted much heated debate and discussions, with allegations and rejections of the guiding features of the manufactured philosophy of perennialism within its translation. *The Study Qur'an* is a product of a team effort, with four editors, all of whom are specialists in Islamic Studies and sufism (Joseph Lumbard, Maria Massi Dakake, Caner Dagli, and Mohammad Rustom) taking the duty of translating different parts of the Qur'an, with Syed Hossein Nasr, leader of the little-known tariqa Marayama, as the overall editor-in-chief. *The Study Qur'an*, an ecumenical project, attempts to bring together both Sunni and Shiite tradition with the dominant theological creeds. The translators use a total of forty-one classical *Tafasir's* to provide detailed commentary through its multiple footnotes. Majority of commentaries were written before the fourteenth century, with Ibn Ashur and Muhammad Husayn Tabatabai being the most recent (both authors having died in the twentieth century). Each of the verses of the Qur'an includes detailed lines of commentary, the Surah al-Fatihah (The Opening) has over six pages of commentary.

More recent noteworthy translations include the much accessible, *The Qur'an: A New Translation* by M A S Abdel Haleem (2005) and *The Majestic Qur'an* by Musharaf Hussain (2020). This was followed by the much-anticipated Qur'an translation by the Jordanian based American Sufi and author, Sheikh Nuh Keller, *The Qur'an Behold: An English Translation from the Arabic* (2022).

Any reader familiar with the history of Qur'anic studies would recognise the complex theological debates associated with translating the Qur'an. The late Fazlur Rahman reminds us in an article titled *'Translating the Qur'an'* that one of the key debates within Qur'anic studies is associated with the 'inimitability' of the *Qur'an*. The text describes itself as absolute, inimitable and uniquely *Arabic-Qur'an* — in the opening verses of Surah Yusuf - 'these are the verses of the clear book. We have sent it as an Arabic Qur'an' (12:1-2). Whilst all translations are attempts at understanding the divine text revealed in the Arabic language, certain scholars have argued, including Abu Hanifa one of the founders of the Sunni school of thought, that the inimitability of Qur'an lies in its *meaning* and not in its *language*. Indeed, some of the early scholars were reluctant in translating or encouraging people to read the Qur'an in any other language. They argue that any attempt at translating the Qur'an presents an *interpretation* or the translator(s) *attempt* at capturing the meaning of the text. The Qur'an, unlike any other scriptures is more than a literary text; whilst the Qur'an refers to itself as the *al-Kitab*, or as the Book, it is more than *a book,* in the conventional literary sense. More crucially, the Qur'an is an *oral* text before it is a *written* text. Muslim communities embody this tradition through *reciting* the Qur'an in prayer and worship or as part of their daily religious rituals. The hadith tradition reminds us that the Qur'an isn't only meant to be recited and read — in fact it should be *embodied*. The Qur'an as an embodied tradition is clearly articulated in the hadith associated with Aisha when she described the Prophet 'as the walking Qur'an.' This embodied tradition of the Qur'an whereby Muslims *express* cultural symbols, *represent* ethical practice, whilst aiming to *behave* according to religious codes. The Qur'an plays a significant role in the intellectual traditions within Muslim societies, but more so in the West African tradition as highlighted by the

Harvard scholar of Islamic studies, Ousmane Kane, and more recently by the Muslim academic Rudolph Ware, in *The Walking Qur'an: Islamic Education, Embodied Knowledge and the History of West Africa.*

Capturing the oral beauty of the Qur'an has been one of the key challenges of translating the Qur'an. As Ziauddin Sardar reminds us in *Reading the Quran* (2011), 'sound plays an important in the structure of the Qur'an. Before it was a written text, the Qur'an existed as sound: this is why it has been compared to as an epic poem'. Trying to capture the sound of the Qur'an presents a formidable challenge to the translator.

It is a challenge, M.A.R Habib, a renowned scholar of English literature, and Bruce Lawrence, highly respected academic and scholar of Islamic studies, take head on. Albeit with a degree of humility and modesty. They note that Qur'an is more than a conventional book; it's an expression of God's spoken message. The goal, they suggest, is nothing short of trying to hear a faint echo of God speaking – a task which is humanly impossible but nevertheless a responsibility. The product of their ten year's labour, *The Qur'an: A Verse Translation* (2024), is published by W.W. Norton and Company. This is the third Qur'an project published by W.W. Norton; the early projects include *The Qur'an: A Norton Critical Edition* (2017) and the much-acclaimed translation by the American artist, Sandow Birk titled *American Qur'an* (2015).

In addition to being a collaboration between a poet and an Arabist, *The Qur'an: A Verse Translation* uses an *accentual verse* for translation. It is an attempt to capture the various modes (or *tilawat*) of the Qur'an, through the deployment of *Saj*, the distinctive rhymed and rhythmic prose of the Sacred Text. So, the reader can appreciate the melodic beauty of the Qur'an in the English language, thus capturing the rhythm, prose, ascent, and metre – as exemplified in the beautiful recitation of the Senegalese Qur'an reciter, Sheikh Muhammad Hadi Toure. The first challenge the translators faced was *how* to capture the rhythmic prose of the Arabic into the English language – especially given that the Qur'an is 'as much an oral text as a written one'? The second obstacle was how does one navigate the deeply poetic character of the Qur'an with the categorical rejection of the text as a work of poetry? As seen in several Qur'anic verses (26:224; 52:30; 69:41), including the following opening verse of Surah Ya Sin (36:69), the Qur'an categorically rejects its poetic status:

We have not taught poetry
to the Prophet, nor is it fitting for him
This is nothing but a reminder
and a clear Qur'an.

Most Qur'anic commentators, including the thirteenth-century Andalusian polymath Qurtubi, Maliki jurist and the author of *al-Jami' li-ahkam al-Qur'an*, rejected the accusation that the Prophet was merely a poet. Prior to the advent of Islam, it was argued that a poet *(Sha-'ir)*, was a person who composed verse and also belonged to supernatural fraternity including 'madmen' and soothsayers, who had the ability to 'communicate' through the medium of the Jinn's with the forces of the unseen world. It was widely accepted, in the so-called 'Age of Ignorance', the pre-Islamic period, that the imaginative powers of the poets were somehow associated with the unseen realm. Responding to the claim that the Prophet Muhammad was mere 'poet', the Qur'an tells the listeners in Surah Tur (52:29):

So, remind them, Prophet –
for, by the grace of your Lord
you are neither a soothsayer
nor a madman.

Whilst the Qur'an detaches itself from the works of poetry, it is clear to anyone who has recited or listened to the Qur'an in Arabic that it has a distinguishable formal beauty which reflects the highest poetic eloquence. It is also critical to note that the cultural connotations of poets within pre-Islamic Arabia does not resonate within the contemporary features or functions of a poet. For example, according to Fakhr al-Din al-Razi, the thirteenth-century author of *Tafsir al Kabir*, pre-Islamic poets would often verbally mocked or harassed people through their spoken word.

Habib and Lawrence recognise that 'not only is the Qur'an aesthetical and musical in nature, but its meaning is inseparable from its sound. Its sound is more poetic than prosaic, even in the later legislative Medinan suras'. The underpinning point of translating the Qur'an through prose, is based upon the recognition that the Qur'an is *not* a work of poetry; indeed, it is *more* than poetry. In order to capture the beauty of the Qur'an, the translators use the established principle, of *saj;* whilst *saj* is often translated into English as 'rhymed prose', it is important to state that this loose translation fails to capture the complex and sophisticated role *saj* plays in the Qur'an. To fully appreciate the firm foundation of the *Qur'an: A Verse Translation,* one has to have an appreciation of the underpinning recent scholarly work around *saj* in the academic literature. In particular, the recent works of Marianna Klar, in her much-cited essay, 'Preliminary Catalogue of Qur'anic Saj' Techniques: Beat Patterning, Parallelism and Rhyme', which appears in her book 2021 book, *Structural Dividers in the Qur'an.* Drawing upon the works of the medieval rhetorician, Ibn al-Athir, who argued that 'majority of the Qur'an is in saj, including the Qur'an's rhetorical features are also informed by the rules of saj. Indeed, Klar uses detailed analysis of Ibn Athir's work to demonstrate 'the omnipresence of saj in the Qur'an'.

A clear example of how both Habib and Lawrence use saj is provided through the opening verse of Surah al-Duha (Surah 93). Surah al-Duha is a relatively short Surah with only eleven verses. It is an early Makkan Surah, said by the early commentators to be fourth, or seventh, verse to be revealed within the chronological order of revelation. The surah responds to the momentary pause (some maintain it was twelve days others say it could be up-to-fifty days) in the early revelation. A group of Meccans declared, 'surely Muhammad's lord has forsaken him and despised him'. Responding to this, Surah al-Duha was revealed, to reassure the Prophet. The underpinning message of this surah is the overall hope, consolation, and God's providence given to the believers.

There is a great deal of variation in how the title of the surah, al-Duha, is itself translated. We can read it as 'The Morning Brightness' (Abul Haleem and Nasr), 'Blazing Morning' (Sheikh Nuh), and 'Glorious Morning Light' (Muhammad Ali). Lawrence and Habib's chose to use 'Morning Light', which in my opinion, captures the essence of the surah. After all, it deals with the light of rising sun, or as Ibn Kathir maintains, *al-Duha* refers to way the light of the sun illuminates the whole day. Other commentaries, such as al-Qurtubi (1272) seek to extend 'light' to reference the whole of creation. Anyway, here is the surah:

Wa-l-duha

first *saj* unit: one beat by the morning light

Wa-l-layli / idha / saja

second *saj* unit: three beats by the night/when/it is still

Ma /wadd 'aka/ rabbuka /wa-ma /qala
third *saj* unit: five beats not/ abandoned you /your Lord
And not / abhor

In order to capture the above verse by using the relative lengths of the three units in English, Lawrence and Habib offer the following rendition, which has the ability to capture the rhythmic beauty.

> By the morning light
> in its brilliance
> by the darkening night
> in its stillness
> your Lord has not abandoned you,
> nor is He abhorring [you].

To appreciate the beauty of Lawrence's and Habib's translation it is helpful to offer a comparison with other translations of the same verse in the English language. For example, following verse taken from *The Quran: A New Introduction* by Abdel Haleem doesn't capture the rhythmic prose of Surah Duha.

> By the morning brightness, and by the night when it grows still, your Lord has not forsaken you [Prophet], nor does He hate you.

The Qur'an: A Verse Translation is not going to be the last Qur'an in the English language. But it is truly a monumental achievement. It has undoubtably made a significant contribution to an already rich compendium of translations, especially given its focus on capturing the poetical and rhythmic beauty of the *Qu'ran* through the richness of the English language. Perhaps one of the many lasting features of *The Qur'an: A Verse Translation* will be the broader cultural contributions that will allow Muslims to *think* Islamically in the English language.

ET CETERA

ON TRANSFORMATIVE JUSTICE

Naomi Foyle

In the context of genocide, language, as scholars of the Holocaust have taught us, disintegrates.

Chantal Kalisa

If there must be a last word on the inexpressible trauma of genocide, 'justice', surely, is a strong contender. Yet how can a crime of unfathomable magnitude, one that divides and destroys whole nations, leaving countless survivors suffering lifelong grief and pain, ever truly be redressed? Must we not concur with the eloquent conclusion of Zarir Merat, head of mission at Avocats Sans Frontières: 'genocide is too heavy for the shoulders of justice'?

In a profound sense, yes. The horror and scale of genocide mitigates against an adequate legal response and, for many survivors, can crush all sense of faith in other people – a faith that, once pulverised, may never be reconstituted. After genocide, the moral scales can never be rebalanced. Still, though, supported by collective recognition, human beings have a remarkable capacity to heal from even the most terrible of wounds. And from early cuneiform tablets to the Nuremberg Charter, the rule of law represents a vital curb on authoritarian power without which the world would be entirely prey to war lords and bad actors. At the very least, our inherent human sense of fairness demands some kind of juridical response to mass human rights violations. Perhaps the best we can say, for now, is that through the limited successes and obvious failures of attempts to respond effectively to genocide, our concept of earthly justice is slowly evolving to become less imperfect.

The crime of genocide clearly calls for retributive justice. Leaders of the violence must be punished, warning other political and military figures that mandating this worst of crimes will have personal consequences. Since Nuremberg various types of courts, from the International Criminal Court (ICC) to International Tribunals and national courts, have emerged as forums for trying the generals and foot soldiers of genocide; and, at the International Court of Justice (ICJ), of holding states to account. While most people would wish to see leaders capable of inspiring entire societies to commit unmitigated evil safely behind bars, if not executed, such trials are not without their detractors. From the proto-genocide Nuremberg trials to the current South African-led ICJ case against Israel's actions in Gaza, genocide prosecutions are routinely criticised as cynical exercises in bias and 'victor's justice', or hopelessly flawed utopian projects, utterly inadequate to the scale of the task. Not just Nazis and their lawyers have noticed that Allied powers had clearly committed criminal acts under the Nuremberg charter yet were spared prosecution. The ICC took fourteen years to open an investigation outside Africa. And even when convictions themselves cannot be argued with, most perpetrators escape justice. Only 140,000 of the estimated 200,000 Nazi perpetrators have been brought to trial, a process resulting in under 7,000 convictions. In twenty-two years, the ICC has issued eleven convictions and four acquittals. The ICJ will likely take ten years to decide if Israel's currently on-going assault on Gaza constitutes genocide, and its interim ruling did not halt the killings.

Even if one could convict all offenders, however, punishment alone cannot deliver the kind of justice that many people feel is required, not just to pay for a crime, but to ensure that a cycle of violence is not repeated. When it comes to genocide, thanks in good part to the example set by the South African Truth and Reconciliation Commission (TRC), a courts-based inquiry into the crimes of the apartheid era, modern nations have largely settled on a post-conflict legal framework based on principles of restorative justice – defined by TRC chairperson Archbishop Desmond Tutu as a process mainly concerned 'with correcting imbalances, restoring broken relationships, with healing, harmony and reconciliation'. There were pragmatic reasons for this approach. Tutu was convinced that in South Africa's still volatile situation of a military stalemate, Nuremberg-type trials of political leaders would have resulted in a bloodbath. But there was also an underlying humanist ethos at work. Established to implement the Promotion of National Unity and Reconciliation Act No 34 of 1995, the TRC was founded on the belief that:

> the telling of the truth about past gross human rights violations, as viewed from different perspectives, facilitates the process of understanding our divided pasts, whilst the public acknowledgement of 'untold suffering and injustice' (Preamble to the Act) helps to restore the dignity of victims and afford perpetrators the opportunity to come to terms with their own past.

Adam Sitze, Professor of Law, Jurisprudence and Social Thought at Amherst College, Massachusetts, calls this faith in 'truth-telling' a largely Western belief, and not substantiated by evidence, a point I will return to later. Tutu, however, declared that Act No 34 was founded in the spirit of the African concept of ubuntu – 'togetherness'. Accepted by many South Africans, the TRC implemented its aims through three subcommittees: the Amnesty Committee, granting amnesty to perpetrators if full disclosure was made of an illegal act committed for a political purpose, proportionate to its aims; the Human Rights Violations Committee, which invited victims to testify; and the Reparation and Rehabilitation Committee, which recommended ways to provide 'fair and adequate compensation' to victims – a right denied them by the amnesty process – and to rehabilitate hurt communities, including reintegrating perpetrators into the social fold.

The validity and success of this approach remains hotly contested. As Annelies Verdoolaege, cultural memory expert from Ghent University, observes, from the outset, prominent South African political actors felt the TRC was biased – either toward the ANC or the National Party government. Many victims felt badly let down by the amnesty provisions, including the loss of the right to pursue their own cases: the family of murdered anti-apartheid activist Steve Biko filed a constitutional challenge against the TRC on these grounds. And though Tutu stressed the importance of reparations to a 'victim-centred' restorative justice process, reparation and rehabilitation efforts fell far short of expectations. Above all, the TRC was widely seen to have failed at its central task of truth-telling. Apartheid-era government records had been destroyed. Perpetrators lied, or told half-truths, or simply didn't turn up. According to Michael Ignatieff, 'all the truth commission could achieve was to reduce the number of lies that can be circulated unchallenged in public discourse'. In its defence, however, the TRC never believed it could deliver perfect justice, stating that it saw its role as 'kick starting' the process of reconciliation. In her close study of the Human Rights Violation Committee, Verdoolaege argues that its work did facilitate some powerful individual experiences of feeling heard and valued, even of genuine reconciliation; and cites scholars who argue that through the establishment of a 'collective memory' the TRC created a shared national identity that had not previously existed between black and white South Africans.

Distinguishing post conflict programmes from restorative justice approaches to more ordinary crimes, the international framework of 'transitional justice' has now emerged. This approach too has its critics. Sitze argues that the field's focus on moving forward obscures the hidden dependence of the TRC's concept of 'amnesty' on historical colonial practices of indemnity, which excused the occupier's violence on the basis that it was necessary to 'maintain order'. The academic field is also narrow in other ways, its mainstream proponents excluding cases of established democracies contending with their colonial legacies. Colin Luoma, human rights lecturer at Brunel University, challenges this view when he defines Canada's National Inquiry into Missing and Murdered Indigenous Women and Girls (2016–2019) as a transitional justice project, arguing that both the Inquiry, and Canada's preceding Truth and Reconciliation Commission (2007–2015) – which investigated the state's notorious residential school system – are signs of Canada's attempt to transition 'from a violent and unjust relationship with indigenous peoples to one that is at least less violent and more just'. The MMIWG Inquiry had a broad mandate to investigate historical and current crimes and concluded that Canada's epidemic of violence against First Nations women and girls was an ongoing 'race, identity and gender-based genocide'. Luoma praises the Inquiry for foregrounding the issues of cultural harm and structural violence, which mainstream transitional justice programmes sideline in favour of redressing discrete civil and political rights violations. Thus far, however, the Canadian government has not demonstrated a keen commitment to meaningful change. As the Assembly of First Nations reports, the Inquiry's two hundred and thirteen Calls for Justice – addressing eighteen areas in need of reform, including education, policing, and health – have largely met with inaction. As of 2024, only two had been completed and over half had not been started. Of the ninety-four Calls to Action made by Canada's TRC, only thirteen had been completed and eighteen had not been started – at which rate it will take fifty-eight years to implement them all.

A more conventional transitional justice process was the Rwandan response to its 1994 genocide, in which up to a million Tutsis, politically moderate Hutus, and long marginalised Twa people were slaughtered in one hundred days by Hutu militias, other Hutus and some Tutsis and Twa – a proportion of the civilians joining in to save their own lives. Post genocide justice in the country is controlled by the country's new government, the Tutsi-dominated Rwandan Patriotic Front, led since 2000 by Paul Kagame. Retributive justice was delivered in the nineties via an International Criminal Tribunal, which tried the leaders, and by the National Courts, which judged the most serious crimes – including some cases of rape. But the legal system was in ruins, many judges and lawyers had been killed, and at the turn of the millennium, over 100,000 genocide detainees remained in prison at a huge cost to the country's coffers. Deeming a national truth commission culturally inappropriate, Kagame repurposed the country's traditional gacaca courts (pronounced ga-cha-cha) to try perpetrators in their local communities, offering to halve their sentences if they publicly confessed and asked for forgiveness in front of their neighbours. As Lars Waldorf, Professor of Law at Northumbria University, elaborates, despite this emphasis on national customs, in practice and in its slogan – 'Inkiko Gacaca: Ukuri, Ubutabera, Ubwiyunge' ('Gacaca Courts: Truth, Justice, Reconciliation') – gacaca functioned very much within the mainstream transitional justice model, and was largely resented by the very people it was supposed to serve.

That is not to say the process was worthless. Survivor Rose Marie Mukamwiza believed that gacaca does do some good. The trials of the accused sometimes provide information about where and how people were killed, and where their bodies were dumped'. And, as in South Africa, some individuals did find peace and reconciliation during the process, or at least believed it was necessary to prevent another 'storm'. But gacaca's flaws were manifold. To start with, participation was mandatory, meaning peasant Rwandans who could barely afford to eat were punished if they missed gacaca to work in their fields. Partisanship was obvious: although ethnic categories had been officially abolished, Tutsis were now all considered survivors, Hutus potential perpetrators, with no consideration for individual experiences or for the Twa. This arrangement meant that no government soldiers could be tried. Many rape cases, although classed as among the most serious – ended up being tried in gacaca by non-professional judges who could not be relied upon to maintain confidentiality. Other basic norms of justice also suffered, as poorly trained and badly compensated judges, forced to quickly process a high number of cases, did not allow sufficient examination or cross-examination of witnesses, and, according to Waldorf, 'rarely set forth their reasoning and evidentiary findings'. As in South Africa, survivors were not permitted to pursue compensation from perpetrators – many of whom were insolvent in any case. Instead, reparations were made from the FARG (Genocide Survivors Assistance Fund), a fund into which all Rwandans – including victims – contribute through their taxes. Over the years FARG has been charged with embezzlement, corruption, and shoddy construction of the houses it built for survivors. Ultimately, Waldorf concludes, the goals of truth and reconciliation were not only not served but actively undermined by gacaca.

According to Waldorf, and bolstering Sitz's criticisms of the South African TRC, the palpable lack of truth telling in gacaca was evident in silence, lies, score-settling, contested testimony, insincere requests for forgiveness, and local micropolitics including pacts in which a person was paid to confess to others' crimes. This lack of cooperation, partly stemming from natural human fear of punishment or desire for revenge, was compounded by Rwanda's long acknowledged 'culture of secrecy', a pervasive sense of mistrust expressed in ways including refusals to respond verbally to authority figures, and a preference for living in scattered houses rather than villages. Deciding to arrive at truth in this context was a convenient expediency. As for reconciliation, Waldorf claims 'gacaca did not just fail to reconcile; it actually made it more difficult, as the uneasy coexistence among neighbours was up-ended by accusations and counteraccusations' – and, in fact, the murders of hundreds of survivors and witnesses during the trials.

This sobering conclusion is substantiated by the research of Susan Tomson, who built trust with thirty-seven Rwandan peasants and documented their individual acts of resistance to the RPF project of 'national unity and reconciliation', which most perceived as a form of 'social control'. National Mourning Week, for example, obliges Rwandans to engage in public displays of grief for only Tutsi victims, which many Hutu and Twa survivors resent, and Tutsi survivors can find humiliating. Survivors are not permitted to bury their dead, victims' bodies having been dug up and reburied in official cemeteries, which are kept locked, or even cost money to enter. At one of the reburial ceremonies, Séraphine, a Twa survivor, defied this edict by:

> Sneaking a bone. A big bone, like my husband had. The official looked away, and I grabbed it and hid it in my skirt. My friend helped me because we knew that I could go to prison or worse for grabbing a bone. She distracted him, and I grabbed it.

Séraphine gained a small measure of peace by burying the stranger's femur on her land, planting a banana tree to disguise the grave. Other survivors remain deeply embittered. One Hutu man complained he had dutifully attended the new ingando reeducation camps only to be 'left to rot'. Many Rwandans also resent being forbidden their own ethnicity. Ethnicity being inferable in other ways, including the place of registration of one's ID card, this governmental decision does nothing to allay Hutu suspicions that innocent Hutus are being denounced and punished to keep the RPF in power.

Ultimately, Tomson concludes, 'justice' in post genocide Rwanda mainly serves the interests of the political upper classes – a national unity project for a one-party state, in which impoverished survivors must sacrifice their wellbeing for the benefit of the urban elite. The RPF has appropriated peasants' land and in 2006 made it mandatory to wear covered shoes in city centres, meaning most rural people are unable to come to the state-sponsored markets that are now the only legal venue for their wares. 'Reconciliation is for people who can afford to eat' said her interviewee Espérance, while Béatha was hopeful of national unity, but wondered, 'is it really peace if I can't take care of my kids?' Challenging not just the RPF, but the founding principle of restorative justice, Thomas believed that reconciliation would only be possible if 'the government stops telling us to tell our truth. We [Hutu and Tutsi] need time to heal'.

If retributive, restorative, and transitional justice are all deeply compromised processes, then how might the global community better address the crime of genocide? Answers lie in expanding the remit of transitional justice beyond the narrow frame of civil and political rights, to include economic, social, and cultural rights (ESCR). States repeatedly reaffirm all human rights to be 'indivisible', but in practice often neglect ESCR – to the peril of justice. In relation to genocide, Tomson observes that true reconciliation is impossible when people feel constrained to say what they think their economic benefactors – be that the state or a 'charitable' neighbour – want to hear. And while reconciliation must involve some degree of trust, evidence exists that economic inequality actively generates mistrust: political scientist Eric Uslaner, as cited by Marek Kohn, found that economic equality 'is the most important social determinate of trust ... a cause of trust, not just an association'. But in national justice processes run by elites, true economic justice is wholly absent and what social justice exists is generally delivered through poorly or unfunded grassroots organisations, such as the Rwandan widows groups that sprang up to provide mutual aid to women left struggling with physical and emotional wounds, homelessness, childcare, and high rates of HIV infection. As for cultural rights – which 'promote, protect and preserve the rights of individuals and communities to develop and maintain their cultural identities and practices' – these are generally invisible in transitional justice models, and, indeed, as Luoma observes, due to their supposed 'definitional ambiguity' are 'overlooked and underdeveloped' in most human rights instruments.

Cultural rights, however, figure prominently in The UN Declaration of the Rights of Indigenous Peoples. As Canada's MMIWG Inquiry well understood, the right to culture is inextricable from other indigenous rights, including environmental rights, while destroying a culture is a powerful way of killing a people. The Inquiry, Luoma argues, went further than any other truth commission in holding a state to account for its failure to uphold cultural rights, including 'through the disruption of relationships with land, the separation of families, the impoverishment of communities, and the lack of access to traditional knowledge, language, and practices that would have contributed to a sense of cultural safety.' In relation to genocide, culture should be actively promoted for its healing qualities –

for First Nations people, culture is an expression of spirituality, while art, theatre, music, dance, storytelling, and literature provide ways for all people to experience catharsis, give testimony and rebuild trust. For Palestinians, poetry has been a vital form of cultural resistance to a genocide decades in the making. As the late Chantal Kalisa explored, in Rwanda, primarily an oral culture, theatre has done much of this work:

> genocide by definition annihilates everything, including the myths, symbols, and language that define a community and its people. Theater has the potential to encourage performers and the audience to envision new imagery and new language, as well as to reconnect with rituals.

When national reconciliation projects refuse to promote economic, social, and cultural rights, they fail not only survivors, but future generations: poverty, social injustice, and cultural repression are major drivers of violence. Incorporating ESCR into the transitional justice model brings it closer to 'transformative justice': not just a new term but a new paradigm with the goal of prevention at its core. As developed by Queer, Black, Indigenous, and Latinx communities in North America, transformative justice is an abolitionist, community-led process that builds alternatives to state justice institutions and actively works to not just respond to violence but end it. When applied to the practices of transitional justice, Paul Gready and Simon Robin propose, transformative justice 'emphasises local agency and resources, the prioritisation of process rather than preconceived outcomes, and the challenging of unequal and intersecting power relationships and structures of exclusion at both local and global levels'. Given the way the world currently works, transformative justice is unlikely to replace retributive justice as a response to genocide, but when the ICJ and ICC move at what would be a glacial pace if the glaciers weren't melting faster each year, local initiatives that empower survivors and genuinely build community resilience feel far more likely to deliver heartening results. As the dark clouds of war gather and rage, only intensifying the climate crisis, all those who insist on a comprehensive human rights based response to genocide hold up lamps of compassion and reason we desperately need to chart our way through the storms ahead.

Finally, given the failures of earthly justice, it is not surprising if genocide survivors put their shattered faith in divine justice. To use the plural pronoun – said by some Quranic commentators to convey God's majesty and authority – God's ways might seem mysterious, Their verdicts veiled, but Their essential commandments are clear. In this sombre and weighty issue of *Critical Muslim*, it seems fitting to give the very last word on genocide to Allah:

> You who believe, be steadfast in your devotion to God and bear witness impartially: do not let hatred of others lead you away from justice, but adhere to justice, for that is closer to awareness of God. Be mindful of God: God is well aware of all that you do. (The Qur'an, 5:8)

EIGHT PEACEFUL CO-EXISTENCES

After even a minor study of genocide one could not be blamed for losing hope, even pondering if genocide is the ultimate fate of human societies. Indeed, this is all heavy stuff. And in the history of the rise and fall of civilisations and empires, a whole lot of what can be classified as genocide (or something almost as horrific) tends to rear itself at the bookends of each chapter. Erased and forgotten peoples left behind in the wake of every new 'advancement'. Those rare groups of people who have come and gone without a touch of genocide often did so under mysterious circumstances. And such enigmas fan the fires of conspiracy theory, some purporting that, actually, this group or that group was annihilated by another civilisation or, more likely, by cryptids, aliens, or a combination of these malevolent forces. Definitely not a good look for the human race.

In the early phases of putting together this issue, there was an idea of using 'The List' to feature all the genocides throughout history. But that would have been a laborious task. But also a controversial one as it is almost certain that your favourite genocide would, of course unintentionally, be left out. Abandoning this task, we took on a greater challenge. Let us look instead for those brief moments in the history of humanity where instead of violence and targeting killing, peaceful co-existence ruled the day.

1. Indus Valley Civilisation – 3300 BC

The Indus Valley Civilisation existed between 3300 BC and 1300 BC along the Indus River in what is modern day Pakistan, India, and Afghanistan. It is also known as the Harappan Civilisation, named after one of the earliest archaeological sites discovered by the British Raj in the nineteenth century. The Indus Valley Civilisation existed parallel to the time of two other great riverine civilisations, Mesopotamia between the Euphrates and Tigris

Rivers and Ancient Egypt around the Nile River. While many mysteries still surround details of the Indus Valley Civilisation, solid archaeological evidence demonstrates that the civilisation was advanced, having buildings that were not just residences, settled agricultural land, networks of trade, a centralised governing structure, and even a written language and religious memorabilia. Most striking is the claims that the Indus Valley Civilisation was a peaceful people as no weapons or indications of an organised military have been found. An old hypothesis held that an Aryan invasion from Indo-European tribes lead to the downfall of the Indus Valley Civilisation. But further examination of the skeletons demonstrates that their deaths came about naturally, not through violence, thus it is unlikely any foreign invaders appeared on their lands. What seems more likely is that climate change led to a decrease in the fertility of the Indus River basin land and that most of the people migrated eastward towards the Ganges River. Where the Indus Valley Civilisation was once thought to be one of the 'lost civilisations' that disappeared suddenly, this idea has been disproven as much of their culture remains in successor peoples throughout the Indian Subcontinent. In fact, elements of the Vedic tradition can be traced back to the peoples of the Indus Valley Civilisation. So, perhaps there is indeed still potential that a thriving, peaceful, and integrated society could again take root in the Subcontinent. We do live in hope!

2. Pax Islamicus — Medina — 622

In the century prior to the Prophet Muhammad's arrival in Medina, the city was a pretty rough place hosting numerous conflicts between largely its Jewish and pagan inhabitants. Brought in first as an arbitrator amongst the clans, upon emigrating to Medina, the Prophet drafted the Constitution of Medina that specified the duties and rights of all citizens of the city, regardless of their background. In the constitution he noted the important relationship amongst all 'Peoples of the Book' setting up a sort of federation, allying all the peoples of Medina under the Prophet's rule. Importantly, the document set faith ties above blood ties and focussed on individual responsibility advancing the systems of justice in the region and putting an end to innumerable retribution-based disputes. The constitution unified institutions of justice, effectively establishing order where it had not yet existed. The Constitution of Medina stands as an important model for multi-faith and multi-ethnic systems of governance so that all the citizens of a municipality can live together peacefully and in tolerance of one another. The model has been used, with varying levels of success, throughout the history of numerous Islamic societies, notably in the Ottoman Empire. But Muslims, being Muslims, have always managed to find disputes, discord, and dissension. But, once again, we live in the hope that the constitution of Medina will become a standard bearer for the ummah! Some hope, some will say, given our history!

3. Al-Andalus — 711

At the far northwestern reach of the Umayyad Caliphate, the Muslim controlled region of the Iberian Peninsula was called Al-Andalus. For over 700 years, Al-Andalus was a focal point for some of the greatest architecture, art, and thought to have come out of what today we call the Islamic Golden Age. Throughout the existence of Al-Andalus, Muslims, Jews, and Christians all had to live amongst one another, further divided by numerous ethnic groups who called the region home. Trade and free movement of peoples throughout the Umayyad Caliphate saw a rich diversity of peoples living together in what was referred to as *La Covivencia*, where the peoples of Al-Andalus lived in relative peace and each tradition had their own legal system. Al-Andalus advanced though between the east and the west to heights rarely seen since producing such polymaths as Ibn-Rushd, Ibn Tufail, Ibn Bajjah, and Maimonides. *La Covivencia* fell apart due to internal strife and fighting during the latter days of Al-Andalus as it fragmented and began to fall apart. By 1492 and the wave of Reconquista, Iberia went to the Christian kings of Europe and the Al-Andalus model has been an unattainable dream since.

4. The Iroquois Confederacy — The Six Nations 1722

The Iroquois Confederacy existed in what is today the northeastern United States and southeastern Canda between the mid-fifteenth and mid-seventeenth centuries. In what is today the state of New York, five indigenous nations, the Mohawk, Oneida, Onondaga, Cayuga, and Seneca came together under the Great Law of Peace, an oral constitution said to have originated from the Deganawidah the Great Peacemaker, Hiawatha, and Jigonsaseh the Mother of Nations, founding the confederacy. The peace lasted for more than 200 years and even brought in a sixth nation, the Tuscarora. The confederacy stands as a model of peaceful coexistence through binding a common territory, using a common language, and under a Parliament-like system called the League that was governed by a Grand Council. Not only did the Confederacy maintain peace amongst the nations that comprised it, but also played a major role brokering agreements with the first European colonists to begin arriving in the seventeenth century, particularly the French, Dutch, and English. Although they remained neutral in most European conflicts in the 'new world', they could not help but be dragged in to the larger conflicts, and Europeans were not above using other tribal communities with an axe to grind with the Iroquois as political pawns. Since most of their official agreements were made with the British Crown, after the American Revolutionary War, most of the Iroquois Confederacy territory was lost. The Treaty of Paris, which ended the war, was only signed by European participants in the war. No land claims or promises were given to the Iroquois. Their decline continued under the expansion of the United States. They virtually disappeared by the War of 1812.

5. The Antarctic Treaty System – 1959

Between 1957 and 1958 a joint scientific research project, coined as the International Geophysical Year, saw twelve nations undertaking active research operations on the continent of Antarctica. This project also saw an end to a shutdown of scientific exchange between the Eastern and Western Blocs that developed since the beginning of the Cold War. In Washington, D.C., these twelve nations signed the Antarctic Treaty on 1 December 1959. This treaty was the first in a system of treaties that established a freedom of scientific activity and banned any and all military operations on the southern continent. Antarctica was defined as any land or ice shelves south of 60°S latitude. The treaty was also the first arms control agreement of the Cold War. Today, over fifty-five research stations have been established on the continent and fifty-seven parties are signed onto the

Antarctic Treaty System. Peace indeed is possible. We suppose it helps when a piece of land has no native population and for the most part is a pretty inhospitable place.

6. ASEAN – 1967

In the midst of the Cold War Thailand, the Philippines, and Malaya came together to form the Association of Southeast Asia (ASA) in 1961. It was a stand against rising communism after the fallout of the Korean War and with Vietnam descending quickly into a state of chaos. On 8 August 1967, Singapore and Indonesia joined the effort founding the Association of Southeast Asian Nations (ASEAN). Beyond standing as a united force against communism, ASEAN also stood for a more collective approach to social and economic development in the region and added cultural preservation and increased education to its aims. After the Cold War, ASEAN stood to uplift the international position of Southeast Asia, and to curb China's influence in Asia and the Pacific. Today, the union is composed of ten states and has two observers, Timor-Leste and Papua New Guinea, but looks to bring in these observers as well as Bangladesh. But ASEAN is not without its own issues. Border disputes have always plagued the organisation and with China making sea claims, these issues continue to simmer. A strongly abided policy of not interfering in each other's affairs keeps the peace but prevents intervention when things go south, an occurrence not totally infrequent in the region's history. The crises in Myanmar and Bangladesh, and genocide of the Rohingya in Myanmar have caused fractures. Moreover, with both China and India expanding their influence in the region, and with ever-present economic woes, ASEAN has to work harder and harder to keep the peace they have worked tirelessly for.

7. The European Union – 1993

As the dust settled on the Cold War, with Germany reunified, and with a great deal of tension released, there was a renewed drive for a more integrated Europe – a dream germinating since the end of the Second World War. By the end of 1992, the Maastricht Treaty got the ball rolling calling for a shared European citizenship, triggering a process that would unify the currency, and unifying foreign and security policies amongst member states. The formation of a customs union that unified the currencies under the Euro as well as a body and process, that blends both the federal and confederal frameworks, for legislation and a legal framework have drawn the union together, giving it the strength to stand out today. The EU has been relatively successful in maintaining a peace not common to the continent which has witnessed almost an endless cycle of war from the days of imperialism to the founding of contemporary nation-states through the end of the Cold War. But now standing at twenty-seven member states, that is without the United Kingdom thanks to Brexit, that peace has never been more tenuous. The rising tide of contemporary fascism and various separatist movements (from future Brexits to the breaking up of the present member states) mixed with the war between Russia and Ukraine, it is not hard to imagine a breaking point. The question remains: will the EU be able to weather the choppy, stormy waters ahead?

8. High Seas / Global Oceans Treaty – 2023

One of the more recent attempts at international cooperation is rapidly developing at this very moment. Again, the most successful peace attempts tend to stick at places without populations. This time, the high seas. As part of the United Nations Convention on the Laws of the Sea (UNCLOS) a legally binding instrument for conservation and sustainability was established under the United Nations Agreement on Biodiversity Beyond National Jurisdiction (BBNJ), also known as the High Seas Treaty or Global Ocean Treaty. The agreement was adopted by the UN General Assembly on 19 June 2023. The agreement sets up the fair and equitable sharing of marine genetic resources (MGRs) and their digital sequence information, establish marine protected areas, to carry out environmental impact studies on the world's oceans, and build the agreement's capacity for marine technology sharing. The agreement does not mention specific measures to combat climate change but lays the groundwork for ecosystem protection and carbon sediment storage potentials. Greenpeace has hailed this as the 'biggest conservation victory ever'. Ninety-two countries were listed as signatories on the agreement and, so far, sixty states have ratified the agreement.

Beyond these eight examples, it was difficult to find further examples throughout history of peaceful co-existence. Indeed, the Ottoman Empire example can be expanded, but that did not come without its own loss of innocence and towards its end, it was not exempt from partaking in some of Europe's games of daggers and shadows. Likewise, when one looks into the term 'peaceful coexistence' the former Soviet Union Premiere Nikita Khrushchev will top many google searches. Indeed, Khrushchev did a great deal of work to make peace amongst the Warsaw Pact nations, and even made strides in maintaining peace between NATO and the Warsaw Pact, this largely remains the 'official' story of history. Proxy wars and shadow conflicts continued, nonetheless. And when peace is maintained by the mere fact that buttons capable of destroying the world multiple times over existed within the high offices of Washington, D.C. and Moscow, it does not sound like a very 'authentic' or genuine peace.

So, exhausted of ideas, the list cannot continue and instead we must hope that new ways of being and existing can be imagined and created in the near future. Peaceful coexistence cannot only be a feature of the history books. It must also be a lived future. For it is a desired future we need direly as existential doom, beyond that which we place upon each other via violence and destruction, requires our attention. Now!

CITATIONS

Genocide, Then and Now by Maha Sardar

The Convention on the Prevention and Punishment of the Crime of Genocide' can be accessed at: un.org. See also: Paola Gaeta, *The UN Genocide Convention, A Commentary*, edited by (OUP, 2009); International Court of Justice, *Reservation to the Convention on Genocide*, ICJ Report (1951); Tatiana E. Sainati, 'Toward a Comparative Approach to the Crime of Genocide', *Duke Law Journal*, 62, 161 (2012), 161-202.

Raphael Lemkin's definition of genocide is from *Axis Rule in Occupied Europe*, (Carnegie Endowment for International Peace, Washington, 1944); it can be downloaded from: http://ereserve.library.utah.edu/Annual/POLS/5450/Yavuz/Lemkin.pdf.

Winston Churchill quote is from his 24 August 1941 broadcast following a meeting with President Roosevelt. Text available online at https://www.ibiblio.org/pha/timeline/410824awp.html.

On the politicisation of genocide, see K E Smith, 'Avoiding an emotions-action gap? The EU and genocide designations' in the *Journal of European Integration* 46(5) (2024), 615-634, discussing the EU's caution in designating atrocities as genocide, motivated by a fear of its rhetoric outstripping its willingness to act.

The quotations are from: Samuel Totten and Paul R. Bartrop, "The United Nations and Genocide: Prevention, Intervention, and Prosecution," *Human Rights Review* 5,4 (2004): 8–31, p 9; Donald G Dutton et al, *Extreme mass homicide: From military massacre to genocide* (Elsevier 2004), quotes from p.445-446, p448, p446-447; James Butler, 'Trivialised to Death', *London Review of Books* 46(16) (15 August 2024); Raja Shehadeh, *What does Israel Fear from Palestine* (Profile Books, 2024) p. 105; Elif Shafak, *How to stay sane in an age of division* (Profile Books, 2020) p. 9; Eric Heinze, 'The Rhetoric of Genocide in U.S. Foreign Policy: Rwanda and Darfur Compared', *Political Science Quarterly*, 122, 3 (2007), 359-383, p366; Hanin Majadil, 'Kahane's spirit of Jewish supremacy lives on – in mainstream Israel'. *Haaretz* 5 September 2024; Gideon Levy, 'In Gaza, Israeli's Dehumanization of the Palestinians has reached a new height'. *Haaretz* 14 August 2024; Arwa Mahdawi, 'Israeli podcasters are laughing about genocide. What would it take to stop?', *The Guardian* 6 September 2024; N Sultany, 'A threshold crossed: on genocidal intent and the duty to prevent genocide in Palestine' in the Journal of Genocide Research (2024).

On Rwanda, see the March 1999 Human Rights Watch report Leave None to Tell the Story: Genocide in Rwanda, and the discussion in G H Stanton, 'Could the Rwandan Genocide Have Been Prevented?' (2004) 6(2) *Journal of Genocide Research* 211; and Rwanda: Genocide Archives Released' Human Rights Watch (2 April 2024). https://www.hrw.org/news/2024/04/02/rwanda-genocide-archives-released

On the Uyghurs, see: Human Rights Watch, "Break Their Lineage, Break Their Roots": China's Crimes against Humanity Targeting Uyghurs and Other Turkic Muslims', 19 April 2021 and 21 August 2023. https://www.hrw.org/report/2021/04/19/break-their-lineage-break-their-roots/chinas-crimes-against-humanity-targeting United Nations OHCHR, 'Assessment of human rights concerns in the Xinjiang Uyghur Autonomous Region, People's Republic of China', 31 August 2022, 7. https://www.ohchr.org/sites/default/files/documents/countries/2022-08-31/22-08-31-final-assesment.pdf

On Ukraine, see: Ukraine's proceedings alleging genocide against Russia in the ICJ, https://www.icj-cij.org/case/182, supported by many states including the USA, https://www.icj-cij.org/sites/default/files/case-related/182/182-20220907-WRI-01-00-EN.pdf.

On Cambodia, see: Tatiana E. Sainati, 'Toward a Comparative Approach to the Crime of Genocide', *Duke Law Journal*, 62, 161 (2012), 161-202; https://www.bbc.co.uk/news/world-asia-46217896 (16 November

2018); and Donald G Dutton et al, *Extreme mass homicide: From military massacre to genocide* (Elsevier 2204) p.445-446

On Bosnia, see ICTY press release, 'Radislav Krstic becomes the First Person to be Convicted of Genocide at the ICTY and is Sentenced to 46 Years Imprisonment' (2 August 2001), https://www.icty.org/en/sid/7964; *Application of the Convention on the Prevention and Punishment of the Crime of Genocide,* https://www.icj-cij.org/case/91; https://www.nytimes.com/1999/11/16/world/un-details-its-failure-to-stop-95-bosnia-massacre.html

On Rwanda, see: https://www.un.org/en/preventgenocide/rwanda/assets/pdf/exhibits/Panel-Set2.pdf Dutton p. 446-447; the March 1999 Human Rights Watch report Leave None to Tell the Story: Genocide in Rwanda, and the discussion in G H Stanton, 'Could the Rwandan Genocide Have Been Prevented?' (2004) 6(2) *Journal of Genocide Research* 211; Rwanda: Genocide Archives Released' Human Rights Watch (2 April 2024). https://www.hrw.org/news/2024/04/02/rwanda-genocide-archives-released; and Eric Heinze, 'The Rhetoric of Genocide in U.S. Foreign Policy: Rwanda and Darfur Compared', *Political Science Quarterly*, 122, 3 (2007), 359-383, 366.

On the death toll in Gaza, see reports by Reuters (https://www.reuters.com/world/middle-east/gaza-death-toll-how-many-palestinians-has-israels-campaign-killed-2024-07-25/) and Al Jazeera (https://www.aljazeera.com/news/longform/2023/10/9/israel-hamas-war-in-maps-and-charts-live-tracker), and analysis published in the Lancet journal (https://www.thelancet.com/journals/lancet/article/PIIS0140-6736(24)01169-3/fulltext). On famine, see reporting by the OHCHR (https://www.ohchr.org/en/press-releases/2024/07/un-experts-declare-famine-has-spread-throughout-gaza-strip), and on destruction of property, homes and schools see AP News (https://apnews.com/article/un-report-gaza-destruction-housing-economy-recovery-4f61dcca7db3fd5eb3da5c6a2 5001e12), reporting by the OHCHR (https://www.ohchr.org/en/press-releases/2024/04/un-experts-deeply-concerned-over-scholasticide-gaza), the European Commission (https://civil-protection-humanitarian-aid.

ec.europa.eu/news-stories/news/palestine-statement-attacks-medical-and-civilian-infrastructure-gaza-and-west-bank-2024-05-20_en), the UN (https://news.un.org/en/story/2024/03/1147272), Al Jazeera (https://www.aljazeera.com/news/2023/12/31/israeli-bombardment-destroyed-over-70-of-gaza-homes-media-office) and the Wall Street Journal (https://www.wsj.com/world/middle-east/gaza-destruction-bombing-israel-aa528542?mod=hp_lead_pos7).

On Israel's and international responses to the ICJ ruling, see https://www.telegraph.co.uk/world-news/2024/01/26/israel-gaza-genocide-case-icj-stops-short-calling-end-war/, https://www.theguardian.com/world/2024/jan/26/israeli-officials-accuse-international-court-of-justice-of-antisemitic-bias, and https://www.jpost.com/israel-news/article-811060. The ICJ decision in question, published 19 July 2024, can be accessed online: https://www.icj-cij.org/sites/default/files/case-related/186/186-20240719-adv-01-00-en.pdf.

On Israel's impossible evacuation demands, see https://news.sky.com/story/gaza-evacuation-why-getting-people-out-in-less-than-24-hours-is-impossible-12983748. On bombing of evacuation routes and safe zones, see https://www.theguardian.com/world/2023/oct/14/gaza-civilians-afraid-to-leave-home-after-bombing-of-safe-routes, https://www.doctorswithoutborders.org/latest/urgent-need-ceasefire-israeli-forces-attack-safe-zones-rafah; and https://www.aljazeera.com/gallery/2024/5/27/photos-israel-bombs-yet-another-gaza-camp-it-had-declared-a-safe-zone. On the targeting of aid deliveries, see https://www.reuters.com/world/middle-east/gaza-is-choked-off-aid-since-crossing-closures-un-agencies-say-2024-05-07/, and https://www.amnesty.org/en/latest/news/2024/02/israel-defying-icj-ruling-to-prevent-genocide-by-failing-to-allow-adequate-humanitarian-aid-to-reach-gaza/. On the targeting of hospitals and other civilian infrastructure, see https://fxb.harvard.edu/2024/04/09/press-release-new-study-of-satellite-data-shows-israels-assault-on-hospitals-schools-and-water-infrastructure-in-the-gaza-strip-was-not-random/, https://www.ohchr.org/en/press-releases/2024/02/widespread-destruction-israeli-defence-forces-civilian-infrastructure-gaza, and https://www.hrw.org/news/2024/05/14/gaza-israelis-attacking-known-aid-worker-locations.

On destruction of civilians' possessions, see https://edition.cnn.com/2023/12/15/middleeast/israeli-soldiers-burningfood-gaza-intl/index.html. On starvation in Palestine, see https://www.theguardian.com/world/2024/feb/27/un-israel-food-starvation-palestinians-war-crime-genocide.

On recognition of apartheid in Israel, see https://www.amnesty.org/en/documents/mde15/5141/2022/en/ and https://www.icj-cij.org/sites/default/files/case-related/186/186-20240719-adv-01-00-en.pdf.

For a full analysis of genocide in Gaza, see https://www.humanrightsnetwork.org/genocide-in-gaza.

All the legal documents on the case for genocide in Gaza can be found in the International Court of Justice website: icj-cij.org. Some reports in the press:
https://www.aljazeera.com/news/2024/8/15/israel-kills-more-than-40000-palestinians-in-gaza-16456-of-them-children
https://www.ohchr.org/en/press-releases/2024/07/un-experts-declare-famine-has-spread-throughout-gaza-strip
https://www.thelancet.com/journals/lancet/article/PIIS0140-6736(24)01169-3/fulltext
https://www.ohchr.org/en/press-releases/2024/04/un-experts-deeply-concerned-over-scholasticide-gaza.
https://civil-protection-humanitarian-aid.ec.europa.eu/news-stories/news/palestine-statement-attacks-medical-and-civilian-infrastructure-gaza-and-west-bank-2024-05-20_en#:~:text=%22Since%20the%20start%20of%20the,today%20completely%20out%20of%20service
Emma Farge, 'UN expert says Israel has committed genocide in Gaza, calls for arms embargo', *Reuters*, 26 March 2024. https://www.reuters.com/world/middle-east/un-expert-says-israel-has-committed-genocide-gaza-calls-arms-embargo-2024-03-26/
Ed Pilkington, 'Top UN official in New York steps down citing "genocide" of Palestinian civilians', *The Guardian*, 31 October 2023. https://www.

theguardian.com/world/2023/oct/31/
un-official-resigns-israel-hamas-war-palestine-new-york
https://www.theguardian.com/world/2024/feb/27/
un-israel-food-starvation-palestinians-war-crime-genocide

On the portrayal of Arabs as terrorists, see Ziauddin Sardar, *Orientalism* (Open University, 1999), the Sut Jhally documentary 'Reel Bad Arabs: How Hollywood Vilifies a People', 2006, and on the contrast with portrayal of Ukrainians in the aftermath of Russia's invasion, see https://www.theguardian.com/commentisfree/2022/mar/02/civilised-european-look-like-us-racist-coverage-ukraine

On the expulsion of Jews from medieval England, see Joshua Trachtenberg, *The Devil and the Jews: The Medieval Conception of the Jew and its Relation to Modern Anti-Semitism* (Jewish Publication Society 2002, reprint of original edition of 1943).

See also Jean Paul Sartre, *On Genocide* (Beacon Books, 1968); Orlando Patterson, *Slavery and Social Death* (Harvard University Press, 1982).

Gratuitous Acts of Evil by Richard Appignanesi

The references to quotations in my text, in order of appearance, are as follows:
Jean-Paul Sartre, *Search for a Method*, trans. Hazel E. Barnes, Vintage Books, Random House, 1968, p.152, p90; Email from Professor Merlin Donald, received 19 February 2024; Aristotle, *Poetics*, 1451bl-6 p6; Walter Benjamin, 1931, in *One Way Street and Other Writings*, trans. Edmund Jephcott and Kingsley Shorter, New Left Books, London, 1979, p.159; André Breton, *The Manifestos of Surrealism*, trans. Richard Seaver and Helen R. Lane, University of Michigan Press, 1972, p.125; reports of Stockhausen's comment can be found variously online. See also Anthony Tomassini, 'Music: the Devil Made Him Do it', *New York Times*, 30 September 2001: https://www.nytimes.com>2001/09/30>arts-music-t

Mikhail Bakhtin, *Problems of Dostoevsky's Poetics*, trans. Caryl Emerson, University of Minnesota, 1984, p. 293; André Gide, *Dostoevsky*, New Directions Paperback, New York, 1961,m p.164, 166, 167.

Aleksarnder Pushskin's 1986 letter is quoted in Andrei Tarkovsky's screenplay *Mirror* in *Collected Screenplays*, trans. William Powell and Natasha Synessios, Faber and Faber Ltd., London, 1999, pp.291-292. Albert Camus's first quote is from
Open Culture, https://www.openculture.com/2017/01>albert-camu, and the following form Albert Camus, *The Myth of Sisyphus and Other Essays*, trans, Justin O'Brien, Vintage Books, New York, 1960, p.3, 78-83, p.83.

The quote from Gide's *Journal* is from Enid Starkie, *André Gide: The God That Failed. Six Studies in Communism*, Hamish Hamilton, London, 1950, p176, other quotes from André Gide, *Return from the USSR*, Alfed A. Knopf, New York, 1937; and *Afterthoughts. A Sequel to Back from the USSR*, Martin Secker& Warburg Ltd., London, 1937. Sartre's quote on Gide is from Nicola Chiaramonte, 'Letter from Paris', *The New Republic* 7 May 1951; André Gide, *Madeleine (et nunc manet in te)*, Justin O'Brien, Elephant Paperbacks, Ivan R. Dee, Chicago, 1989, p..45-46, p.16-20, p. 53-54; and Peter Sloterdijk, *God's Zeal: The Battle of the Three Monotheisms*, trans. Wieland Hoban, Polity Press, Cambridge, 2009, pp. 15-17.

Letby's guilty verdict has been challenged. Campaigners allege her innocence but forensic evidence submitted by Dr Dewi Evans, a neonatal expert for 30 years, and her presence on duty at the death of all the infants have been maintained by the Crown Courts that handed down whole-life orders.

Genocide Denial by Abdelwahab El-Affendi

Samantha Power quoted is from, 'A Problem from Hell. America and the Age of Genocide, (New York, Basic Books, 2013P, p. 35. Didier Fassin quotes from his 5 Feb 2024 article: 'The Rhetoric of Denial: Contribution to an Archive of the Debate about Mass Violence in Gaza', *Journal of Genocide Research*, DOI: 10.1080/14623528.2024.2308941; and A. Dirk

Moses references are from 'Genocide as a Category Mistake: Permanent Security and Mass Violence Against Civilians.' *Genocidal Violence*: 15; and 'Replacing "Genocide" with "Permanent Security" via Genealogy', *Global Intellectual History*, (04 Sep 2023): DOI: 10.1080/23801883.2023.2253010

The open letter by Jurgen Habermas and his colleagues can be found at: https://www.resetdoc.org/story/habermas-israel-principle-solidariety/

See also: Abdelwahab El-Affendi,. 'The futility of genocide studies after Gaza.' *Journal of Genocide Research* (2024): 1-7; and, editor, *Genocidal nightmares: narratives of insecurity and the logic of mass atrocities* (Bloomsbury Publishing USA, 2014).

Championing Bosnian Genocide by Sean Goodman

The references, in order of mention, are as follows: The Trial of Ratko Mladić: FRONTLINE PBS https://www.youtube.com/watch?v=HJh8fuaqslo; Milošević's St. Vitus Day Speech: http://www.slobodan-milosevic.org/spch-kosovo1989.htm; American Renaissance Vol. 6, No. 7 https://www.amren.com/archives/back-issues/july-1995/ and Vol. 10, No. 6; https://www.amren.com/archives/back-issues/june-1999/ Kosovo, The Alamo of Europe http://www.louisbeam.com/kosovo.htm and Kosovo and the Far Right https://www.splcenter.org/fighting-hate/intelligence-report/1999/kosovo-and-far-right

On 'remove kebab' meme, see 'Jewish/Muslim lies about Srebrenica "genocide"' https://www.stormfront.org/forum/blogs/u233200-e2886/ and 'Biggest Kebab Removers in History': https://www.stormfront.org/forum/t1307551/

The Balkan Insight report: 'The "Awakening": American Right-Wing Extremists Find Allies in the Balkans' https://balkaninsight.com/2022/04/13/the-awakening-american-right-wing-extremist-finds-allies-in-the-balkans/; and for comparison of Gendrom and Torrant manifesrtos, see ADL: https://www.adl.org/resources/article/striking-similarities-between-gendron-and-tarrant-manifestos. An incomplete digital archive of Living Marxism can be found here: https://www.marxists.org/history/etol/newspape/living-marxism/index.htm

The mentions include, Alexander Reid Ross *Against the Fascist* Creep (AK Press, 2017); John Pilger, 'The Bogus "Humanitarian War on Servia': https://consortiumnews.com/2016/08/24/the-bogus-humanitarian-war-on-serbia/

Michael Parenti *To Kill a Nation: The Attack on Yugoslavia* (Verso Books, 2000); English translation of Milošević preface http://www.slobodan-milosevic.org/news/parenti.htm and Jeremy Scahill talk, 'The Myth of Humanitarian Intervention' is available on YouTube: https://www.youtube.com/watch?v=WXQMNYPbcQM&t=244s

Other quotes are from Samantha Power: *A Problem From Hell: America in the Age of Genocide* (Basic Books, 2002) p p264; nd Dale C. Tatum, *Genocide at the Dawn of the 21ˢᵗ Century* (Palgrave Macmillan, 2010.) p123

Catastrophe Upon Catastrophe by Liam Mayo

The transcript of Piers Morgan with Bassem Youseef can be found at: https://scrapsfromtheloft.com/tv-series/israel-hamas-war-piers-morgan-bassem-youssef-on-palestines-treatment-transcript/

The following texts are mentioned in the essay: Theodor Adorno, *Negative Dialectics* (Routledge, 2003); Walter Benjamin, 'Theses on the Philosophy of History,' in *Illuminations*, edited by Hannah Arendt, translated by Harry Zohn. (Harcourt, 1968) pp 253–264; Hannah Arendt, *On Revolution* (Penguin, 1990) and Walter Benjamin, *The Storyteller: Tales out of Loneliness* (Verso 2016); Marshall Berman, *All That is Solid Melts into Air: The Experience of Modernity* (Penguin, 1988); Bill Clinton, *My Life* (Knopf 2004); Fedrick Jameson, *The Ideologies of Theory: The Syntax of History*, Vol. 2 (University of Minnesota Press, 1988); Ziauddin Sardar, *Postmodernism and the Other: New Imperialism of Western Culture* (Pluto Press, 1998); Ziauddin Sardar 'The Smog of ignorance: Knowledge and Ignorance in Postnormal Times' *Futures* 120 102554 (2020); and Ziauddin Sardar, editor, *Emerging Epistemologies: The Changing Fabric of Knowledge in Postnormal Times* (IIIT/CPPPFS 2022); William Gibson *Pattern Recognition* (Penguin, 2004); and Vilem

Flusser, *Language and Reality*, translated by Rodrigo Maltez Novaes, University of Minnesota Press, 2018 (original 1964).

Nokhchi-chuo by Marat Iliyasov

Books mentioned: Marlène Laruelle: *Is Russia Fascist?* (Cornell University Press, 2021); Abdurakhman Avtorkhanov, *The killing of the Chechen and Ingush people* (in Russian, Moscow, 1992); Alexander Solzhenitsyn, *Gulag Archipelago* (Harvell Press, 2003).

See also: Mark Galeotti, *Russia's Wars in Chechnya* (Osprey, 2024); Anna Politkovskaya, *A Dirty War: A Russian Reporter in Chechnya* (Harvell Press, 2001); and Venora Bennett, *Crying Wolf: The Return of War in Chechnya* (Pan Books, 2001).

God's Shadow on Earth
by Robert Zayd KiaNouri-Zigmund

The Qur'an commentary comments are from: Seyyed Hossein Nasr, editor, *The Study Quran: A New Translation and Commentary*. First edition. New York, NY: HarperOne, 2015, 40:26c and 30:41c.and George Archer, Maria Massi Dakake, and Daniel A. Madigan, eds. *Routledge Companion to the Qur'an*, 1st ed. Routledge Religion Companions, New York: Routledge, 2021, p423, p110-130

Khaled Abou El Fadl. *The Search for Beauty in Islam: A Conference of the Books*. Lanham, Md: Rowman & Littlefield, 2006, Chapter 23; Khaled Abou El Fadl, *The Prophet's Pulpit: Commentaries on the State of Islam. Volume II*, Usuli Press, 2023, p218-219, p219; Khaled Abou El Fadl, *Rebellion and Violence in Islamic Law*, Cambridge University Press, 2001, p113; and Khaled Abou El Fadl, *The Great Theft: Wrestling Islam from the Extremists*, HarperSanFrancisco, 2005, p198

Quotes on Saudi Arabia are from: Meulen, D. van der. *The Wells of Ibn Sa'ud*. The Kegan Paul Arabia Library. London; New York: Kegan Paul International, 2000, p65-68; Joseph Kostiner, *The Making of Saudi Arabia*,

1916-1936: From Chieftaincy to Monarchical State, Oxford University Press, 1993, p119

On Shia theology and thought, see: Muḥammad Ḥusain aṭ-Ṭabāṭabā'ī. *Shi'ite Islam*. Edited by Ḥusain Naṣr, State University of New York Press, 1977; and Mehran Tamadonfar, *Islamic Law and Governance in Contemporary Iran: Transcending Islam for Social, Economic, and Political Order*, Lexington Books, 2015.

Other citations from: Ibn Taymiyya, Majmu' al-Fatawa, IV: 440-1, 444, 450-2; Ja'far SubHani. *Al-A'immah al-Ithnay 'Ashar*, n.d., 411; Hugh Kennedy, *The Prophet and the Age of the Caliphates: The Islamic Near East from the Sixth to the Eleventh Century*, Pearson Longman, 2008, p132-133; Hamid Dabashi, *The Persian Prince: The Rise and Resurrection of an Imperial Archetype*. Stanford, California: Stanford University Press, 2023, p133, p70-73.

On Hamza Yusuf, see: Abdullah Feras, 'Hamza Yusuf & The Sultan: A Case Study in the Misuse of Prophetic Traditions » IDI.' *Islamic Discourse Initiative* (blog), September 16, 2019. https://www.islamicdiscourseinitiative. com/politics/hamza-yusuf-the-sultan-a-case-study-in-the-misuse-of-prophetic-traditions/ and Walaa Quisay, 'Hanson, Hamza Yusuf.' In *Oxford Research Encyclopedia of Religion*, 2023. https://doi.org/10.1093/acrefore/9780199340378.013.838.

On Donald Trump, see: 'Golan Heights: Trump Signs Order Recognising Occupied Area as Israeli.' March 25, 2019. https://www.bbc.com/news/world-middle-east-47697717; Al Jazeera. 'World Leaders React to US Embassy Relocation to Jerusalem.' Accessed November 8, 2024. https://www.aljazeera.com/news/2018/5/14/world-leaders-react-to-us-embassy-relocation-to-jerusalem.

On Saudi fatwas: 'A Fatwa From The Council Of Senior Scholars In The Kingdom Of Saudi Arabia Warning Against Mass Demonstrations.' Accessed March 27, 2024. https://www.islamopediaonline. org/a-fatwa-from-the-council-of-senior-scholars-in-the-kingdom-of-saudi-arabia-warning-against-mass-demonstrations/; Carnegie Endowment for

International Peace. 'State-Sponsored Fatwas in Saudi Arabia.' https://carnegieendowment.org/sada/75971#:~:text=religious%20authority.%20In-,one%20such%20fatwa,-from%20March%202016.

On Guantanamo Bay, see: Adayfi, Mansoor, and Antonio Aiello. Don't Forget Us Here: Lost and Found at Guantánamo. First edition. New York: Hachette Books, 2021, p40.

On oppression in Iran, see: Al Jazeera. 'Executions in Iran Hit 8-Year High in 2023.' Accessed May 1, 2024. https://www.aljazeera.com/news/2024/3/5/iran-executed-834-people-last-year-highest-since-2015-rights-groups. Al-Ihya, 'On Hijab and Changing Conditions of Time and Place'Sayed Kamal Al-Haydari, 2020. https://www.youtube.com/watch?v=PlUMcjiX6eU and Ziryab Jamal. Abdulaziz Al-Qattan Defends Kamal al-Haydari & Highlights His Plight Under House Arrest, 2021. https://www.youtube.com/watch?v=-yKi1Y_IK-c.

See also: Ezzeddin Ibrahim Nawawī, *An-Nawawi's Forty Hadith*, translated by Denys Johnson-Davies, Jakarta, Dar al-ilm, 40:34; Saïd Amir Arjomand, 'The Constitution of Medina: A Sociolegal Interpretation of Muhammad's Acts of Foundation of the 'Umma." *International Journal of Middle East Studies* 41, no. 4 (2009): 555–75. https://www.jstor.org/stable/40389306, p563, and p562-563; and Martin S. Kramer, editor. *Shi'ism, Resistance, and Revolution*, Routledge, 2019; and The Usuli Institute. 'The U.S. Government Is the Most Influential Imam in World Today,' October 14, 2022. https://www.usuli.org/2022/10/14/the-u-s-government-is-the-most-influential-imam-in-world-today/ and 'The Power of Moral Unison: Confronting the Bid'ah of Despotism,' February 2, 2024 https://www.usuli.org/2024/02/02/the-power-of-moral-unison-confronting-the-bid-ah-of-despotism-usuli-khutbah-by-shayan-parsai/.

Birth of Bangladesh by Ali Nobil Ahmad

Books mentioned in the article include: Karrar Ali Agha, *Witness to Carnage 1971* (Salman Art Press, Lahore, Pakistan, 2012); Iftikhar-Ud-Din Ahmad, *Memories of a Lacerated Heart* (Trafford, 2017); Bina D'Costa, *Nationbuilding,*

Gender and War Crimes in South Asia (Routledge, 2011) (Interview with Geoffrey Davis); and Yasmin Saikia, *Women, War, and the Making of Bangladesh* (Duke University Press 2011).

Two superbly researched and well written blog posts by Imran from Ontario and Tufail Qaiser:
Imran "A Nishan e Haider at Kala Pul, A Grave that got moved, and a Monument that never existed" blogpost, at Mani Junction, August 20 2019: https://www.meemainseen.com/2019/08/rashid-minhas/
Tufail Kaiser, "Bluebird-166 is Hijacked" blogpost, 03 October 2012, available at: https://kaiser-aeronaut.blogspot.com/2012/10/bluebird-166-is-hijacked_8656.html

Eyewitness accounts by Murray Sayle, Anthony Mascarenhas and others consulted in *Bangladesh Documents*, edited by Sheelendra Kumar Singh (Indian Ministry Of External Affairs, New Delhi, 1971); also Rounaq Jahan's 'Genocide in Bangladesh' in Samuel Totten, Wiliiam S. Parsons and Israel W Charny (eds) *Century of Genocide* (Routledge 2004); and Jenefer Coates, 'Bangladesh: the Struggle for Cultural Independence', *Index on Censorship* Volume 1, issue 1, March 1972.

Rohingya by Kaamil Ahmed

My book *I Feel No Peace: Rohingya Fleeing Over Sears and Rivers* is published by Hurst, (London, 2023). See also: Azeem Ibrahim, *The Rohingyas: Inside Myanmar's Hidden Genocide* (Hurst, London, 2018); and Habiburahman, *First, They Erased Our Name: A Rohingya Speaks* (Scribe, 2019)

Heba Abu Nada by Luke Wilkinson

I would like to thank Somaia Abu Nada for providing the photo of her sister and for taking the time to speak with me.

Heba Abu Nada, *Oxygen is not for the dead*, Dar Diwan for Publishing and

Distribution, Kuwait, 2nd ed., 2021; and Palestine Cultural Platform, https://www.almanassa.ps/page-4425.html

Heba Abu Nada, 'A message to everyone who wants to die in Gaza', Al Jazeera, 30/08/2017.

Fady Joudah, 'A Palestinian Meditation in a Time of Annihilation', Literary Hub 1st November 2023, [https://lithub.com/a-palestinian-meditation -in-a-time-of-annihilation/].

Heba Abu Nada, posts on Facebook, 07/10/2023 – 20/10/ 2023, [https://www.facebook.com/profile.php?id=100002457890081]. '"Not Just Passing": A Poem by Hiba Abu Nada', [https://arablit. org/2023/11/27/not-just-passing-a-poem-by-hiba-abu-nada/]. Somaia Abunada, 'In Gaza, grieving our loved ones is a privilege amid Israel's genocidal war', Middle East Eye, 04/12/2023, [https://www.middleeasteye. net/opinion/israel-gaza-grieving-loved-ones-privilege-genocidal-war].

Remembering and Forgetting by Robin Yassin-Kassab

I highly recommend Edina Bećirević, *Genocide on the River Drina* (Yale University Press, New Haven and London, 2014). As well as being a detailed study of the Bosnian genocide, it contains ideas and information relevant to genocide in general. I came across Taylor Branch in the Bećirević book. The full version of his notes on the Clinton presidency is here: Taylor Branch, *The Clinton Tapes: Wrestling History with the President* (New York, Simon and Schuster, 2009). Other works mentioned: Jasmin Mujanović, *The Bosniaks: Nationhood After Genocide* (Hurst, London, 2023) and Amir Telibećirović and Sabaha Colaković, *The Siege of Sarajevo 1992- 1996*, (Vrijeme, Zenica, 2019).

The Gaza Prison by Hassan Mahamdallie

Mohammed al-Hajjar, 'In Gaza, you don't only see death. You smell it. You breathe it', *Middle East Eye*, 14 January 2024: https://www.middleeasteye. net/opinion/gaza-dont-only-see-death-smell-breathe- it#:~:text=Gaza%20is%20under%20constant%20siege,people%20 with%20semi%2Ddecomposed%20bodies.

BBC, 'More wounded Palestinians tell BBC the Israeli army forced them on to jeep', BBC 30 June 2024: https://www.bbc.co.uk/news/articles/cw4y91032d1o#:~:text=Two%20more%20Palestinian%20men%2C%20injured,at%20speed%20%E2%80%93%20along%20village%20roads.

Last Word: On Transformative Justice by Naomi Foyle

Chantal Kalisa is quoted from her article 'Theatre and the Rwandan Genocide' in *Art from Trauma: Genocide and Healing Beyond Rwanda*, edited by Rangira Béa Gallimore and Gerise Herndon (University of Nebraska Press, 2019). The book is dedicated to the memory of Kalisa, who lost maternal relatives in the Rwandan genocide, and who died at the age of 50, after a brief illness. Zarir Merat is quoted by Lars Waldorf in his article '"Like Jews Waiting for Jesus": Posthumous Justice in Post-Genocide Rwanda' in *Localizing Transitional Justice: Interventions and Priorities after Mass Violence*, edited by Rosalind Shaw, et al. (Stanford University Press, 2010), also cited later in the essay. Statistics in paragraph three of the Last Word are taken from a CNN article and from the ICC website: https://web.archive.org/web/20230702085149/https://www.cnn.com/2018/12/14/europe/germany-nazi-war-trials-grm-intl/index.html and https://www.icc-cpi.int/about/the-court. Arguments for and against the ICC can be widely read on the internet, including at https://theconversation.com/20-years-on-the-international-criminal-court-is-doing-more-good-than-its-critics-claim-186382 and https://newint.org/sections/argument/2014/12/01/international-criminal-court-racist

Archbishop Desmond Tutu is quoted from his Foreword to *The Report of the Truth and Reconciliation Commission*, which can be accessed at https://omalley.nelsonmandela.org/index.php/site/q/03lv02167/04lv02264/05lv02335/06lv02357/07lv02398/08lv02403.htm. In the Foreword (Chapter One of Volume One of the Report), Tutu states that Act No 34 endorses 'the need for understanding but not for vengeance, a need for reparation but not retaliation, a need for ubuntu but not for victimisation.' Adam Sitze is quoted from his book *The*

Impossible Machine: A Genealogy of South Africa's Truth and Reconciliation Commission (University of Michigan Press, 2013), Annelies Verdoolaege from her study *Reconciliation Discourse: The case of the Truth and Reconciliation Commission* (John Benjamins Publishing Company, 2007).

Colin Luoma is quoted from his article 'Closing the cultural rights gap in transitional justice: Developments from Canada's National Inquiry into Missing and Murdered Indigenous Women and Girls' in *Netherlands Quarterly of Human Rights* (Volume 39, Issue 1, March 2021). The article can be accessed at https://journals.sagepub.com/doi/full/10.1177/0924051921992747.

The Missing and Murdered Indigenous Women and Girls Final Report and the reports of the Canadian Truth and Reconciliation Commission can be accessed online at:
https://www.mmiwg-ffada.ca/final-report/ and https://nctr.ca/about/history-of-the-trc/truth-and-reconciliation-commission-of-canada/ The Assembly of First Nations fifth anniversary progress report on the MMIWG Inquiry can be downloaded at https://afn.ca/all-news/press-releases/assembly-of-first-nations-afn-marks-the-fifth-anniversary-of-national-inquiry-into-missing-and-murdered-indigenous-women-and-girls-mmiwg-with-progress-report-on-the-implementation-of-the-calls-for/

Rose Marie Mukamwiza is quoted from *We Cannot Forget: Interviews with Survivors of the 1994 Genocide in Rwanda*, edited by Samuel Totten and Rafiki Ubaldo (Rutgers University Press, 2011). Susan Tomson and her interviewees Séraphine, Espérance, Béatha and Thomas are quoted from Tomson's book, *Whispering Truth to Power: Everyday Resistance to Reconciliation in Postgenocide Rwanda* (University of Wisconsin Press, 2013). As far as I can judge from the contextual information given by the researchers, who included a Rwandan genocide survivor (Rafiki Ubaldo), these interviews were conducted ethically and with great sensitivity to the needs of the survivors. More information on FARG can be found at: https://www.justiceinfo.net/en/40610-rwandan-reparations-fund-breaks-ground-but-is-still-not-enough-say-victims.html

Marek Kohn cites Eric Uslaner in his book *Trust: Self Interest and the Common Good* (Oxford University Press, 2008). An introduction to transformative justice, written by Mia Mingus, can be found at:
https://transformharm.org/tj_resource/transformative-justice-a-brief-description/. Paul Gready and Simon Robins are quoted from their edited volume *From Transitional Justice to Transformative Justice* (Cambridge University Press, 2019).

CONTRIBUTORS

• **Ali Nobil Ahmad**, journalist and political consultant, is currently an Iméra Resident Fellow at the Institute for Advanced Study, Aix-Marseille Université • **Kaamil Ahmed** is the author of *I Feel No Peace: Rohingya Fleeing Over Seas and Rivers* • **Richard Appignanesi**, writer, editor, and philosopher, has just published a collection of his poetry, *Recordances* • **Ruth Cuthand** a Canadian artist of Plains Cree and Scottish ancestry, won the 2020 Governor General's Award in Visual and Media Arts • **Abdelwahab El-Affendi** is President and Provost of the Doha Institute for Graduate Studies, Qatar • **Naomi Foyle** is a well-known poet and science fiction writer • **Sean Goodman** is a scholar of far-right extremism • **Tam Hussein** writes for *New Lines* magazine • **Marat Iliyasov** is Visiting Scholar at the Global Academy of George Washington University • **C Scott Jordan** is Executive Assistant Director of Centre for Postnormal Policy and Futures Studies and Deputy Editor of *Critical Muslim* • **Adrianne Kalfopoulou**, poet and essayist, is the author of *On the Gaze: Dubai and its New Cosmopolitanisms* • **Celine Kasem** is a Syrian researcher and activist • **Robert Zayd KiaNouri-Zigmund**, scholar of Islamic law, theology and human rights, serves as an editorial associate for The Maydan • **Hassan Mahamdallie**, playwright and theatre creative, is Director of the Muslim Institute • **Liam Mayo** is a seasonal lecturer in social sciences and humanities at the University of the Sunshine Coast in Australia • **Shamim Miah**, Senior Lecturer in Sociology at Huddersfield University, is Reviews Editor of *Critical Muslim* • **Michal Rubin** is an Israeli psychotherapist, Cantor, and poet living in South Carolina • **Carol Rumens** is an award-winning British poet, playwright and translator • **Maha Sardar** is a human rights barrister • **Zain Sardar**, a philosopher, is programme manager at the Aziz Foundation, London • **Andleeb Shadani** is a poet, essayist, and short story writer from Lucknow, India • **Martin Shaw**, Emeritus Professor of International Relations and Politics at the University of Sussex, is the author of *War and Genocide*, *What is Genocide?* and *Genocide and International Relations* • **Luke Wilkinson** is pursuing a PhD in Theology and Religious Studies at the University of Cambridge, and working on the history of Muslim-Christian relations in Malta, where he grew up • **Robin Yassin-Kassab** is Deputy Editor of *Critical Muslim*.